Last years new projects

6 new 747 400's
② 10 new A340 600's.
Ordered 5 new A380XX's - biggest plane in world
Opened Game reserves in Africa Recognized as amongst the very best
Bought 5 miles Mayorcan Coastline for new hotel Started Kasbar in hills of Marakesh
Launched low cost airline Australia - Virgin Blue - that caused Quantas shares to drop 25% - and air fares even More.
Sold 5000 cars through Virgin Cars Dot Com fastest growing on line Car Company
Signing up 15000 new customers a week to gas/electricat □ d a mill in mobile phones
Secured site for largest cinema in World in Tokyo.
Launched Virgin Mobile in Australia 100000 will be sold by Octobar
Opened first megastore in Beirut. September Dubai.
Sold 200000 mortgages.
Trainline - Sold 10 million tickets through 4 million customer
Set up Virgin Travelstore.
Set up Virgin Wines Dot Can - most successful wine web site
Secured permission to fly to Trranto/Lagos. Did so
Bought or built 100 Virgin Active Centres both in Britain and South Africa. Average size 30000 sq feet.
Launched complete new interiors and exteriors on all Virgin Atlantic fleet - introduced new seate
won bid with other airlines for how to run Air Traffic Control.
Put in best plans for East Coast Mainline - same country 4 billion High speed line plans trains up East Coast. SRA take up plan
Introduced new Voyager Trains on Cross Country network on time - one every 5 days

Business Stripped Bare

By the Same Author

Losing My Virginity: The Autobiography

Screw It, Let's Do It: Lessons in Life and Business

Business Stripped Bare

Adventures of a Global Entrepreneur

Richard Branson

Published by Virgin Books 2008

2 4 6 8 10 9 7 5 3

Endpapers designed from extracts from the personal notebooks of Richard Branson

First published in Great Britain in 2008 by
Virgin Books
Random House, 20 Vauxhall Bridge Road,
London SW1V 2SA

www.virginbooks.com
www.rbooks.co.uk

Addresses for companies within The Random House Group Limited
can be found at: www.randomhouse.co.uk/offices.htm

The Random House Group Limited Reg. No. 954009

A CIP catalogue record for this book
is available from the British Library

Hardback ISBN 9781905264438
Trade paperback ISBN 9780753515020

The Random House Group Limited supports The Forest Stewardship
Council [FSC], the leading international forest certification organisation.
All our titles that are printed on Greenpeace-approved FSC-certified
paper carry the FSC logo.

Our paper procurement policy can be found at www.rbooks.co.uk/environment

Mixed Sources
Product group from well-managed
forests and other controlled sources
www.fsc.org Cert no. TT-COC-2139
© 1996 Forest Stewardship Council
FSC

Typeset by www.carrstudio.co.uk
Printed and bound in Great Britain by
CPI Mackays, Chatham ME5 8TD

I'd like to dedicate this book to
all the wonderful people – past and present –
who have made Virgin what it is today.

Contents

Acknowledgements

Writing *Business Stripped Bare* has been another life lesson for me. I've been able to remind myself of many of the business escapades that I've been involved in over the years. I know some of my Virgin colleagues are decidedly nervous about what I might be saying – and whether I might go 'off message', as the politicians say – but a real strength of the Virgin Group is that they are prepared to let me talk candidly about the business.

Of course, any lapses in memory about events are purely my own. What do they say at the end of television true-life dramas – that 'some names and dates have been changed'? Not really necessary in this case, but my intention is not to embarrass or disparage anyone.

The Virgin story has been a phenomenon – building a global business in one lifetime – and it still has a long way to go. We have packed so much in. Over the years there have been so many outstanding and committed people steering our Virgin businesses. I really should thank them all individually but if I did, this book would be twice the size and the publishers wouldn't be too happy with me. So I shall save my thanks for those who have had a direct influence on the business in recent years.

I'd like to acknowledge the work and assistance of Stephen Murphy, Virgin's chief executive, who gets little credit for the magnificent job he does; Gordon McCallum, Mark Poole, Patrick McCall and Robert Samuelson; Jonathan Peachey and Frances Farrow in America; Andrew Black in Canada; Brett Godfrey in Australia; Dave Baxby in Asia-Pacific; and Jean Oelwang at Virgin Unite, our charitable enterprise. At Virgin Atlantic Airways, Steve Ridgway has been a great friend and confidant for many years, while Alex Tai at Virgin Galactic has shared a lot of adventures with me, and his colleague Stephen Attenborough is working hard on our exciting new space venture. Thanks to Tony Collins at Virgin Trains, Jayne-Anne Gadhia at Virgin Money and Matthew Bucknall at Virgin Active; to our legal team, led by Josh Bayliss, who have kept us on the straight and narrow path; to our PR gurus Nick Fox and Jackie McQuillan; to my perfectly formed personal team of Nicola Duguid and Helen Clarke, based here on Necker Island; and to Ian Pearson for looking after the Virgin Archives in Oxfordshire.

I'd like to thank Will Whitehorn, the president of Virgin Galactic, and a long-term adviser and friend, for steering this book project. At Virgin Books, now part of Random House, I'd like to thank Richard Cable, Ed Faulkner and Mary Instone for their hard work in defining the shape of the book. Thanks also to my good friends Andy Moore, Andy Swaine, Adrian Raynard, Holly Peppe and Gregory Roberts for their friendship and feedback.

I'd like to record my appreciation of journalist Kenny Kemp, my collaborator and researcher on this text, who chased me around the world and grabbed time away from my busy business schedule to help me with my thoughts, and Simon Ings who helped me to craft those thoughts so well.

And, finally, a wonderful thanks to my wife, Joan, my children, Holly and Sam, and my dearest mum and dad for all your love and support.

Richard Branson
Necker Island, August 2008

Introduction

I spoke to him nearly every day, using him as a sounding board. He seemed to me the kind of business expert who could enhance our thinking. He gave us good advice on the Virgin One account. His name was Gordon McCallum. He used to work for the business consultancy McKinsey & Co., and I knew he'd been doing some work for Wells Fargo – to do with consumer banking and financial services and major retailers including JC Penney. I trusted him. I knew a lot about him – but it suddenly dawned on me one day: 'Gordon? Do you work for us?'

'Yes,' he replied.

'I mean, are you an employee?'

'No, Richard, I'm not. I'm still working as a freelance consultant at the moment.'

Oh.

'Well,' I said, 'you'd better come for a job interview. See you tomorrow at the house.' And I put the phone down.

I can't remember much about that night but I must have had fun; when Gordon turned up at my place in Holland Park, at 9 a.m. sharp,

I was still in bed. In fact, I couldn't seem to get out of it. So I tucked myself under the sheet and called him up and said: 'Well, I'd like to offer you a full-time job.'

It was not the kind of meeting he had expected, but he rose to the challenge. 'What kind of job?'

'What kind of job would you like?'

Finally Gordon cracked. In all his years at McKinsey he had never come across this technique as a way of identifying corporate talent. He burst out laughing, but he wasn't put off. 'I'd like to help Virgin develop a much clearer business strategy for the brand and help you expand it further internationally.'

This made a lot of sense. It was what I'd been hoping for. 'What would your title be?' I said, and leaned over to grab my dressing gown.

He thought about it. 'Something like Strategy Director?'

'Fine – we'll call you the Group Strategy Director of Virgin.'

We sorted out the money, and the deal was done – and I went off to have a shower.

Is this any way to do business?

Absolutely.

At its heart, business is not about formality, or winning, or 'the bottom line', or profit, or trade, or commerce, or any of the things the business books tell you it's about. Business is what concerns us. If you care about something enough to do something about it, you're in business, and you'll find ideas in this book that will help you. This is a business book for everyone, whether or not they imagine themselves to be 'business people'.

Making the most of Gordon's considerable talents and playing fair by him was not a 'business decision' I had to make – it was simply my business, my concern, my affair. I'm no less a businessman when I'm in a dressing gown – and I'm certainly not more of one when I put on a suit.

This was brought home to me pretty sharply in July 2007, during an hour-long session at the Aspen Ideas Festival. I was being interviewed by Bob Schieffer, the former CBS news anchorman of the *Evening News*. This is the man who moderated the 2004 presidential election debate between George W. Bush and John Kerry. Bob knows his stuff, so I expected a grilling. He could see that underneath my brash exterior I still harbour some nervousness about speaking in public, so he started off warm and generous, getting me nice and relaxed, conversing about all kinds of matters from terrorist extremism to space tourism, before he delivered his sucker punch. I had left school at fifteen to set up a student magazine, and Bob asked me *why I had gone into business.*

I just stared at him. I suddenly realised I had never been interested in being 'in business'. And, heaven help me, I said so, adding: 'I've been interested in creating things.'

Now, feeble as that sounded on the stage at Aspen, that's the gist of my thinking about business. It shouldn't be something outside of yourself. It shouldn't be something you can stand away from. And if it is, there's something wrong.

Over the years, the Virgin Group has made it its business to run railways, build a spaceship, launch a new airline in Africa, and help fight Aids and HIV. These are our concerns. Not all of them are 'businesses' in the usual sense – and the journalists who have accused the Virgin Group of making no business sense are right, but in the wrong way. *The greatest and most unusual achievement of the Virgin Group is that, unlike most businesses, it remembers what it's for.*

Business is creative. It's like painting. You start with a blank canvas. You can paint anything – *anything* – and there, right there, is your first problem. For every good painting you might turn out, there are a zillion bad paintings just aching to drip off your brush. Scared? You should be. You start. You pick a colour. The next colour you choose has to work with the first colour. The third colour has to work with the first colour and the second. The fourth colour . . . You get the idea. You're committed now. You absolutely cannot stop. You've invested. There is no reverse gear on this thing. People who bad-mouth businessmen and women in general are missing the point. People in business who succeed have swallowed their fear and have set out to create something special, something to make a difference to people's lives. Are the colours just right? Are the planes polished? Do the crew look good? Are they comfortable? Are the seats OK? What's the food like? It costs *how* much . . .?

And whether you're a surrealist or a CEO, there are always bills to pay and money always arrives later than you ever dreamed possible. In the teeth of a downturn, petty financial hassles can turn into major, life-changing crises, and tough decisions often have to be made. This is the side of business that journalists like to write about – but it's the least exciting, least distinctive part of business. It's secondary. It's dull. What really matters is what you create. Does it work or not? Does it make you proud?

When I meet people around the world they often say to me I must have a wonderful life. They're not wrong. I am a very fortunate person. I have my own island in paradise, a wonderful wife and family, loyal and entertaining friends who would walk over hot embers for me, and I for them. I travel a great deal and I've had many life-affirming adventures and experiences. Even George Clooney once let slip that he'd swap his life for mine – much to the excitement of my wife!

Success has made much of this possible. Would I have been happy without my successes in business? I'd like to think so. But again, it depends on what you mean by business. Would I have been happy had I not found concerns to absorb me and fascinate me and engage me every minute of my life? No, absolutely not, I'd be as miserable as sin.

Today the Virgin Group spans the world. It is truly an internationally recognised brand name, trusted and enjoyed by many hundreds of millions of people across the continents of the world. Could it collapse overnight? Almost certainly not: we've built it to contain any amount of damage, by organising it into around 300 limited companies. I think we've proved that a branded group of *separate* businesses, each with limited liability for its own financial affairs, makes sense. We're never going to have a Barings Bank situation where a rogue trader is able to bring down the whole Virgin Group. One disaster isn't going to cause 50,000 job losses worldwide. Forty years' worth of work isn't going to be flushed down the toilet overnight. And although the combined Virgin Group is the largest group of private companies in Europe, each individual company is generally relatively small in its sector. And so we have the advantage of being the nimble 'underdog' player in most markets.

At the time of writing, we are sailing straight into a brute of a storm. More than a year ago now, tens of thousands of poorly advised families in America ran out of money to pay their mortgages. They lost their homes. Their misfortune is now being visited upon the rest of us on a global scale, as the sub-prime mortgage crisis convinces bank after bank to reduce its lending. One major UK bank has already collapsed. Some global financial institutions have needed massive government refinancing. It's not a disaster – yet. But the price of oil is going through the roof, and consumers throughout the world are noticing the difference to their fuel and heating bills. Their response is perfectly sensible: they're not buying things. But this in turn could spell real trouble for the consumer businesses on which many national economies depend.

Like any business, the Virgin Group has to steer around all these obstacles. In *Business Stripped Bare* I'll be looking at the key elements that have brought success to our companies, despite poor economic conditions and changing markets.

In business, as in so many other creative endeavours, the idiots' guides are for idiots. Like you, I've scanned the airport bookshelves. Like you, I've browsed the business books. Like you, I've felt my heart sinking. There are exceptions – I'll mention the ones I've enjoyed as I go – but in general these business writers are a dreary bunch. Most of them seem to be writing about what business is like from the outside – not about what it's like to actually *do*.

They're writing, in some abstract way, a prescription for how to paint a picture. They've got nothing to say about painting a bad picture, or about how to tell a good picture from a dozen bad pictures, or how to let go when a good picture turns out to be bad, or how to live with yourself when you realise you've thrown a good picture away, or . . .

You get the idea. Every business, like every painting, operates according to its own rules. There are many ways to run a successful company. What works once may never work again. What everyone tells you never to do may just work, once. There are no rules. You don't learn to walk by following rules. You learn by doing, and by falling over, and it's because you fall over that you learn to save yourself from falling over. It's the greatest thrill in the world and it runs away screaming at the first sight of bullet points.

Most of what I have done with the Virgin Group is about my own gut instinct. I've never analysed what I do in any formal way. What would be the point? In business, as in life, you never step into the same river twice.

So all I can do for you now (and I firmly believe that this is all anyone can honestly do) is map the territory I've seen. The good news is, I've covered a lot of territory.

On 11 November 1999, surrounded by near-naked women, I announced Virgin Mobile from inside a giant see-through mobile phone in Trafalgar Square, London. Three years later, in Times Square in July 2002, I paid homage to the hit British film *The Full Monty*; wearing only a cellphone to cover my shame, I unveiled Virgin Mobile's partnership with MTV. The point of these hugely enjoyable stunts was that, with Virgin, what you see is what you get.

Well, there are no stunts here (the editor tells me we can't afford a pop-up section), so I'll just have to rely on the title to get this book's message across. I've stripped Virgin's businesses bare. Rather than banging on about how successful they are, I've written about what my companies are actually about. What were our intentions? How well, or how badly, did we realise our early hopes? I've gone through my notebooks and diaries, hunting for common themes and ideas, and I've divided what I've found into seven sections. I'll be looking at:

People

The brand

Why delivery is vital

What we learn from our mistakes and setbacks

Innovation as a driver for business

The value of entrepreneurship and leadership

The wider responsibility of business

I think of our brand as one of the premier 'way of life' brands in the world. Whether you're in the United States, Australia and New Zealand, Japan, South Africa, India, Europe, Russia, South America or China, the Virgin brand means something. The Virgin brand is about enjoying life to the full. By offering customers excellent value for money in so many areas of their lives, we aim to make them happier.

These values do not come cheap. These values must be paid for. Our Virgin Mobile business in America still holds the record as the fastest company to generate revenues of over a billion dollars. That's faster than Microsoft, Google and Amazon. We've created more business multimillionaires than any other private company in Europe – and we're among the top twenty in the United States. Business requires astute decision-making and leadership. It requires discipline and innovation. It also needs attitude, a good sense of humour and, dare I say it, luck.

We turn entrepreneurial ideas into outstanding businesses. We receive hundreds of business ideas every month, often directly via our website. We employ a gatekeeper – a corporate development assistant

– whose job it is to record, log and classify all ideas as they arrive. She then passes them on to our experts. They read through and research the best of them. A tiny number are passed to our investment professionals – whole teams of them, working in London, Switzerland, New York, Shanghai and Sydney – and they are more forensic about business than the detectives on *Crime Scene Investigation*.

What if we like your idea? If you've seen the BBC's *Dragons' Den* – or *American Inventor*, its US equivalent – then you know what's coming. We will strip you bare.

We normally invite people to come along to Virgin's Investment Advisory Committee and present their plans in London, New York or Geneva; and sometimes in the Far East, in Japan or China. At these weekly meetings we have a team of six Virgin managers we can pull in to help examine projects. So that our own vested interests don't blind us to new opportunities, none of the committee runs a Virgin business on a day-to-day basis – but they work closely with all of the top people who run our businesses and bounce ideas off them all the time.

Our global chief executive, Stephen Murphy, who operates in Switzerland, and Gordon McCallum (our UK chief executive), ask some very tough questions. They will rigorously push and pull your business plan about to see if there is a profitable business underneath. Facing the committee can be daunting for the uninitiated – and you are normally expected to be well prepared, with the facts at your fingertips. But these people don't bite, and (unlike some of their television counterparts) they are not remotely rude. They can ask for more meetings so that deeper questions can be answered. Often the committee meets several times before a final decision is given. We look at spending plans, income forecasts, the marketing budget, and when the company is likely to break even. We work out our exit strategy – will it be a sale, or a flotation on a stock market? And, above all, we look at the key managers who will be running the business. This is the holy grail for us, because it's the people that make a great business idea work.

More often than not, after all things are considered, they'll recommend that we don't invest in your business. The possible reasons for this are so many and various, they're not even worth agonising over. Dust yourself off. Learn what lessons you can. Make your next call.

The Virgin team acts just like any other commercial venture capitalist organisation. It assesses your potential, whether it fits with the group's ambitions and strategy, and of course brand values, and what the possible returns and profits will be. Then it works out what kind of stake the Virgin Group should take. In return, the new company gets the full range of Virgin's expertise – and I'll agree to help raise the profile, make key introductions and offer any advice that I can.

The Investment Advisory Committee are my trusted lieutenants and they know almost everything there is to know about the Virgin global business. I'm rarely at their meetings – the team don't like my interruptions and interference. I know this because they have a nickname for me. They call me Dr Yes – a parody of the wonderful James Bond movie *Dr No*.

If I like your idea, but the investment committee have concerns, then I usually ask them to go and find solutions to the problems they've identified. I prod these people constantly. I remember, before we developed our mobile phone business, I was on to them every week saying: 'Why aren't we in this yet?' The committee didn't want to launch Virgin Blue, either, but in the end they saw sense!

But, you see, I have an ace up my sleeve. If I believe in your business idea, I can be quite persuasive in getting people to accept my point of view. I never do this lightly – but, as I've said, usually go with my gut instinct, disregarding whole volumes of painstaking research. I would love to be able to tell you that every ace I've played has turned out to be a Virgin Blue or a Virgin Mobile. But I can't – which is why I make my senior colleagues at Virgin very, very nervous!

Should we decide to go ahead with you, we sign up as branded venture capitalists (occasionally, as unbranded investors), take a stake in the company, and then look for a return on that investment after about two to five years.

And that, the cynics will say, is that. Of course, businesses also have a duty of care for the health and well-being of their people (and you will hear what we have done in South Africa for our staff with HIV/Aids). Beyond that, though, business is 'just business': a scramble for profit. Right?

Well, that might describe crime; it certainly doesn't describe business.

Ethics aren't just important in business. They are the whole point of business. We're in business to make things. And when you decide what to make, that, right there, is an ethical decision.

The more successful you get, the bigger and harder the ethical questions become. I spent the first half of my career creating businesses that we could be proud of, that paid the bills and ensured that the Virgin Group was strong and survived. It has been our aim to establish Virgin as the 'Most Respected Brand in the World'. It has to be one that is trusted in each and every marketplace. I think once the Virgin Galactic space programme starts, we have a chance of being the most respected brand in space too!

On the back of that work, I've built the second half of my career, creating what I call 'war rooms', to tackle environmental problems and disease, bringing together global leaders to form the Elders – compassionate people who wield their huge influence for the good of humanity. The entrepreneurial skills we use to get these projects up and running are the same ones we used to create Virgin Records and Virgin Atlantic. Why would they be any different? Business is about getting things done. No, scratch that: business is about getting *better* things done (whilst building profits) and setting up a not-for-profit 'social' business is not really any different to setting up a commercial business.

Make no mistake: being better is hard to do, and only gets harder the bigger you get. If you've got a brand with 300 companies, you've got to be diligent and make sure that nobody makes a mistake that damages the business's reputation. That means no bribes, no backhanders and no hidden payments to oil the wheels of commerce. It means treating people fairly and equitably.

Now the stakes are even higher. The threat of climate change is the biggest challenge we face as a planet. Virgin is, among many other things, a transportation group. A rail travel company. An air travel company. With a space tourist start-up. So we're making things worse – right?

Well. We cannot unmake air travel – or space travel for that matter. No one in business can unmake anything, any more than a band can unmake a song. Can you unmake your hangover? Your indigestion? Your children? Your last week's work? No. Welcome, then, to the first law of entrepreneurial business: *there is no reverse gear on this thing*.

Virgin is dedicated to developing new renewable fuels and energy sources and greener technologies in rail, air and space to cut all our carbon footprints. It is responding to the current crisis decisively, the only way a business can: by making things. Virgin is trying to do a credible job for the environment. By making better things, it's making things better – and in this book, I hope to show you how.

I've enjoyed an incredible life – and I hope there is much more to come. I'm planning to work till I drop and I'll continue to challenge myself as long as I enjoy good health and still have my marbles. And I hope that the fortune that I have been granted can bring enormous opportunities to other people and make a real difference.

I hope you find *Business Stripped Bare* a useful read. My experiences may even shake up your ideas about what business is. They've certainly shaken up mine.

1 People

Find Good People - Set Them Free

'Mr Richard! Mr Richard! Do you have a minute, please?'

I was visiting Ulusaba, our private game reserve, close to the stunning Kruger National Park in South Africa. It's an enchanting piece of bush and, thanks to Karl and Llane Langdon, a well-managed one. The previous owners had planned to fence it in – all 2,060 hectares of it – to protect the local wildlife from poachers. We decided, on the contrary, to take the advice of our rangers, and have allowed our leopards, lions, elephants, cheetahs and rhinos to move and migrate freely between our land and the neighbouring Kruger.

The reserve had cost me nearly $6 million in 1999 – a testament to the salesmanship of the South African president, Nelson Mandela, who persuaded me to keep faith with his homeland. Even when times have been hard for the Virgin Group and I needed liquid cash, I could never bring myself to sell it.

'Mr Richard!'

I stopped and turned round and stood there, dazzled by one of the most winning smiles I've seen in my life.

'Mr Richard.' It was a woman from the village, dressed in a KwaZulu gown of bright reds and yellows. 'I've heard you are a very generous man. Can you lend me money to buy a sewing machine?'

At this time Virgin Unite, our charitable foundation, was busy at work in the villages in and around the reserve. The villagers had been walking a long way to Sand River for water that was not particularly safe to drink. So the foundation had sunk boreholes to provide the villagers with a nearby source of clean water. It taught skills, helped with the school and built a medical clinic. It created play areas for kids, and huts from which the villagers could sell their goods to tourists.

The tourists were our business too. For nearly ten years, Ulusaba has been a magical place, especially loved by people who come here to rent our upmarket lodges, one perched on the summit of a granite outcrop with stunning eagle-eye views across the bush, the other a tree house overlooking the Mabrak riverbed, where many animals come to drink and frolic.

I've been asked for money hundreds of times over the last thirty years, but rarely with such directness. You've heard of the elevator pitch? This was the elephant-pool pitch.

She told me she was a talented seamstress but that she needed cash to buy a sewing machine to get her business going.

'So how much do you need?'

'Three hundred dollars would be enough,' she explained. 'And, what is more, I'll repay it within three months and employ six people full-time.' The woman's determination and ambition were fantastic. So was her focus: she knew exactly what she wanted, and why. She got her $300.

And as I walked away I said to myself: That's money I'll probably never see again.

I wasn't being cynical. I simply had experience of how the odds were stacked. At Ulusaba – which means 'place of little fear' – I had come to know many local people who were working on the game reserve and looking after our visitors. And believe me, they have big fears. Malaria, tuberculosis and HIV/Aids stalk their daily lives.

Three months later I was invited back to the village to open some of the community projects supported by Virgin Unite, including crèches, orphans' homes and an Aids-awareness clinic. When I got there, six women came up to me, and gave me a gift of the most exquisite cotton pillows and tribal clothes which they had made. And, to complete my surprise, they returned the $300.

But where was the original entrepreneurial seamstress? I asked.

'Mr Richard, she is so sorry she can't be here personally to see you. She is off to the market selling the products,' they told me.

I've thought of her often since that day: a confident, direct, intelligent woman, using a sewing machine to better her own and others' lives. Never mind *Dragons' Den*: if you want to meet entrepreneurs, come to Africa. It's a continent full of opportunities for the creation of wealth, enterprise and future prosperity.

Since the mid-1970s, the economist Professor Muhammad Yunus has been saying much the same thing about the women of Bangladesh. But how do we foster entrepreneurism in communities that, whatever their potential, have virtually nothing?

Muhammad Yunus started his Grameen Bank as a practical economics project in 1976. He won the Nobel Peace Prize in 2006 for pioneering an economic system in which small, low-interest loans are extended to people who are unable to obtain a loan from a traditional bank. Grameen's rule of thumb is to keep the interest rate as close as possible to the prevailing market rate in the commercial banking sector rather than moneylenders' exorbitant rates. It has transformed the lives of millions and the bank now has 2,400 branches, and 7.5 million borrowers. The default rates – at 2 per cent – are lower than those of any other banking system. Every year, 5 per cent of Grameen borrowers move out of poverty. His work has spawned a global movement.

Muhammad is a proponent of 'social business'. He said in an interview with the *Santa Barbara Independent*:

> *Ordinary businesses are aimed at making money ... there is no consideration of how people benefit, it is all about making profits. Social business, on the other hand, is all about social benefits, not personal gain. Profits are important to social businesses, which seek to sell products at prices that make it self-sustaining. A social business is not a charity – but profits are not its ultimate goal. When a social business turns a profit, the original investors are repaid, but the rest of the profits stay with the company in order to achieve its long-term social goal of helping the poor.*

His view is that many of the problems of the world remain unresolved because capitalism is poorly understood and poorly practised. The issue, he says, is not in the capitalist system itself, but in the hash that people repeatedly make of it. He completely rejects the common view, that capitalism is all about the bottom line.

He says: 'In this narrow interpretation we create a one-dimensional human being to play the role of entrepreneur. We insulate him from other dimensions of life, such as religious, emotional, political dimensions ... Everyday human beings are not one-dimensional entities, they are excitingly multidimensional and indeed very colourful.'

Muhammad thinks capitalism can – and should – enrich the whole person.

I'm not good at theory. Almost everything I've learned, I've learned by doing. However, Muhammad's opinions excite me. They confirm a lot of the gut feelings I've developed about business over the years. And topping my list of gut feelings is this: *business has to give people enriching, rewarding lives, or it's simply not worth doing.*

Later on, we'll be returning to Virgin's African adventures, and some of the wider political questions this story throws up. For now, though – since we have to start somewhere – let's start at home. Let's start with you. Wouldn't it be wonderful if your company were full of people like the seamstress who accosted me that day in Ulusaba? Think what you could achieve.

Well, there's no reason why it can't be, and in this chapter I'm going to tell you how Virgin tries to foster the entrepreneurial spirit at every level of its business.

First of all, take a cold, hard look at your present surroundings.

Are you really going to be able to empower the people around you? I ask because, for all I know, your workplace may be a sink of despair. And while we've had a few notable successes in this area, it is, I would say, superhumanly difficult to change a company's existing culture.

Virgin learned this the hard way in 1996, when we acquired Euro Belgian Airlines and turned it into a cheap, cheerful, go-getting budget airline called Virgin Express. Well, that was what Virgin Express was supposed to become. We rebranded the airline and floated 49 per cent of its stock on the Brussels and NASDAQ stock markets. We knew it wouldn't be easy, because we'd be in competition with solid low-cost airlines such as easyJet, Ryanair and Go, with all the benefits they had of being based in the UK. Not only that, we would be based in *Belgium* (remembering how much it cost us to operate there brings tears to my eyes to this day). Nevertheless, I believed that with a quick transfusion of the Virgin spirit, we could make a go of it.

Boy, was I wrong.

Our Brussels-based low-cost carrier was one of the toughest challenges we have faced. Debilitating European regulations on the thirty-five-hour working week and high fixed costs meant that there was little room for radical changes. This is a nightmare when you are trying to run a low-cost operation and arrange rosters and crew patterns. But if it was bad for us, imagine what it was like for the staff. They were cynical about the business, for the very good reason that there was no fun, no camaraderie and no real sense of ownership.

We set about changing all that – or tried to – and landed feet first in a can of worms: strict union regulations, tortuous pay negotiations, constant strike threats. I had to go in myself and try to sort it out, and it taxed my own legendary reserves of karma. The crucial lesson I learned was: *avoid taking on someone else's legacy.* In June 1999 I wrote in my notebook with reference to the turmoil at Virgin Express: '*Almost for the first time in my life I can't sleep at night. Fighting the outside world is easy. Trying to make peace among one's own staff is hell. We must never allow another company to get into this mess.*'

As life turned out, shortly after that diary entry we made Neil Burrows the CEO and he set about turning the business around with incredible hard work and great leadership. However, just as Neil had got the costs into line with the most competitive in Europe and finally turned Virgin Express into a credible people business which worked, 9/11 bankrupted our biggest partner SABENA. Eventually, in March 2006, Virgin Express and SN Brussels Airlines merged to create Brussels Airlines and Neil went on to lead the combined businesses merging the two cultures and creating what is today a very successful airline in the capital of Europe. It was a salutary experience, and the business message is clear: if you're in the mood to buy a new business – wait. It can take a long time to change a business culture. Are you sure you wouldn't be better off starting one from scratch? So many business acquisitions end up being disasters because the people involved fail to understand the real challenges involved with getting different types of people to all work together and share the same goals. They look only at the numbers.

This lesson can be applied more widely, and that's what I want you to do now. Look around you. If the people you're responsible for have already been crushed beyond recognition, and if your bosses are more interested in putting you right than in listening to what you have to say, you are better off hunting out more promising surroundings for yourself.

Even better, start from scratch. Seek out people with the right spirit, bubbling just beneath the surface, and get working with them.

The people you need are rare, but they're not hard to spot, so let's start with them.

You will find the 'Virgin type' of person all over the world. I bump into them frequently in bars, cafes, hotels and small businesses, in libraries, post offices, in hospitals, at the jetty in the Caribbean, even in government offices and the civil service. Virgin types pop up everywhere, and in every nation. These people don't know they're special, but they are; they are out there, and you can spot them.

If you're in charge of a company, or a human resources department (I hate this description – I call them 'people' departments!), you should be searching for them, too. These people, by their nature and their outlook on life, enjoy working with others. They're attentive. They smile freely. They're often lively, and fun to be with. I don't underestimate qualifications – I just don't assume they're going to tell me anything about a person's character. Having 'savvy' is much more important than having a formal education. The things you learn can only complement who you are – and in my book, who you are counts for a whole lot.

I am always on the lookout for talent – it's not easy to find energetic and enthusiastic people with the right attitude. We look for people who can grow into their work, and respond with excitement when we give them greater responsibility. Jobs, after all, can be learned. Recently, we noticed two guys doing a brilliant job of running the water-sports activities at a rival hotel. Everyone loved them. We didn't need water-sports people. But we needed managers: and we asked these guys to run our island home in the Caribbean, Necker. In business, someone who can stay cool and calm under pressure is an asset. This is especially true for the Virgin Group, as so much of what we do involves dealing directly with the public. Today's consumer can be very demanding, especially when things aren't going according to plan.

I want to keep the Virgin Group fresh. So I have tried very hard to re-create, in every company, the atmosphere of Virgin's early years.

There's no rule book. The past is the past. We can't preserve it; it would be silly for us to try. But what we can do is look for the next generation of the right sort of people. Like everybody else, we're looking for dedication, and belief, and a willingness to go that extra mile for colleagues and customers. But we keep certain other thoughts in mind, too. It seems to me that when you love what you do, you're too busy to stand on your dignity. When you're good at what you do, you don't worry so much about your image. So I think it's a positive sign when people don't take themselves too seriously.

Good people have always been at the heart of the Virgin business, and that's largely because we have tried to keep our businesses small, and our management teams tight-knit. I feel that small, compact companies are, generally, better run. This is partly because people feel more connected in smaller companies.

In an ideal business environment, everybody should have a rough idea of what everyone else is going through. People should be free to talk. Banter is essential. Anonymous, over-formal, regimented surroundings produce mediocre results. Niggling problems either fester, or they end up on your desk. No one runs that extra mile for you.

And there's another thing you should take into consideration: if your people aren't talking to each other, how are they ever going to get ideas? It was the physicist Albert Einstein who said: 'What a person does on his own, without being stimulated by the thoughts and experiences of others, is even in the best cases rather paltry and monotonous.'

There are few places more depressing than a room full of people who have nothing to say to each other. *So put people together in a way that will have them bouncing ideas off each other, befriending each other, and taking care of each other, and suddenly they are coming to you, not with gripes and problems, but with solutions and great ideas.*

Of course, there'll be friction. People working in small teams, in close proximity with each other, will rub each other up the wrong way from time to time. But nothing festers. Nothing stalls. People get over their problems. They come into work curious about what the day will bring. They're not having to contend with that dreadful, low-level headache that comes from not quite connecting with the people with whom they're spending most of their day.

As a manager, you're going to need a modest amount of psychological insight to build great management teams. But practice pays off, and you don't have to agonise over finding exceptional 'characters'. Given the right conditions, exceptional people will reveal themselves. The buzz of Virgin's early years was generated by a diverse mixture of incredible characters. I remember the brilliant Simon Draper, a student from South Africa who became the music buyer for our fledgling business. At Virgin Records, he was our musical sounding board. He was hip, cool, loved music and therefore had an unerring ability for finding fantastic music. He signed some of our best bands, and the music he fostered was the bedrock of our success.

There's another thing about teams: they don't last for ever. Think of a team as being like the cast in a theatrical play. Actors who work too long together on the same show for too long grow stale. When the business lets you, shake things up a little.

In the early days, when one of our Virgin companies ended up employing more than a hundred staff, I would ask to see the deputy managing director, the deputy sales manager and the deputy marketing director. I would say to them: 'You are now the managing director, the sales manager and the marketing director of a new company.' Then we would split the company in two. And when either of those companies got to a hundred people, I would once again ask to see the deputies and split the company again.

Virgin Records birthed nearly twenty different companies in the Notting Hill area of London. Each one would be independent and competing in the marketplace, but they would share the same accounts and invoicing department. Being the managing director of something small – rather than the assistant to the assistant MD of something big – gave people more clout. They were able to take pride in their successes, and they had to learn quickly and well from their failures. They were offered incentives according to how well they did. Although each company was relatively small, collectively the group turned into the largest independent record company in the world, and the most successful. If we'd kept everyone in the same building, I don't think we would have generated the ideas that led to our success.

Even today, each Virgin company is relatively small, although our airlines and train businesses, by their very nature, have grown significantly. I can't say that I know everyone's name now – indeed, it's been a while since that was the case, but we have tried to retain a culture of intimacy. If we set up a new airline we create a completely separate, stand-alone entity. Virgin Blue in Australia, Virgin Atlantic and Virgin America are independent companies. Our new airline in Russia will be independent, as is Virgin Nigeria, although we have pulled in technical people from Virgin Atlantic to help establish it. We pass and exchange expertise at arm's length. This makes the Virgin Group a fascinating environment for people who work in the airline businesses. One year Virgin people might be working in Britain or South Africa, the next spending time down under in Australia. This is a wonderful way of keeping hold of good people for longer. At Virgin, secondment is a way of life. There has to be a bit of give and take because some of our companies have different ownership structures. But our managing directors usually realise their people can benefit from a cross-fertilisation of ideas and culture.

There is nothing more demoralising than to work your pants off, only for strangers to be promoted to the senior positions you aspire to. At Virgin, we keep business in the family wherever we can, and we promote from within. The woman who was the managing director of Virgin's recording division started work for Virgin at the Manor Recording Studios; she was the cleaning lady. The manager of the Kasbah, our hotel in Asni, Morocco, first demonstrated her winning ways with people as a masseuse on Virgin Atlantic.

By 1995, I estimated some thirty people had become millionaires or multimillionaires as a result of starting Virgin businesses – and this didn't include the hundred or so musicians who became millionaires through record sales. Since then we can probably say that another eighty Virgin people have become millionaires in our businesses. This reward is just a by-product of success in business.

It's a fact of business life that people come and go. The offer of better prospects or career advancement elsewhere will naturally draw good people away from time to time. But what about the others – the ones who leave in order to do much the same thing, for much the same money, elsewhere? What went wrong?

Managers often assume it's a question of pay. This is lazy of them. Yes, money is important. It's essential to pay people fairly for the job they do, and to share out the profits of a company's success. But throwing money at people isn't the point. When people leave a good company, it's often because they don't feel good themselves. They feel marginalised. They feel ignored. They feel underused. Few people spend every spare hour scouring the jobs pages hunting for a higher salary. Most are driven back into the jobs market by frustration. Their bosses don't listen to them.

If you have a strong business idea and it falls on stony ground, there is only one possible response: 'Sod it, I'm fed up with this lot. I'm getting out of here.'

So – managers should listen more?

It wouldn't do any harm. At Virgin Blue, our Australian domestic air carrier, founder Brett Godfrey's management method dictates that all of the management team have to get out once every three months and 'chuck bags'. This means that they turn out at 4 a.m. and do a full shift with the baggage people. That way they get to understand the problems and the hassles of the job. And because turnaround time is so vital, he also wants to involve and reward the baggage handlers too. Brett has given them bigger incentives to help with getting the planes back on the runway again. He calls them the 'Pit

Crew' and has decked them all out in Ferrari red. In some airports baggage handlers have been viewed as the lowest of the low. Not at Virgin Blue.

For my own part, I always make it a rule, when I'm in a city, to stay, if possible, where the cabin crews hang out. I'm a regular at the Holiday Inn at Potts Point, Sydney, which has certainly enjoyed better days, but its location is superb. I'll stay there with 200 of our cabin crew, so I can spend time with them and hear how they're doing, and if there's anything we should be looking into.

But we're still missing the point. Maybe your manager *is* a good listener. Maybe your manager is listening too much, to too many people at once, in too much detail. The thing is, if you have a good business idea, why should you have to ask permission every time? Why can't you just carry it out? Why can't you show it off to your manager in action? Why won't people give you the freedom to try, to succeed, even (horrors) to make mistakes?

At Virgin, we try as far as we can to make people feel as if they are working for their own company. Our more senior people have share stakes or options in the companies they run and, as a result, we've created a lot of very successful people over the years. But however our staff are employed, every one of them should feel that, in some respect or other, they own their own work.

Within reason, this is more important to people than their salary. I'll give you an example: Qantas's cabin crew earn $66,400 a year on average based on 'seniority'! Virgin Blue's much younger crews get $40,000. Our crews clock in for over 700 hours a year. Qantas's work for just 660 hours. This difference is likely to be eroded over time as the business matures, but in the meantime Virgin Blue's customers are reaping the advantage in lower fares.

How is this possible? Are Virgin Blue's staff of poorer quality?

Not a bit of it. Some people think airline hospitality is an easy job, and maybe it is – on paper. I've tried being an airline steward for a few days and I know just how hard it is. To get it right and have people come back again and again, the staff have to be absolute perfectionists in terms of their customer-service ability. So whereas at some airlines you could literally go into a pub on a Saturday night, hand out some business cards, train a few people up and that would be it, Virgin Blue puts its guest-facing crew through a rigorous five-stage recruitment process.

Why would they go through all that for a lower salary? Because Brett has introduced a reward system on Virgin Blue. Instead of creating a climate of fear, he has set things up so that the cabin attendants can take responsibility for their actions. He calls it 'First to Know, First to Fix', so that if cabin crew sort things out and it is recognised then they get a free flight ticket, which they can give out to anyone. This is typical of Brett's approach. Another point he insists on is that people with self-discipline don't need to be treated like naughty school-children. It is important not to hammer people who make mistakes, provided they were made with honest intent.

After all, we only live once, and most of our time is spent at work, so *it's vital that we are allowed to feel good about what we do.* Throwing yourself into a job you enjoy is one of life's greatest pleasures – but it's one that some leaders of industry seem determined to stamp out at all costs.

Enjoyment at work begins where all other enjoyments begin: in good health. I write this with no small twinge of conscience, as I do get unfit from time to time. Week after week goes by and I hardly seem to leave the air or airports. I think of Nelson Mandela: during his years in captivity, he kept himself fit with press-ups and sit-ups. He kept his brain alive with a daily routine of exercises. Recently I spent about four months travelling back and forth to Australia, and I could have done with some of Mandela's spirit. I think I only managed an hour's surfing during a one-night stop-off in Bali; at least the buzz from that kept me going for days.

There is no denying, it's easier to stay fit in pleasant surroundings. Our Virgin health clubs make the experience as pleasant as possible, but it's a lot easier to spend an hour chasing rays in the shallows off Necker than it is to slog up and down in a swimming pool. Still, exercise is a bullet worth biting, whatever your surroundings and whatever the pressures of the day. The more energy we can bring to our working days, the better.

It's important, if you see someone overdoing it, to say, 'Go on a holiday.' If someone has lost a family member, let them take as much time off as they need. *There's no point in having people working under unmanageable stress. You've got to give people time to mend.* It's the decent thing to do, it makes practical sense and, when you're in the kind of business we're in, it may even, one day, save a life. Remember, we run airlines. We run train companies. We take people's money and in return we hurtle them about the globe at hundreds of miles an hour. Our chief engineers need to ensure that their engineers are contented, fulfilled and enjoying their work. This is the only sure-fire method we know of inculcating a culture of safety and routine excellence – and Virgin's safety record is, as a result, second to none.

While we're on the subject, I might as well mention another one of our safety measures. You've probably noticed that all our trains and planes have names. By giving these huge, powerful, potentially lethal machines names, we help our people remember where they were working yesterday, or last week, or last month. We help them recall specific problems and gripes with individual engines, coaches or aisles. We make communication easier. People don't have to reach for their diaries every time they're asked about some niggling detail. We never forget that our engineers and flight crew are people, and we'd much sooner personalise our machinery than mechanise our staff.

I find it extraordinary that so many managers pay no attention to the fabric of their workplaces. How are people supposed to believe in your company when all they see of it, day after day, is a couple of dying pot plants and a fire extinguisher? At Virgin, we give people the tools they need to do their job properly. How else are they ever going to feel pride in where they work? Virgin people have told me that at the end of a tiring day, when they are off duty, having a drink in the pub, or a meal, they're occasionally asked where they work. When they say, 'With Virgin,' the enquirer usually replies, 'Lucky you! That must be a great place to work.'

Our staff usually agree.

For many of our companies, the work environment is also public space. On our planes, for example, we make sure that our seats are the most comfortable in the air, the food is excellent, the uniforms are the best and the planes are modern, safe and efficient. On board a plane, customer service and staff satisfaction are pretty much the same issue. They should be handled as one.

But a concern for surroundings is part of the general Virgin philosophy. It runs through all of our businesses, whether or not they deal directly with the public. We're not talking about glitz or vast expense. We're talking about providing people with the right tools for the job. Do that, and your employees will approach every day with freshness and enthusiasm. If you file and forget them in some kind of stationery museum, the keenest heart will wilt.

It occurs to me that so far in this chapter, I've been giving you a lot of 'don'ts'. Don't micromanage. Don't ignore people's needs. There's a better way of looking at the manager's role, and I can best express it by telling you about the first time I met Gordon McCallum.

Virgin Atlantic's inaugural flight landed in San Francisco in 1996. As we celebrated, I was buttonholed by an extremely vivacious Irish marketing executive who worked for McKinsey & Co. She invited me to talk to a group of the company's analysts and consultants at their California Street offices.

McKinsey's consultants spend most of the working week in the offices of their client companies. As a consequence, they don't get much time with each other. So they have made Friday lunchtime their chance to get together: a bonding session over a brown-bag lunch of chicken-mayo subs and fruit juices. Usually, they have a guest to talk about business. Now it was my turn. I got my invitation on the Wednesday; I turned up on the Friday.

Was I prepared? I was not. I cannot for the life of me remember what I said. Whatever it was, though, Gordon made the effort to keep in touch. Years later, I asked him what I said at the meeting that had hit a nerve with the McKinsey people.

'No idea.'

'Really?'

'Not a clue.'

'So why did you stay in touch?'

Gordon shrugged. 'You turned up with a sandwich and a fruit juice,' he said. 'You made time for us.'

When I was twenty-one, someone described Virgin as an 'unprofessional professional organisation', which for my money is just about the best backhanded compliment anyone in business could ever receive. We run our companies professionally and we make sure that everyone does their job to the highest standards. But the way we make sure is to *see that people are having fun*. Fun is not about acting stupid. It's the feeling you get when you're on top of things. We try to make sure that the people who come into contact with a Virgin business end up with a smile on their face (not always easy).

Formality has its place when it simplifies things: when it lets people know what's going on and what to do. We can't be continually reinventing the wheel every time three people meet in a room. That said, I dislike formality. For every time it oils the wheels of business, I can point to fifty more occasions when it gummed things up, made people feel miserable and stifled communication. It says something about the state of business when people are *surprised* that I walk into a room and eat a sandwich with them.

The best Virgin manager is someone who cares about people and who is genuinely interested and wants to bring out the best in them.

A manager should basically be a considerate person who is as interested in the switchboard operator and the person who cleans the lavatories as he or she is in the fellow managers. In my view, a boss who is willing to party with all of their people – and pay attention to their personal concerns – has the makings of a great leader.

They will earn their colleagues' loyalty and trust, for a start. But just as important, they will make friends. Remember what I said earlier, about business being, first and foremost, about concern? Business is not something you can stand away from. So it hardly surprises me that, over the years, I've befriended the people I've worked with, and found business to do with my friends.

It saddens me how rare it is that people want to go on holiday with the people they work with. When I work with people, I really want to get to know them personally. I want to meet their families, their children, I want to know their weaknesses and their strengths, and above all I want them to know mine. That way, we can do more together.

It can go wrong. I remember there was one situation many, many years ago when a very close friend came to run a division of Virgin. We were both so happy about it. Then, a little while later, his life was thrown into turmoil and some of the other managers were coming to me to say that he wasn't working out. I had to persuade him that he was trying to deal with too much and that he should step down. It was a really difficult moment, and it put a massive strain on our friendship. But the fact is we were friends, we dealt with the problem the way friends do, and we stayed close. Attending the twenty-first birthday of his triplets, I felt thankful that, at Virgin, we had found a way to factor friendship and decency into our internal dealings, which had saved this friendship. I know it makes us happier; and I believe strongly that it benefits our work.

Across the whole Virgin Group, we encourage people to take ownership of the issues that they confront in their working lives. In a service-led industry especially, this kind of attitude pays huge dividends. I think if people are properly and regularly recognised for their initiative, then the business has to flourish. Why? *Because it's their business; an extension of their personality. They have a stake in its success.*

Herb Kelleher of Southwest Airlines in the US once said: 'It's difficult to change someone's attitude – so hire for attitude and train for skill.' I've talked a little bit about what I look for in people, but there's one key quality I haven't mentioned yet, and this might surprise some people: it's discipline.

In his book *Good to Great*, the business guru Jim Collins says all companies have a culture but few have 'a culture of discipline'. This doesn't mean that people are tied to a tree and whipped if they don't work well, or have their wages docked if they're five minutes late. It's not that kind of discipline I'm talking about. It is to do with having disciplined people. And we have disciplined people right across our Virgin businesses. After all, if you're going to let people get on with and even develop their jobs, you need people you can trust.

Some people are a bit startled when I sing the praises of self-discipline, and I think it's because they associate self-discipline with formality, with rigid thinking – with a slave-like, machine-like devotion to duty.

They have in mind an airline pilot. The pilot sits down in the cockpit surrounded by an array of complicated computers and gauges. Step by step, the pilot and his co-pilot begin their preflight checks. It is disciplined and methodical. Then, before take-off, the pilot speaks to air traffic control, and, following precise instructions, proceeds to the runway. The pilot then waits to be cleared for take-off, keeping in contact with the control tower. After approval, the pilot decides how the plane should take off. Once airborne, the pilot does everything needed to keep the aircraft, passengers and crew safe and then, when it approaches its destination, brings the aircraft down – often in foul conditions – into the airport. The pilot operates with great discipline within a very strict and highly regulated system. Pilots are not expected to be creative or entrepreneurial. They mustn't do anything out of the ordinary. Right?

Well, not quite.

It's 5 November 1997. Bonfire Night – when people in the UK traditionally have bonfires and firework parties. At Heathrow, staff are awaiting the arrival of Virgin Atlantic's A340-300 Airbus, *Maiden Tokyo,* from Los Angeles. I'm here waiting to board a flight to Boston on this windy and blustery morning when I get the call. Only one set of wheels had dropped down from the landing gear of Flight VS024.

Maiden Tokyo is coming in for an emergency landing.

At the helm is Captain Tim Barnby – a very modest person and one of the best and most experienced pilots in the UK. On board are 114 people – 98 passengers and 16 crew. I'm listening in on my mobile, keeping my mouth firmly shut as the operations crew and Tim run through their options. It doesn't sound good. A four-engined Airbus landing on one set of wheels in strong crosswinds has all the makings of a major incident.

Tim can't see if the landing gear is down or not so he flies the plane low over the tower of air traffic control to help them visually assess the situation. It just gets worse and worse: not only are the left set of wheels not down – the undercarriage door hasn't opened, either.

Four people now stand between a plane full of people and disaster: Tim, and his two co-pilots, Andrew Morley and Craig Matheson – and our own chief pilot Robin Cox on the ground talking them in.

Tim and his colleagues brought the plane down the runway on one set of wheels. Then right at the end of the runway, he gently dropped the wing on to the ground. Fire crews sprayed the plane with foam and passengers used the emergency chutes to get out on to the tarmac. Nine people were treated for minor injuries but all the passengers got off safely. And the plane? Tim landed it so gently, so carefully, that a month later it was back in the air.

I use this example because it is more dramatic, but the lesson I want to draw from it could just as well apply to a train driver, a customer-service operator, or indeed anyone throughout our business. *A self-disciplined employee will have the patience to conduct routine business routinely, the talent to respond exceptionally to exceptional circumstances, and the wisdom to know the difference between the two.* In some settings, this is easy to do. For airline pilots, it is incredibly, even crushingly difficult. Pilots operate according to a strict framework, but they cannot afford this strict routine to dull their senses or flatten their reactions.

After the emergency landing, I invited Tim and the whole crew to Necker, our private island in the British Virgin Islands, to say thank you. I'm pretty sure they had a good time, and I'm pretty sure that working for Virgin is more rewarding than flying for other carriers. In the end, though, we can only rely on Tim and pilots like him to look after themselves: to handle the tedium of routine long-haul flying and still be able to react brilliantly when things pack in around them.

For Virgin, it is fundamentally important to give people with the right temperament the freedom and responsibility to do their jobs properly – and Bonfire Night 1997 confirmed our decision only ever to hire the best pilots we could find.

Virgin Atlantic doesn't take on pilots from scratch. We make sure that they have a long track record of experience in military or commercial flying – often up to ten years' flying with a short-haul airline. Tim's CV is longer than most: among the planes he's flown are Spitfires and B17 bombers. We don't require that all our flight crew are Britain's number-one leading aerobatical display pilot in their spare time – but it helps! It's also one reason why we are now able to recruit spaceship pilots from Virgin Atlantic and Virgin America and so easily find the test piloting and supersonic experience that we need for the unique Virgin Galactic mission.

When I started Virgin Atlantic Airways I appointed as our chief executive Roy Gardner, who had been chief engineer at British Caledonian, a highly respected airline. This emphasised our commitment to having someone at the helm who knew about the planes and was committed to safety. And at the time of writing this (I am never complacent because I understand the nature of mass transportation) Virgin Atlantic and all our other airlines have been in operation for twenty-five years without a major incident and without loss of life. I (like all involved in running an airline) hope I have another twenty-five years of being able to say the same thing.

Remembering who you are: it's the biggest challenge an expanding business ever has to face. Virgin Atlantic is now a quarter of a century old and has worked hard to keep its original essence. I recall at the time, looking around on the very first day, wondering if we would ever be able to keep this up – all this enthusiasm, all this laughter. I wondered if we'd get the chance to be truly different.

Then I remembered Herb Kelleher.

Herb set up Southwest Airlines in Texas in the 1970s, and for nearly forty years his airline has set the benchmark for successful no-frills aviation in the United States. Southwest built its business around two innovations: low fares, and outstanding customer service. Considering the woeful record of many of America's other airlines, this has always impressed me. Looking back, I think Kelleher's thinking made a big difference to how we approached things at our airlines, and particularly in Australia with Virgin Blue.

From day one, Herb and his executive colleague Colleen Barrett focused on developing the company's culture – a way of doing things that would sustain its founding values as the years went by.

We've already met Herb's dictum about hiring for attitude and training for skill. His other 'primary attitudes' are also Virgin's and my attitudes, through and through:

1. *Employees are number one. The way you treat your employees is the way they will treat your customers.*
2. *Think small to grow big.*

3. Manage in the good times for the bad times.

4. Irreverence is OK.

5. It's OK to be yourself.

6. Have fun at work.

7. Take the competition seriously, but not yourself.

8. Think of the company as a service organisation that happens to be in the airline business.

9. Do whatever it takes.

10. Always practise the Golden Rule, internally and externally.

The egalitarian spirit of Southwest Airlines has driven its success. Even in the first quarter of 2008, with a weak economy and soaring jet-fuel prices, it achieved record operating revenues – a staggering $2.53 billion – and its net income actually went up – by 30 per cent! – to $43 million. You don't achieve results like that without the loyalty of a huge number of happy and satisfied customers.

Herb and Colleen and the managers of Southwest understood, better than most in this industry, that employee satisfaction and customer service are two sides of the same coin. They have maintained their culture of customer service by employing people who are right for the business, and by giving them the tools and incentives to do their work well. Until recently, they had no serious rivals. Now, I'm proud to say, they've got Virgin America to contend with: a younger, fresher organisation. This is going to be a memorable tussle, but a tussle rather than a fight because the real enemies are the huge, heavily protected legacy carriers in the United States who have fed off barely disguised subsidies from Congress for nearly a decade whilst letting their planes age, service standards collapse, prices rise and people become demoralised.

*

Every once in a while, the vast Virgin Group has to remind itself who it is. This is never a one-man job. Stephen Murphy's arrival as chief executive was part of a major overhaul of Virgin's operations. Along with colleagues such as Gordon McCallum, Robert Samuelson, David Baxby, Frances Farrow, Patrick McCall, Mark Poole and Will Whitehorn, Stephen and the team have helped reshape and redefine where we wanted to be as a business.

Now, that paragraph probably struck fear into your heart. Restructuring is a pretty bloody process, right?

It can be. If your business has ossified to the point where you haven't a clue what's wrong, and in desperation you've called in a bunch of management consultants who charge by the hour, then, let's face it, your troubles began some while ago.

I'm not saying for a second that the Virgin Group finds structural changes painless. But we do have this advantage over most businesses: we're modular. We can shed limbs and split functions without turning the whole operation upside down. Over the years we've been criticised for turning ourselves into a ragbag of unconnected businesses. Our critics miss two important points. First, they're not assigning enough importance to the Virgin brand. (I'll try to explain our brand philosophy, and how it has helped us thrive in diverse businesses, in the next chapter.) The second point is: *so what?* Ending up as a ragbag of assorted companies now and again is no disadvantage to a group that does its housework regularly and keeps its businesses as small, independent and entrepreneurial as possible.

Circumstances and opportunities change. The world *changes, come to that. The only constant is change itself.* When I started in business, the standard one-liner about commercial short-sightedness was 'People will always need hats'. Oh, how we tittered, as we stuffed those LPs in big brown envelopes and lugged them to the post office. These days the line to raise a youthful sneer is probably 'People will always need rock albums'.

Companies aren't change-proof, and no company will last for ever. And in the Virgin Group particularly, they come and go. What's wrong with that? Companies do things. They are tools designed for a particular purpose – or they should be. If they are superseded, or surplus to requirement, we shed them. We try our level best not to shed the people, or the know-how, but the company itself is not something we allow ourselves to get too nostalgic about. When Virgin renews itself, critics who tut-tut at all the leaves falling to the ground have failed to spot the tree.

And in the mid-1990s and early 2000s, we did lose leaves. We lost whole branches. We began to look carefully at what worked for us and what didn't. We cooked up the Investment Advisory Committee – a more formal structure for considering fresh business projects and monitoring the performance of our existing businesses. (Dr Yes was peeved, but he bit his tongue.)

And not long after, on 14 February 2007, we had the chance to show what a leaner, more clear-headed Virgin Group could do. The combined company of NTL, Telewest and Virgin Mobile relaunched in the UK as Virgin Media, creating the largest Virgin company in the world.

Now, have you heard the story of the dog who chased the car? Chasing the car was great fun – but now that he's caught it, what the devil does he do with it? This was pretty much my dilemma as I contemplated Virgin Media's 10 million customers and 13,000 employees across the UK. Up till then I'd always thought of myself as a 'small is beautiful' kind of entrepreneur. Virgin Media was not by any measure small. It wasn't beautiful, either. There were acute issues that had to be addressed, and this would mean months of hard work. This time, James Kydd, Ashley Stockwell and our senior brand and customer service people were on hand to remind us who we were, reshaping the company so that it maintained and contributed to the Virgin brand.

The NTL part of our business, in particular, was in a very sorry state. We needed to make drastic changes to its levels of customer service. For one thing, the people dealing with complaints didn't seem that interested in helping people.

We found out why: it turned out that they were spending their entire working lives reading from scripts.

These went straight in the bin. We told our call-centre people to solve problems with one call if possible, and we reallocated resources to the front line to improve customer operations.

We wanted to keep things simple for the customer and for our own people, and it seemed to us that the best way of doing this was to let people just get on with their jobs. There was scepticism at first. What would happen if one of our customer-service people overstepped the mark? What if people started offering customers too much?

My response to that was pretty much 'Live and learn'. I don't think anyone should be criticised for being overly generous when handling a disgruntled customer. If one or two of our people got themselves into a tangle, it just meant that they'd do better next time.

In the airline business, you learn very quickly not to skimp on the goodwill gestures. They let people know that, whatever the difficulty, you're still working for them. Even better is quick, accurate information. As we know, 'quick' and 'accurate' almost *never* go together, but we do what we can, and in the meantime, our gestures go a long way to reassure some seriously inconvenienced people. Of course, families who've been waiting for many hours could be let into the business lounge. Yes, of course we can make you more comfortable: would you like a massage? You've been fantastic, and we'd like to say thank you: here's a flight upgrade for next time. None of this is in the service manual, because you can't dictate attitudes from on high. All you can do is hire the right people and empower them to sort things out as they happen.

If someone has paid you for something, and it goes wrong, being cagey or defensive will kill you stone dead. You will never see that customer again, nor their family, nor their friends. *If someone has a lousy experience at your hands, they will warn people.* The knock-on effect of this destroys businesses. If, on the other hand, you are able to sort out your customers' problems better than they expected, then they will be your loyal friend for life.

We began this chapter by discussing entrepreneurship, and we're finishing with thoughts about customer service. A curious combination, no?

I feel very strongly indeed that young, independently minded businesses can provide customers with great service: it's the monoliths and the business establishment that make customers' lives a misery. I think this because the values of the Virgin brand are all about customer service; we are focused on the customer in a way that most businesses aren't.

But I also want to make a wider point.

In the 1970s, when we set up Virgin Records, no one in the UK used the word 'entrepreneur' any more. Or if they did, they considered it something unsavoury. A businessman running a number of firms was seen as a 'chancer' – the television comic stereotype was Del Boy, the wheeler-dealer on the outside of the law, in *Only Fools and Horses*, or *Minder*'s Arthur Daley, the gin-drinking spiv played brilliantly by George Cole. In earlier days I was regularly dismissed as a 'Del Boy' myself (this always puzzled me; I thought I was more like Rodney). In fact, throughout history the entrepreneur has always been a favourite villain. From Ancient Greece to Shakespeare's *Merchant of Venice* right through to the film *Wall Street*, entrepreneurs represent 'money-making' and 'capitalism' – and in some sections of society those are still dirty words.

The UK media's view of business people has changed – but not nearly enough. Some elements of the British press still can't quite get their heads around the idea that business is a worthwhile pursuit, which actually provides most of the tax revenue, employment and wealth of the whole nation. Entrepreneurs have taken the risk in starting companies, innovating products and offering the services that make people's lives easier, better and safer.

As my friend Jon Butcher puts it, 'Entrepreneurs have literally destroyed poverty in the Western world as the rest of the world knows it, and as history knows it. No other social system can compete with the entrepreneurial free market system in terms of productivity, raising standards of living and creating permanent prosperity. Asia has exploded out of poverty in my lifetime thanks to entrepreneurs. Huge chunks of poverty should be taken out of Africa in the next ten years thanks to up-and-coming entrepreneurs. So capitalism actually works. Communism and true socialism are no longer taken seriously because they simply don't work. They actually hurt people. They've kept entire generations in poverty. They are disastrous though well-meaning systems that have ruined hundreds of millions of lives. Yet somehow there are elements of our culture that still associate profit-making with vice.'

Entrepreneurs are also the greatest philanthropists, from Andrew Carnegie in the nineteenth century to Bill Gates today. Carnegie, who made his vast fortune in the US steel industry, paid for almost every library in the Western world built in the nineteenth century, which brought about an educational revolution.

So, let me spell it out. Entrepreneurship is not about getting one over on the customer. It's not about working on your own. It's not about looking out for number one. It's not necessarily about making a lot of money. It is *absolutely not* about letting work take over your life. On the contrary, it's about turning what excites you in life into capital, so that you can do more of it and move forward with it. I think entrepreneurship is our natural state – a big adult word that probably boils down to something much more obvious like 'playfulness'. I believe that drudgery and clock-watching are a terrible betrayal of that universal, inborn entrepreneurial spirit.

For centuries – and certainly since the Industrial Revolution in the eighteenth century – industry has swallowed lives and, in turn, helped to give business a bad name. Men and women have had to conform to a mechanical model of work. They have been treated like cattle (literally, in many cases). Within my lifetime, upheavals in politics, science and technology have changed the nature of work, especially in the developed world. For some of us, it is our incredible good fortune that we are all having to think less like employees, and more like entrepreneurs. The era of 'jobs for life' is over – at last!

Inspire your people to think like entrepreneurs, and whatever you do, treat them like adults. The hardest taskmaster of all is a person's own conscience, so the more responsibility you give people, the better they will work for you.

For thirty-five years, the Virgin Group has steered clear of rote mediocrity and steamed full-speed ahead into a world of pleasurable scheming, spiked with the occasional cock-up. The way we have worked has allowed us to live full lives. I can't give you the formula for this, and you probably wouldn't follow it anyway. After all, you're having to respond to the circumstances you're in, while doing the job that you're doing. I hope this book will give you some ideas about how you can empower your employees – and empower yourself, come to that. But you really have to find the solutions that work for you.

Here is the good news: *the more you free your people to think for themselves, the more they can help you. You don't have to do this all on your own.*

Brand

Flying the Flag

When I was sixteen I was approached by a woman called Patricia Lambert who offered me £80,000 to sell *Student* – the magazine I had started at school – to IPC, now the Trinity Mirror stable of newspapers and magazines based in the UK.

It so happened that I had found a tiny island off Menorca which I was thinking of buying and living on. It was a beautiful place with one very small whitewashed house that had a loo which dropped its waste down the side of a cliff. Living in splendid isolation in the middle of paradise seemed like an attractive proposition at the time because, while our music mail-order business was taking off, running the magazine just got harder and harder. Until I'd sold the advertising I had no regular money to fund the printing and paper costs. It was edge-of-the-seat stuff at first but it had begun to wear me down.

IPC were not only offering me a lot of money; they wanted me to stay on as editor. *Student* wouldn't, strictly speaking, be my magazine any more, but I would get to keep a job I still enjoyed doing.

So I decided to accept, and I went along to lunch at IPC in Holborn, just off Fleet Street. They had all the directors around the table. And once we had shaken hands on the deal, I started to talk about my vision. I told the directors I wanted to set up Student holidays, a Student travel agency, Student record shops, Student health clubs – even a Student airline? I could see eyebrows being raised. After the lunch I got a call thanking me for coming – but the directors had changed their minds about the investment, cancelling the plan to buy my magazine. They were far too courteous to say so, but the writing was on the wall: they thought I was mad.

Many years later Patricia was good enough to write me a delightful letter telling me just how much they had been kicking themselves over the years as they watched Virgin stir up sector after sector, almost exactly as their young would-be magazine editor had predicted.

I suspect they were right in not dealing with me. IPC were and are in the publishing business. They are publishers. They know who they are, and they didn't need some kid, however promising, telling them all the other things they could be. The last thing they wanted was a wasp in the room, batting itself against their windows and getting more and more frustrated, and that, surely, is what I would have become.

Most businesses concentrate on one thing, and for the best of reasons: because their founders and leaders care about one thing, above all others, and they want to devote their lives to that thing. They're not limited in their thinking. They're focused.

The conventional wisdom at business school is that you stick with what you know. Of the top twenty brands in the world, nineteen ply a well-defined trade. Coca-Cola specialises in soft drinks, Microsoft's into computers, Nike makes sports shoes and gear.

The exception in this list is Virgin – and the fact that we're worth several billion dollars and counting really gets up the noses of people who think they know 'the rules of business' (whatever they are).

We're the only one of the top twenty that has diversified into a range of business activities, including airlines, trains, holidays, mobile phones, media – including television, radio and cable – the Internet, financial services and healthcare. And believe me when I say this really upsets people. I remember in July 1997 London's *Evening Standard* covered our advance into America with an article headlined 'WHEN BRAND STRETCHING STRETCHES CREDIBILITY'.

I think this says more about the business community generally than it says about Virgin. How far must we fly before pundits of one sort or another stop predicting our fiery descent? Our proposition isn't hard to understand: *we offer our customers a Virgin experience, and we make sure that this Virgin experience is a substantial and consistent one, across all sectors of our business.* Far from 'slapping our brand name' on a number of products, we carefully research the Achilles heels of different global industries, and only when we feel we can potentially turn an industry on its head, and fulfil our key role as the consumer's champion, do we move in on it. The financial services industry is an eloquent example. In three years, Virgin Direct acquired 200,000 investors and was managing £1.6 billion. As a result of its entry into the market, much of the rest of the industry brought their charges down too to compete.

Incredibly or not, Virgin has thrived by weaving its magic through many seemingly unrelated sectors. Between 2000 and 2003, Virgin created three new billion-dollar companies from scratch, in three different countries. Virgin Blue in Australia took 35 per cent of the aviation market and reduced fares dramatically. Virgin Mobile became the UK's fastest growing network. Virgin Mobile in America was America's fastest ever growing company, private or public. Our revenue per employee – $902,000 – is the best in the world, and we've got the highest customer satisfaction record too, with 95 per cent of our five million customers recommending us to a friend. Over the last thirty-five years we at Virgin have created more billion-dollar companies in more sectors than any other company.

And right now, as everyone is battening down the hatches and preparing for the twenty-first century's first really big global recession, Virgin turns out to be ready for the storm as well. Because its risks are spread, the failure of one part – even a major part – will not ruin the whole. (Imagine if we hadn't diversified and if we had just stuck with the record and music industry, which today faces huge challenges because of the digital download revolution – we might well have disappeared!)

So here's the question: if Virgin has more fun when times are good, and weathers well when times are bad, why doesn't every company try to 'do a Virgin'? And why are the business teachers still telling young entrepreneurs to stick to what they know?

Well, I think the business teachers are *right*. You *should* focus on what you know. You *should* also focus on what gets you up in the morning. And for most people, that means you *should* focus on one core business.

The odd thing about Virgin – and this is what people often have difficulty with – is that Virgin's particular focus made it *absolutely imperative* that it diversified into many businesses. Contrary to appearances, Virgin is as focused as any great company. Its oddness comes from what it focuses *on*. We might have hit upon the exception that proves the rule: our customers and investors relate to us more as an idea or philosophy than as a company.

Virgin's success upsets people because it seems to contradict the wise rule that you should stick to what you love. Where's its focus? Where's its centre? *Something* must be getting that Branson bloke out of bed in the morning – but what the devil is it? We thought it was music, but then it was air travel, which we sort of understood because of his ballooning, but then it was trains, money and mobile phones, and what is it now? Healthcare? Space? Oh *help*!

I've never made any secret of what gets me out of bed in the morning. *It's the challenge. It's the brand.* Maybe it's something to do with my surname. I remember a journalist from the *Daily Telegraph* magazine did some research into the root of my name and discovered that, yes, 'Branson' was originally 'Brandson': my distant ancestors made their living branding cattle!

For me, the brand is central. Whenever I say this to people, however, an awful lot of them feel their eyes misting over. 'What the devil does he mean, *the brand*?'

I'll try to explain. Let's start simply with a quick sketch of what a brand can do.

IPC, as we know, publishes magazines. What I want you to do is name three of its titles. If you're in the industry, you'll have no problem reeling off a dozen. (They're very successful.) If you're not in the industry, you won't have a clue. Why would you? The IPC brand means plenty to the industry, but nothing to the punter. The punter wants the flavour, tone and content of the magazine, not its purse-holder. The punter cares about the magazine's brand; the owner's brand would merely get in the way.

Who published the last novel you read? Which production company made the DVD you watched last night? You probably don't know, the companies know you don't know, and you know what? – nobody minds.

Brands exist as a means of communicating what to expect from a product or service – or to highlight the family likeness between different products and services. An established brand on a new product is a guarantee that what you're getting will be, in its own way, like something you've enjoyed before. This is not always a good thing. Readers of Mills & Boon romances may want the same kind of story again and again; families look forward to taking their kids to see the new Pixar movie, regardless of whether it's about animals, toys or cars. On the whole, though, novelty and discovery count for a lot in the entertainment sector, and the last thing you want to do is stick some galumphing great label over everything you do, suggesting to your audience that your new thing is just like your old thing.

At the other end of the spectrum – perched in splendid isolation in the far, far infrared – there is Virgin. The Virgin brand tells you that using *this* credit card is rather like using *this* airline, which, in turn, is rather like using *this* health spa, and listening to *this* record, and paying into *this* pension fund.

What's the family resemblance? What resemblance could there be between these diverse goods and services?

Pretty obviously, it has something to do with the customer, because when you look at the range of things we're involved in, the customer is about the only factor common to all of them.

And that really is all there is to it. The Virgin brand is a guarantee that you'll be treated well, that you'll get a high-quality product which won't dent your bank balance, and you'll get more fun out of your purchase than you expected – *whatever it is*.

You see, what gets me up in the morning is the customer, and the idea of giving the customer a good time. No other brand has become a 'way-of-life' brand the way Virgin has. And we achieved it, not by clinically deciding one day to become a way-of-life brand, but simply by following our appetites and the things we were curious about. I've always and continually been interested in learning new things and, equally important, I've always wanted to share what I learned with other people.

Should you follow the 'Virgin formula', and focus your company around the customer's experience? Probably not. Not unless your heart's really in it. Not unless, like me, you wake up of a morning saying to yourself, 'Let's give people some *fun*!' Obviously, I hope you care for your customers. But I can't tell you that your company should be *about* customers. What your business is about is up to you.

The Virgin brand came into existence gradually, to reflect what I was fundamentally interested in. And to my own surprise, it wasn't publishing magazines; it wasn't even music. My driving force, I realise now, was *finding new ways to give people a good time* – ideally, in places where they were least expecting it. Like airports.

While the brand has its roots right back in the seventies with my beliefs and spirit, I think Virgin Atlantic has done more to capture and articulate what the brand stands for and personifies to consumers. Many other Virgin companies have adopted those powerful values of innovation, honesty, caring, value and fun. So I believe it's about great customer service and giving people a good time.

This is why Virgin wears its sense of humour on its sleeve. *We want to inform and entertain people.* You don't have to be a Virgin customer to enjoy our adverts and our publicity stunts. We have found over the years that giving people a good time, and making them feel like they're in on the joke, has been better for the brand than any amount of complex campaigning.

I'll give you a quick example: on Virgin Atlantic flights we had these beautifully designed salt and pepper pots. At least, we had them when we took off. By the time we landed, most of them had disappeared. Our passengers were swiping them and using them at their own dinner tables. What to do? We decided to make a joke of it. At the bottom of each pot we stamped the words 'Pinched from Virgin Atlantic'. We turned an embarrassment into a piece of cheeky loss-leader promotion. We got people onside by bringing them in on the joke. In itself, this was a fairly trivial matter; repeated across our whole group, our fun-loving attitude makes a tremendous difference to our business.

Irreverent humour is one of Virgin's brand values, and this has to do with our wanting to be honest about the ups and downs of our business and to share what we think with the people who matter most to us – our customers. The people who read our adverts are the same people who read about our tussles, our setbacks and our mistakes. So why would we want to pretend the real world doesn't affect us? Everybody knows of our run-ins with BA over the years. When the world's press gathered to watch BA erect their London Eye Ferris wheel on London's South Bank and we heard they were having technical problems, we scrambled our airship. The banner trailing behind it read: '*BA can't get it up.*' We also had a lot of fun when we introduced onboard massages on Virgin Atlantic, running an advertisment in the newspapers saying '*BA doesn't give a shiatsu!*'

When Sydney Airport Corporation (owned by a division of the very successful Macquarie Bank) decided arbitrarily to raise their landing charges, Virgin Blue's CEO Brett Godfrey and I decided to put a slogan on the side of our planes and on the massive billboards lining the road to the airport. '*Macquarie. What a load of bankers!*' It made headlines, and it made a point: the bankers seemed to be after easy cash at the expense of the low-cost market. Eventually Macquarie agreed to renegotiate the fee question. I dressed up as a native American Indian, smoking a pipe of peace, and buried the hatchet with them. (Literally – it's still there somewhere, under the tarmac!) It was one of those 'No hard feelings, mate' moments, and I think the Australian public enjoyed our irreverent approach. Interestingly, as a result, we've now become partners in a number of companies. *Befriending one's enemy is a good rule for business – and life.*

Too many companies want their brands to reflect some idealised, perfected image of themselves. As a consequence, their brands acquire no texture, no character and no public trust. At Virgin, we certainly talk ourselves up, but we are genuinely a real company doing real work in the real world – not some sort of alien visitation.

It may be that Virgin has grown up to be one model of what a modern company should be. It may be that, by making the customer the focus of its business, and by giving good customer service a brand name, Virgin has created something genuinely new in the business world – something future generations can emulate and build upon.

Past a certain age, we all want to be Moses, leading our people into the promised land. Then I look at myself in the mirror in the morning after a heavy night and I think: Oh, Richard, get over it!

Virgin may simply be *odd* – an accident of history. I like fun. I began work in a decade that prized fun. People associate me with that decade and the feel-good factor has stuck with me ever since. Virgin's been a rallying point for that spirit of fun – but would Virgin have worked at any other period of history? Would it work now? The bottom line is, we'll never know.

Good brands reflect the histories of the time and the group of people that made them. They cannot be easily copied. They cannot be recycled. A brand is like an artist's signature (in Virgin's case our brand is literally an artist's signature!) What you make of your brand is up to you. While I hope and expect that there are lessons in this chapter for you, I cannot tell you what your brand should do. What I will do is ask that you take it seriously – as seriously as a painter treats the signatures on his canvases.

A brand should reflect what you can do. You have to deliver, faultlessly and for all time, whatever your brand promises, so it's better to make your offering sound witty and innovative than to pretend you're more than you are. *Get the brand right from the start, by being honest with yourself about what it is you're offering.* A brand will eventually date you, so I think you're better off intelligently evolving it as we have always done than tritely updating it. These rather trivial rebrandings generate a lot of fairly funny adverse publicity, and with good reason: they're a sort of corporate comb-over – and about as effective.

This, anyway, was our philosophy when we came up with the name 'Virgin' – and I had to respond vigorously to the Registrar of Companies Office in the UK when they said the name Virgin was too rude to register. Part of that response consisted of proving that 'Virgin' had been used as a ship's name without complaint as far back as 1699 and indeed one such ship was recorded as having docked at Cadiz on 26 April 1699 in the May edition of the *London Gazette*. It was a bit risqué, I suppose – a bit of fun. But the word wasn't simply plucked out of the air. It reflected the fact that every business we began, we started from scratch. We've been 'virgins' in almost every new business field we've entered. To my mind the name Virgin was the *opposite* of rude: it meant pure, in its original condition, unexploited and never used. Virgin referred to us, because we were all virgins in business. Registering the brand was critical. Defending it in every legal jurisdiction in the world has been expensive. But it's all proved essential for Virgin's success.

A brand's meanings are acquired over time. Some meanings will be the product of serious discussions and years of directed and dedicated effort. Some meanings will just stick to the brand, whether you like it or not. Remember, a brand always means *something*, and ultimately, you can control the meaning of your brand only through what you deliver to the customer.

If I describe to you Virgin's early years, you'll be able to see how the Virgin brand came to mean what it does today. I would like to say that all the things Virgin means to people were the product of masterful business planning. They weren't. Luckily, we did a good job, so the labels that stuck to us were generally positive, whether we intended them or not.

Immediately, however, I am confronted by the fairly frightening fact that I will have to explain to younger readers what music meant to my generation. How else are they going to understand Virgin Records, our first company?

I believe music isn't as central to most young people's lives today as it was back in the 1970s. There's a lot of brilliant music around today – I think about KT Tunstall and Amy Winehouse for starters – but looking back, the 1970s was a unique time, and people then had an incredible passion for rock music.

Partly, it was about choice. In those days, living in England, we didn't have DVDs and mobile phones, and we didn't have an array of TV channels – only BBC and ITV – and computer games were the playthings of superpowers, who used them to target their deadly arsenals of nuclear weapons. So for young people most of their time and energy was spent on music – and that meant buying records. It was the one luxury kids had. Anticipating a new Led Zeppelin, Yes or Queen album kept us going for weeks.

In the 1970s and 80s, album releases were monumental events; and we built a business on the back of them. I think there are some interesting business lessons that still apply today from the creation of Virgin Records. After all, the progressive-rock music business was then in its infancy, and Virgin Records was there from the start.

When we started Virgin Records, mainstream crooner Andy Williams and avant-garde rocker Frank Zappa were in the same alphabetical A–Z racks in Woolworths. While the 1960s had witnessed an eruption in pop music and rhythm and blues groups – led by the Beatles and the Rolling Stones – the old record labels run by big business still dominated. There was no discounting of music, and the industry that existed was very conservative and stuffy. It was presided over by middle-aged guys who listened to string quartets. Most recording studios were sterile and expensive factories set up for only a few recording takes, and music shops with their perforated hardboard sound booths were stuck in the 1950s. There was little excitement attached to buying music. And there were only a few radio shows where you could hear decent rock music.

In the spring of 1970, we decided to create a mail-order service that sold the kind of music we liked: a record company that was outrageous, irreverent and long-haired. That flavour established Virgin, sowing the seeds of what it has become today. From day one, young people identified with it because it was so different.

As well as the American magazine *Rolling Stone*, there were two British weekly music newspapers when we began. *Melody Maker* was a serious rock and pop paper, with reviews that also covered folk music and jazz. Although it was a must-read, the writers were rather worthy and full of their own self-importance. And there was *New Musical Express*, or *NME*, which was more pop-orientated and somehow stuck in the sixties. Then a new arrival, *Sounds*, with its tagline 'Music is the Message', came along.

Sounds was first printed on 10 October 1970 and I was on the phone to the advertising department to secure some cut-price adverts.

I've always believed in trying to get into a new publication that is trying to break the mould. *Sounds* was a magazine that mattered for our success. It was right in our marketplace. It sold 200,000 copies in its first week and gave the opposition, *Melody Maker* and *New Musical Express*, a bit of a fright. *Sounds*' first rock album chart was dominated by Black Sabbath's *Paranoid*, the Rolling Stones' *Get Yer Ya Ya's Out*, *Led Zeppelin II*, *Deep Purple in Rock* and *Cosmo's Factory* by Creedence Clearwater Revival. These would be the albums that our mail-order business would sell. Unfortunately, there were some dreadful anomalies in the charts too, such as *The World of Mantovani*. His world would be banned from Virgin Records. So too was Andy Williams.

For this start-up business there was a basic flaw – we didn't have any credit. We didn't have any references either, which meant the record companies wouldn't supply us. So we took out adverts in the music press and I managed to get a deal whereby I could pay for them a month in arrears. We didn't have any records either, so we went along to Ray Larone's company in Notting Hill Gate. We'd buy them from him at a discount and then mail them out to our customers. That way, we had the cash in from the public before we bought the records and paid for the advertising. This is how we got the business up and running.

When I hear of today's entrepreneurs launching new businesses by putting all their debt on their credit cards, I think that this pretty much parallels what we were doing with Virgin Records. I'm not going to sit here and say, 'Don't do it.' But if you do do it, you have my sympathy. Self-funding your first business is cripplingly difficult.

Ray's tiny shop soon became one of the biggest record sellers in England. The record companies' lorries would turn up with piles of packages of records, and we would have a lorry outside the back of his shop and then take them off to our office, which was in the crypt under a church in Bayswater.

From the first, our image and sales pitch were vital assets. (We had precious few others.) During the early days in South Wharf Road, we all contributed, but John Varnom was the one who made a difference. He was off-the-wall, utterly unreliable, and very creative. He wrote our adverts in a Victorian-gothic style of self-parody but also an early Virgin brand-message of the future: that quality could also mean value for money.

> *'There must be something wrong with them.'*
> *'There isn't.'*
> *'They must be old, bent, cracked, wizened, split, warped, spoilt, scratched and generally too hideous to contemplate.'*
> *'They aren't.'*
> *'They can't be smooth, glistening, perfect, unblemished, miraculous, black and shiny like those you get in the shops.'*
> *'They are.'*
> *'But surely there must be some difference, some gap, abyss, divide, chasm, canyon or other unusual feature?'*
> *'There is.'*
> *'What is it then?'*
> *'They cost less.'*

We all rolled up our sleeves, stuffing brown packages with cut-price Virgin mail-order albums by Led Zeppelin, Pink Floyd, Jimi Hendrix and the Rolling Stones. We were all paid the same, £20 a week, and it all had a very hippy, communal feel. 'Five to fifteen bob off any album on any label' – that was our sales pitch. And we were now working flat out on the mail-order business to cope with demand. The record companies realised we were the mystery behind the huge success of Ray's little record shop – and so they extended credit to us directly.

But we weren't making any money. Over the years I've met a lot of old customers who were in on a scam. Irate people would phone up or write a letter and say they had never received their rock album. We had no proof that it had gone out because in our office it was all so chaotic, and proper accounting methods were unheard of. So we would send out another album. Our profit margin was so tight that doing this regularly – and we did do it regularly – was wiping out any of the money we made. This was one of the biggest business lessons I learned. *Turnover can be huge, but it is the profit margin that matters.*

Still, the Virgin Records brand was getting noticed. Typical sales were several thousand LPs each week. It all had potential. Then disaster struck, and here I learned another key fact about running a business: try to have a plan B.

In October 1970, the postmen and women of Britain began a bitter dispute for more pay. The strike lasted forty-four long and desperate days for us – and our business dried up. We needed to diversify the brand. Fast.

We took out adverts in the music press. A half-page on 6 February 1971 announced that we had now opened a small shop at 24 Oxford Street. I'd managed to secure a decent short-term deal on the rent of the first floor of a three-storey shop, next to a secretarial college, and upstairs from NU Sounds.

To combat the downturn we needed to get people into our shop. We increased the advertising campaign with '*A step-by-step guide to Virgin Records' new joint in Oxford Street*'. The puns continued – '*They are no dopes at Virgin Records. That's because all our customers are cool. They know a swell joint when they see one.*' We offered more than records; we had coffee, cassette tapes, posters and headphones, all within thirty seconds of Tottenham Court Road tube station. Some reckon that our staff sold even more than this, but I don't think I can comment about what they did in their spare time.

By the end of 1971, we were buying full back-page adverts declaring we were: The Firstest, Bestest, Cheapest. Another advert began: '*Ha, ha, ha, ha. This is our managing director giving a customer money. Chap tried to pay full price for a record.*'

In some ways not a lot has changed. In 2008, if you're sitting on a crowded tube train on the Central line in London, you can look up and read our advertising for Virgin Media and it still carries the same tone of gentle irreverence. Even in the early days we were promoting convenience and customer choice – only in a different dimension.

Back in 1971, someone had a bright idea. We should open a recording studio, too. Tom Newman, one of the original crew at Virgin Records, originally suggested we set up a four-track recording studio in the crypt. Meanwhile, I'd met George Martin, the legendary producer of the Beatles albums, to do an interview for a new edition of *Student*. When I told him of my plans, he said that four-track was out of date and that modern recording now needed at least eight-track equipment. I told Tom to flog the four-track we'd already bought and look for an eight-track. We'd spent £1,350. I was learning an expensive business lesson about getting the best equipment you could possibly afford.

By the time of my twenty-first birthday I had a magazine, a mail-order business and now I was contemplating setting up a recording studio. We were £11,000 in debt after the first year from the record business and I was struck down by an ulcer. The doctor advised me to take some time out. Tom Newman and I thought moving our studio to the country might be an option. It would be better for my health at least. I bought a copy of *Country Life* and saw an advert for an old English manor house at Shipton on Cherwell. It looked ideal. I was bowled over the minute I clapped eyes on the place. I desperately wanted to buy it and hatched plans for a 16-track studio. The bank agreed to give me a loan and I bought the Manor on 25 March 1971.

In October 1971, as we advertised waterbeds for sale in our shops, there was an extra little note on our ads: '*We have a quiet studio in the country now, so if you're going to make a sound and you want to relax when you do it, ring us.*' The studio was ready to rock. And it did.

The recording studio began to attract the kind of musicians we liked to hear. The decision to make it a 16-track studio was imperative, as bands were becoming more sophisticated. Instead of simple bass, drums, guitar and vocals there was now more dubbing and overlaying of different sounds and textures. We soon realised we would need to have a 32-track, 20-channel sound desk to meet the increasing demand, as recording technology and the evolution of keyboard synthesisers allowed new forms of musical expression and way-out sounds. We brought in leading sound specialists Westlake Audio from Los Angeles to design the studio – with Dolby sound – and bought only the latest kit. The magic of the Manor was that it was a place where the artists could be relaxed and hang out after coming out of a studio session. It was a stimulating place to stay and we kept the wine cellar stocked up and always went with the flow. If a band wanted a wild party or a blowout, then it was fine with us. That's what helped the juices flow. Since then, throughout our businesses, I have always insisted that Virgin try to create these special places or rooms where people can become inspired and create their best work.

Almost all of the biggest names in rock and pop music carved their reputations in that studio. The Manor taught me how to run a business and handle creative people. I also learned that not everyone gets what they truly deserve in life. I listened to some musicians with a modicum of talent who got a few lucky breaks; others with talent seeping out from every pore who simply didn't make it. I've sat drinking with people who have abused their gifts – and others who have made absolutely the most of some pretty dubious talent.

It is well documented that Mike Oldfield's debut album, *Tubular Bells*, was a breakthrough into the big time for the burgeoning Virgin empire. Mike was (and still is) a genius. But he was also an incredibly hard and fastidious worker – and that's something that takes you a long way in life. I remember first hearing an early tape of his material on our houseboat and being captivated by its haunting beauty and complexity. It was mind-blowing that a fifteen-year-old played all of these instruments so beautifully. We tried to get some of the record companies interested but they all had cloth ears and the dinosaur A&R executives turned him down.

So one afternoon in the pub, I said to our team: 'Let's do it ourselves. Let's set up our own record company and release Mike as one of our first LPs on our own Virgin Record label.'

Everyone thought I'd had one glass too many. We were still primarily a mail-order business, not a record company. But I persevered. I asked Mike for a list of the instruments he needed and went off to Charing Cross Road and rented them all: drums, synthesisers, guitars and tubular bells. We arranged for Mike to have time in the recording studio, between bookings, in the spring of 1973. He worked night and day, playing all the instruments himself, then sat at the mixing desk with Tom Newman to fine-tune the recording. I had never witnessed someone who listened and concentrated so hard or with such acute attention to acoustic detail.

Our decision to distribute the record ourselves was shrewd. But it was by no means certain at the time that the gamble would pay off. Virgin Records was a tiny business and it lacked the clout and the distribution of other major players.

Simultaneously, we were releasing Gong's *Radio Gnome Invisible* and we were promoting an avant-garde German rock band called Faust. (In typical Virgin Records style, we were giving away the album, *The Faust Tapes*, for 48p – an album for the price of a single.) But Gong and Faust were to be mere musical footnotes compared with *Tubular Bells*. Chris Blackwell, who ran Island Records – the company nearest to our way of thinking – loved Mike's music and offered to distribute it for us, and even offered to take it off our hands for a substantial profit.

It was tempting but we decided to do it all ourselves. It was a game-changing decision and it was incredibly bold. I'm always apt to take the greater risk: *a bigger risk for a large chunk of the upside*. That's what I learned then, and I still apply a version of this in business today. It might have been sensible to let Island do all the grunt work:

the advertising, marketing and delivery to the record shops. But I felt that we had placed our faith in Mike, and should do this ourselves.

In June 1973, John Peel played the record on his late-night Radio 1 show, *Top Gear*. This was the first time the BBC disc jockey had ever played a whole side of an LP.

The next morning the phone rang off the hook with people wanting to lay their hands on the album. It never stopped ringing.

John Peel was hugely influential – and so too were the music press. The power of the print medium has always played a major part in building the Virgin brand. But I began to understand and appreciate this fully only during the summer of 1973. While the Gong and Faust reviews were lukewarm, Mike Oldfield's were sizzlingly hot.

The album remained in the charts for five years, selling two million copies in the UK alone. Worldwide this figure was nearer 10 million.

In November 1972, aged twenty-two, I was speaking to my girlfriend when I penned one of my first lists.

1. Learn to fly.
2. Look after me/you/boat.
3. Entertain everybody with me.
4. Invite nice people back.
5. Start getting the small house together at the Manor.
6. Start buying odds and sods for the Manor.
7. Work with me on projects/sort me out.
8. More shops to be found.

But despite these ambitions it was obvious we were still a small company thrashing around. Most of us were still in our early twenties. We needed professional help, and I began a search for a proper accountant in 1973. I penned the advert myself:

Virgin Records have, within three years, built up seventeen shops, two recording studios, a large export company, an import

> *company, a publishing company, an agency, a management*
> *company, licences in every country in the world, a successful*
> *record company and a friendly staff of 150 people. Virgin Records*
> *don't have a shit-hot accounts department.*

Virgin Records grew to become the largest independent record label in the world. And, in 1992, after our abortive time on the stock market in 1987, we sold it to EMI for a billion dollars.

We sailed pretty close to the wind on several occasions in the early days. We just about delivered on our promises, but it was a struggle. Given my time again, though, I'm not sure I would make any changes to the major decisions we took. We were feeling our way into what the brand could deliver. We were waking up to the idea that Virgin's interests lay less in our own enthusiasm for any one business, and more in giving our customers a reason to be enthusiastic about the various things that we did. This, I believe, is why the Virgin model is so devilishly hard for start-ups to copy. Unless you're working in a magical industry to start with – and music in the 1970s was certainly magical – it's hard to see how you can win such loyalty and fellow feeling from your customers as you develop and expand.

That's not to say it can't be done. But the Virgins of the future won't look like anything we ever did. They'll emerge from the gaming industry, or the social-networking sector, or some area quite unknown to me and my generation. They'll look contemporary, they'll look odd, they'll thrill the kids, scare their parents, and they'll take everyone by surprise.

Emma, a sixteen-year-old girl, can't afford a mobile phone contract. She's just left school and has started in a hairdressing salon. She isn't earning a lot but she wants to keep up with her friends. She enjoys flicking through the celeb mags, watching *Friends*, likes Madonna, Janet Jackson and MC Hammer, and she chats regularly to Mark, her steady boyfriend, who's slightly older. He's just landed a labouring job with a building contractor, and he supports a top-flight football club, though he can't afford a season ticket. He enjoys a few pints of lager with his mates. He likes rap and hip hop and wants a heavy sound system for a souped-up Toyota, once he passes his driving test. It's the 1990s. The big phone companies aren't too interested in Emma and Mark – but we are.

Our entry into the mobile phone business remains to this day one of our brand's finest achievements. By offering prepay phones to young people, we were offering a product that was manifestly not a rip-off, to customers everyone else was ignoring. This proposition harnessed the brand values Virgin had acquired in the 1970s and launched them, through a new medium, at a new generation. This was the moment the Virgin brand went truly 'mobile', transferring, almost seamlessly, not simply from one sector to another, but – even more remarkably – from one age demographic to another.

We love starting new businesses in unfamiliar sectors, and later in the chapter I'll tell you how our 'branded market venture capital' model really ticks. This business of leaping generations, however, is something of a miracle to me, and I'm not entirely sure how much of it is design and how much is dumb luck. The fact is, our brand has managed to straddle a couple of generations and is well on the way to capturing the imagination of a third. Market research shows that the Virgin brand is the most admired by parents as well as their children. As I get older, the challenge is going to be to ensure that the next generation admire the brand, so that we get three generations enjoying what we do. By then, the power of seventies nostalgia will be expended – and we'll discover whether the Virgin brand really is timeless!

Our adventures in mobile telephony began in Japan. I was on a visit, and while I was there I asked some young people what the latest thing was. They proudly showed me their mobile phones. The Japanese were streets ahead of the mobile game and NTT DoCoMo, a spin-off of Nippon Telecom, had launched mobile phones with limited Internet access. The enthusiasm with which the young people I met had greeted DoCoMo's online games provided me with a clear idea of where the mobile phone was heading. NTT DoCoMo, Japan's largest cellular firm, was the first to get a mass-market Internet-enabled phone on to the market. We needed to be in this game, too.

Back in the nineties I was becoming acutely aware that our kudos with young people was declining as my own generation was growing older. The kids we once sold records to were buying holidays, pensions, financial services and healthcare. That was OK by us – we sold all these things. But what about their children? Mobile phones – and text messaging – were a booming market. For 16- to 24-year-olds, these things were becoming like an extra limb. From a marketing point of view, therefore, the mobile phone gave us the opportunity to re-establish Virgin in the youth market. We launched first in the UK in 1999.

We knew we had a great product, and we knew how to get it out there. We got our pay-as-you-go vouchers into places where young people found them easy to buy. We courted WH Smith's, Sainsbury's, Tesco, Texaco and BP petrol stations.

But we still had to get young people's attention.

James Kydd, Virgin Mobile's advertising guru, didn't have a generous budget to spend on building the brand. (Mind you, we once asked him to go head-to-head with Coca-Cola, pitting a £4 million budget against Coke's £400 million.) In the mobile battle, the competition was split between four companies – Vodafone, BT Cellnet, One2One and Orange – and so the hill James had to climb *was* a hill and not, as before, Mount Everest. We reckoned the money stacked against him was in a ratio of about 3:1. James told me that 3:1 was doable. I gave him £4 million for the launch.

James aimed specifically at our target market. He found good news stories that the tabloid newspapers and other media would report. He used the emerging Internet channels and viral networks to build a buzz and create a lot of fun.

At the same time, we had to remain in the public's eye as the 'consumer's champion', so we took the other players head-on, challenging Hans Snook, Orange's chief executive, to put his money where his mouth was when he promised to match our tariffs. He didn't. Then Virgin Mobile took some swipes at Charles Dunstone's Carphone Warehouse, urging him to recommend our phones. Charles, a great sailing and skiing buddy of mine, was big enough to laugh it off, but I think our in-the-face campaign caused him some embarrassment at the time.

Vodafone was middle-aged, BT was in decline, One2One was cheap and Orange – regarded as the gold standard – was leaning too much towards the business market. So, when Virgin Mobile addressed the youth market, it had the field pretty much to itself. It filled the space with the kind of attitude, wit and irreverence we had cultivated since our early days at Virgin Records. We offered a blind-dating service which people loved – we even gave them the option of receiving a phone call half an hour into the date so they could make an excuse and bail out – 'So sorry, I have to go – my dog has died!'

Our television adverts were a work of genius. The creatives came up with the idea of our 'Devil Makes Work For Idle Thumbs' series, featuring a string of superstars including Busta Rhymes, Wyclef Jean and Kelis. Each star would have to be prepared to have a laugh at their own expense. We wanted them to be funny. They quickly became a cult: and we were back in tune with urban youth.

The adverts, created by Ben Priest and directed by Bryan Buckley, were sharp and funny and set a cool tone for the business. From early on we knew it was working. A key statistic for us was the acronym ARPU, average revenue per user. This rose and rose until we had the highest ARPU in the prepay industry. By the first quarter of 2003, Virgin signed up more customers than O2, Orange, T-Mobile and Vodafone combined.

Then in May 2004, as we celebrated our 4,000,000th customer, we signed up 23-year-old Christina Aguilera.

The advert, shot in Los Angeles, had her make fun of her own relationship with the paparazzi. Christina is waiting in a plush record company office and her thumb idly moves to the button which operates the 'up' and 'down' motion of the chair on which she is sitting. Her rising and falling in the chair is viewed and misconstrued by construction workers on the other side of the street, who think they have stumbled across the celebrity sex scandal of the year. We knew we'd hit the money when real-life paparazzi snuck in to take pictures of her during filming, generating lurid false reports about the advert before it was even cold in the can. Thanks, lads – you all helped raise our profile!

Publicity is absolutely critical. You have to get your brand out and about, particularly if you're a consumer-oriented brand. You have to be willing to use yourself, as well as your advertising budget, to get your brand on the map. A good PR story is infinitely more effective than a full-page ad, and a damn sight cheaper. I have an absolute rule. If CNN rings me up and wants to do an interview with me, I'll drop everything to do it. Turning down the chance to tell the world about your brand seems just crazy to me, and it astonishes me that the very people who sign off on multimillion-dollar advertising budgets – the CEOs and presidents of huge corporations – are the very same people who hide behind their PAs and turn away all journalists at the door.

There can be no doubt that Virgin Mobile succeeded by delivering on the promise of a unique brand: a brand that appeals not to any particular demographic, but to an attitude of mind. The Virgin brand is about irreverence and cheek. It values plain speaking. It is not miserly, or mercenary. It has a newcomer's voice – and in a world of constant technical innovation, the voice of a company that's coming fresh to things is a voice people find oddly reassuring. It's a brand that says, 'We're in this together.' I think James Kydd did a brilliant job of realising those values for a new generation. Can it be done again? I think so. There's nothing particularly 'seventies' or 'nineties' about the values I've just listed. The attitude is timeless. It's human. I like to think it's pretty acute, psychologically. But I'll concede that if my son Sam, or daughter Holly, decide to join the business – and I would never want to push them – it would make our job easier, because then we could have younger faces launching the products, rather than their middle-aged dad!

Before I tell you about Virgin Blue – a recent big adventure for the Virgin brand – now is probably as good a time as any to talk about me. I mean Richard Branson the public celebrity (or mascot, or scapegoat – I've been all three in my time).

A large part of the Virgin story has been my willingness to be a central character in our publicity. I don't know how many different outfits I've dressed up in during my business life – probably more than Laurence Olivier. I can thank Jackie McQuillan, my director of Media Relations, for a great deal of them. Over the last fifteen years she's dreamed up many costumes and hair-raising stunts for me – from shaving off my beard and donning a wedding dress, to dressing up as an Indian prince and jumping off a building in Mumbai, while playing a drum, to launch our first ever business in India! I believe the public has enjoyed the kind of visual stunts we've pulled over the years. The reason they're enjoyable is that they're very carefully thought through. They have to be witty. They have to make people smile. They have to engage the mind as well as the eyes. They have to work in the telling as well as the witnessing. And they absolutely must convey the qualities of the brand as well as the message. My near-naked appearance in Times Square in July 2002 is a good example: to unveil our partnership with MTV, a division of Viacom, I wore only a cellphone to cover my nether regions. 'I'm here to physically prove that Virgin Mobile USA's national cellphone service has nothing to hide,' I said.

And as we'll see, Virgin's reputation as a have-a-go company has had one unforeseen but highly valuable consequence: when things go wrong with our oh-so-carefully rehearsed stunts, they still convey the brand!

But is it constructive to have so much attention and focus on the boss of a business? It can occasionally work against you. As I'll explain later, all that nonsense in the media about my 'sweetheart deal' with the British prime minister Gordon Brown, just because we were on the same plane, did our bid for the troubled Northern Rock bank no favours. But all in all I think the positives outweigh the negatives. My own high-profile adventures have not just highlighted the brand, they've personified it. I've used my success in business to throw myself into some truly wonderful adventures. The speedboating and the ballooning were great for the brand because they were real challenges, undertaken in a spirit that reflected our brand values. And they were enormous fun. World-record attempts are not everyone's cup of tea, and wouldn't add value to every brand. The trick is to find your own way to personify your own brand values; I think you will feel the advantage.

In general, the media has been extremely fair to the Virgin brand. We've been able to enliven the news, features and comment pages with some of our challenges – and because we have so many consumer-facing businesses there's always a regular stream of news stories to whet the media's appetite. Our press people ensure that journalists are invited along to every product launch and are kept up to speed with our plans. For any business building a consumer brand, speaking to journalists is part of the deal. I've met a lot of business people who shy away from public attention, but I feel the Virgin Group has had a strong relationship with the media over many years. Besides, I started out as a fledgling journalist with *Student*; I enjoy the company of editors, journalists, writers and public relations people.

Having said that, I think it is important for the public relations people to build the profile of individual companies and their leaders within the wider group. Steve Ridgway is the chief executive of Virgin Atlantic Airways and he remains in the background – usually with a smile on his face – when I'm making an announcement or undertaking a media stunt. But Steve is also happy to appear in feature articles and business trade magazines that are relevant to promote the airline. That's the way it should be and I'm pleased that all the chief executives of the Virgin Group companies work hard at promoting the brand.

I was jet-lagged after a fourteen-hour flight and taken straight off the plane. A whirling helicopter was waiting for me on the tarmac at the private aviation centre. I thought for a moment I might be hitching a quick trip to my hotel, but I was mistaken.

One of the Virgin team put a harness around me and over my head, strapped me in tight, and clipped me to a wire rope. I was about to get a bumper adrenalin rush which blew away any lingering yawns from the flight.

My arrival into Australia was bum-tightening. It was the closest I've ever been to flying like a bird. I can assure you it's not the normal route for our Virgin airline passengers arriving at the Kingsford Smith airport and heading to downtown Sydney. I was hauled off the ground, dangling 100 feet underneath the helicopter as we rose higher and higher above the skyline. It was a spectacular way to arrive, like Peter Pan flying over London. Instead of Big Ben and the Houses of Parliament, I could see girls sunbathing on Bondi Beach, and surfers gliding along in the aquamarine waters below. The aerial tour took me over Sydney Harbour Bridge, and I was so close, my shoes nearly scuffed the top of the arch. We went whizzing past the Sydney Opera House, with dozens of people waving up at me, and landed at Custom House Quay, and the waiting pack of media. I was supposed to be telling them about the launch of Virgin Mobile Australia. I took a deep breath.

Every time I go to Australia it's full on. I've waterskied behind an airship in shark-infested water, been rescued by the Bondi Beach babes, bantered with radio host Rosso, of Merrick and Rosso fame, handed out the choc ices at V Festival – all the normal things that a chairman should get up to, but very rarely does.

I'm regularly asked what I've learned about doing business down under. Has the experience of setting up Virgin Blue been different in Australia to elsewhere? The answer is yes; it has been different – and highly rewarding too.

I think Australians warm to the idea of the Virgin brand more than any other nation in the world – and that includes Britain. Even before Virgin Blue took off, the Virgin brand had 94 per cent recognition in the country, perhaps created in some way by my ballooning and powerboating activities and my autobiography, *Losing My Virginity*, which has sold well in Australia. In 2008, Virgin Blue was listed as one of the top ten brands in the Asia-Pacific region, and one of the top five most trusted brands in Australia.

I've tried to work out why the Virgin brand should have struck such a chord with the Australian people, and I think it's because having fun is an unofficial national sport there. The outlook of most Australians isn't parochial. Many have been off backpacking around the globe and doing their own thing before settling down. The Aussies don't like unnecessary regulations or petty officiousness, and they are prepared to work their socks off, then go and party like there's no tomorrow.

I've always tended to think of Virgin as a youthful brand (not a 'youth brand': that's a different, narrower idea). In Australia, though, I don't think Virgin's brand values carry the same connotations about age. I think everyone gets it, straight away, without worrying about whether our offering is for their generation or not.

Given Virgin's growing maturity, and the ever increasing distance we're putting between our current businesses and memories of our progressive-rock roots, Virgin's welcome in Australia is reassuring. It convinces me that our cross-generational appeal isn't a fluke, and that our offering is pretty much universally welcomed.

It's been fascinating to see how the Virgin brand interacts with other aspects of the Australian national character. When you compete against Australians, it's hardball, but usually scrupulously fair. They also like the underdog and most of our businesses in Australia fitted that model, even though Virgin, as a group, now employs thousands of people down under. Part of the Australian sporting ethos is to play tough and during any game drive your competitor into the ground as hard as you can and then have a few beers afterwards with your opponent and celebrate – or commiserate – in friendship. 'No hard feelings, mate,' is a widespread Aussie expression after a tussle. That's the Virgin way, too – though we'd never thought of the brand in quite those terms when we started. So it may be that the Virgin Blue experience is adding a further meaning to the Virgin brand.

The ordinary Australian – and New Zealander – deserves a good deal. They work hard for their pay and hate being ripped off, but for years they knew that Qantas, their national carrier, the now defunct Ansett and Air New Zealand just weren't giving value for money.

I have always said that I love tackling lazy industries: Qantas and Ansett are good airlines but they had a duopoly ripe for challenge. In August 1999 we announced our intention of setting up an Australian domestic airline. We had A$10 million of capital to invest.

At the time of writing, in 2008, Virgin Blue has 32 per cent of the air-travel market in Australia, with over 2,200 flights per week to twenty-two domestic destinations. It has expanded into New Zealand as Pacific Blue, it flies in Tonga, Samoa and Fiji as Polynesian Blue, and is planning to fly to the United States as V Australia.

In under ten years we have built an airline that Australians, New Zealanders and Polynesian islanders really seem to love, and there's an infectious spirit every time I step on board one of our planes.

Virgin Blue was the brainchild of Australian Brett Godfrey, whose dad worked for Qantas, and Rob Sherrard (who set up Sherrard Aviation and gave Brett his first job as an accountant). They jotted their idea on the back of some beer mats in 1993. Brett had walked around with this stack of cardboard in his back pocket for several years before he approached me. It's strange that some of the best ideas in life emerge after some liquid lubrication!

Brett first came to my attention when he wrote a brilliant reply to an article that was hostile to our European carrier, Virgin Express. It encapsulated my thoughts exactly, and stuck in my mind for a long time.

By 1999, Brett was Virgin Express's chief financial officer. We'd gone through three CEOs, and Brett had been acting chief operating officer, so by now he knew all the snags and problems of the airline business up close. He was incredibly hard-working, and had a great way of getting along with people. His force of personality had smoothed over some sticky situations.

So, one Thursday evening, I phoned Brett to offer him the job as head of Virgin Express, staying on in Brussels. He was polite, but turned me down. He said he wanted to quit because he now had two young children, Ryan and Nicholas, with his wife, Zahra, and wanted to return to Australia.

I said: 'If you want to do anything in Australia let me know and we'll see what we can do.'

'Funny you should say that,' was his reply. And he proceeded to tell me about his plan for a low-cost airline in Australia.

'Well, why don't you put a plan together? I'll have a look at it,' I said.

Brett went home that evening, dusted down his proposal, and got one of his colleagues to fly to Oxford next morning to deliver the plan. I read it and phoned him the next evening.

Brett's idea had already been rejected by the Virgin executive team in London. But I believed there was value in this case. He told me I was the first person who shared his vision and that he had almost given up on his idea. I asked him to look at five outstanding issues and then get back to me. My questions were about slots, good aeroplanes, terminals, ticketing and staff and pilots. Brett went off to Australia and returned within a week with all the answers nailed down. After speaking with our team I said: 'Screw it, let's do it.'

There was a handshake. I said I would give him $A10 million, and the next day it was deposited into his bank account. (His bank manager phoned him up, thinking it was a mistake!)

Brett had already garnered support from Queensland's government, led by Peter Beattie, which would help with the marketing of this untapped tourist region. This was a great stroke of luck – all of the regional capitals in Australia were keen for a new airline to be based in their states, but Brisbane, along with Perth, was the fastest growing part of Australia, with the Sunshine Coast a huge attraction. The payroll tax was better than elsewhere, and so too were the beaches. When we launched we had 12,000 CVs from people all wanting to relocate to Queensland!

When the American low-cost carrier JetBlue was set up, it had a budget of $120 million. Brett's budget of A$10 million was extremely tight, but he had done his homework. He knew that Compass, Australia's first budget airline, which was under-capitalised, collapsed and died in December 1991, squeezed out by Ansett and Qantas in a price war. Compass boss Bryan Gray gave us an indication of what to do – and where it all went wrong. We didn't need to repeat his mistakes. And what followed was as perfect an example of Virgin's 'branded venture capitalism' in action as you could want, and also a good illustration of why it is sometimes better to follow a pioneer than be a pioneer.

Rumours started to fly about a new entrant in the domestic airline market, and on 30 November 1999, at a press conference in Custom House Quay, Brett's backer was revealed. It was Virgin. We had kept our deal under wraps brilliantly and caught the market on the hop. A one-way fare from Brisbane to Sydney, which had cost A$150 each way, would now be less than A$100. ASX, the Australian stock exchange, went mad. A$2 billion was wiped off Qantas's stock price. Brett and I joked that if we had thought to take a hedging position on the fall in Qantas's shares, we could have already recouped our start-up costs.

We both knew that Qantas was one of the best-run airlines in the world – but they had become very cosy with their duopoly with Ansett. Virgin Blue simply had to be different. Our culture would be the point of differentiation – and no one could copy the Virgin culture.

From day one, Brett was on the lookout for people with no previous airline experience. The advertising for Virgin Blue was along the lines of: 'If you've got purple hair and you're working in a butcher's shop and you can still smile after a tough day, you're the kind of cabin crew we're looking for.' His whole approach reminded me of the tone we set for publicity at Virgin Music. It was direct, informal and genuinely informative.

And, of course, these were exactly the qualities he was looking for in his people. A genuine smile is impossible to fake for very long, and we needed people who were prepared to smile. The job of an airline cabin crew is arduous. You're standing for ten hours a day, in confined spaces, dealing with the public. At least the pilots get to sit down and don't have to face the passengers. But a cabin-crew member has to have the right spirit to deal with customers who have lost their bags, missed their flights or spilt red wine over their white sundress. On Virgin Blue, Brett and his team called his cabin staff 'guest-facing crew' and he worked hard to get their ethos right. I remember telling him once that his Virgin staff were more Virgin than anywhere else in the business. Admittedly the morning after a great party with them! I would have said the same about Virgin Atlantic staff the morning after the night before!

Once I was asked by an Australian reporter why we had decided to call our new airline Virgin Blue when the Virgin symbol was red. The fact was we'd run a competition, and some people had sent this idea in to take the mickey. Since in Australia a redhead is known as a 'bluey' we thought, Hang on, that's quite clever. Let's make our red planes Blues.

We're by no means the only company to gently mock our own brand, and the strategy is often very effective. You do need years of successful delivery before it's worth doing, but the idea is a sound one. It shows that you're comfortable with your public. Some commentators complain that Virgin's chumminess is a bit hard to take, given our global reach. On the contrary, I think the public are pretty smart. They know how big we are. They see our planes in the sky. I think the public are irritated far more by pompousness and cant, and so it's much better to make gentle jokes at your own expense than to make out you're more important than you are.

Back in March 2000, Brett was still talking about starting slowly, with only a dozen people, including director of communications and third founder, David Huttner. But the momentum took hold. By August we had 350 staff and we were ready to take to the skies. We wanted to be ready in time for the Sydney Olympics, due to start on 15 September, but we were burning through our cash. Manny Gill, the finance director, went to see Brett to tell him there was nothing left in the coffers and they couldn't afford to pay the wages. Brett was shrewd: he had set up a separate account and tucked away a spare million for exactly this eventuality, and Manny was able to run the payroll.

We needed new planes and Brett had to deal with this too. Our first planes were leased but later we also decided to buy ten New Generation Boeing 737s, delivered brand spanking new from Seattle. A few days later I received my daily phone call from Brett. The cheeriness was gone from his voice, and I sensed his nervousness.

'Richard, I've a cheque in front of me for $A600 million. Are you sure you want me to sign it? The biggest cheque I've signed before was for my mortgage.'

'Brett?'

'Yes, Richard?'

'Just sign the bloody cheque.'

Our initial sales projection had us reaching profit within three years, but we overtook those goals sooner than we expected. Brett wanted to enter the New Zealand market after Air New Zealand's subsidiary, Freedom Air, began a service from Tasmania to Brisbane. This allowed us to launch Pacific Blue, operating out of New Zealand and flying from Christchurch to Brisbane.

The idea was simple: to fly directly, point to point, rather than herd passengers unnecessarily through a larger hub airport. This 'hub-busting' approach made life far easier for the customer, and since our new planes were extremely reliable, there were huge efficiency gains. Within four years, Virgin Blue was flying forty-one Boeing 737s, the packhorses of the worldwide expansion of budget flying, and we had 3,000 people on our payroll and more than 30 per cent of the market. It was a considerable achievement.

The day of the launch was 31 August 2000 at 10 a.m. The flight was packed and Brett, Rob and the team took a leaf out of my book and began a tradition of dressing up. They arrived as the Blues Brothers. I wish I could have seen the expression on the face of Geoff Dixon, Qantas's CEO, when he heard that. Here were his only serious rivals, taking the piss out of themselves, and everybody – crew, press and passengers – was loving them for it.

A year in, and we were going head-to-head with Qantas and Ansett. We knew we were hurting them. They were running into a lot of difficulties. Virgin Blue, the new kid on the block, was roughing up the market.

From the start, Virgin Blue was the airline of the Internet. If you wanted to fly, the cheapest way was booking over the Net. Qantas and Ansett, with their legacy systems and relationship with travel agents, took around 2–3 per cent of their bookings on the Net. Virgin Blue's Internet bookings were 60 per cent of the total at the launch, and 92 per cent within six months. The Net was easier to use, and because the transaction fees were minimal for us, this gave us an edge on costs.

Then, in June 2001, we received an unsolicited offer for Virgin Blue. Brett was approached by Gary Toomey, Air New Zealand's CEO, and they had dinner at the Chairman's Club Lounge in Melbourne – an opulent place with its gold-plated toilet seats. They chatted away and Brett said that he would definitely listen to any offer, and wanted to keep the channels open if there was any way they might work together. A few weeks later, Brett was invited to catch up with Gary again at the Crown Casino in Melbourne, a popular haunt for big dealmakers. Before their hors d'oeuvres were ordered, Gary offered him $70 million for the airline. Brett, as quick as a flash, asked if this was US dollars. 'Of course,' replied Gary. That was A$120 million.

When Brett finished supper he phoned me with this info. It meant that at least we had a valuation for the business on the table. As far as the wider Virgin Group's position was concerned, it would have been a good time to realise some of the investment but, in truth, it was far too early to contemplate.

We turned down the offer but it wasn't long before we had another, more significant approach. The chief executive of Singapore Airlines, Dr C K Cheong, called me up. I knew him well. In December 1999, we sold a 49 per cent stake of Virgin Atlantic to Singapore Airlines for £600 million, using the proceeds to invest elsewhere within the Virgin Group.

Singapore Airlines had a 20 per cent stake in Air New Zealand – and Air New Zealand owned Ansett. We knew that Ansett was in deep trouble. Air New Zealand had bought it for too much money, only to discover it couldn't afford the number of planes necessary to replace Ansett's ageing fleet. Given Ansett's troubles, it didn't surprise us that Cheong wanted Virgin Blue out of the way.

What startled us was his offer. 'Look,' he said to me, 'it only cost you A$10 million to launch Virgin Blue last year. Now I'll give you A$250 million for the company. But you have to give me a decision by tomorrow morning. If you don't say yes, we'll put massive investment into Ansett, and put Virgin Blue out of business within six months.'

Cheong was our new partner. And this was a friendly conversation! But Virgin Blue was a fantastic airline. It was really making a difference in Australia. It was a fun airline to have a stake in. It had the best cabin crew, wonderful new planes and everyone thought the world of it. So we had a dilemma. On the one hand we had this amazing offer – it really was a fantastic return on the money we had invested. On the other hand the business had massive potential and the public and the staff relied on us.

Brett understood the position. He knew that I might sell at this stage. We met up in Brisbane and had a long chat. We walked around the hotel room all evening, discussing the different options. There was something fishy in all this. Why were Singapore so desperate to get rid of us? Why were they willing to hurl their money down the bottomless pit that was Ansett, just in order to destroy Virgin Blue? They were our partners. They had taken a stake in Virgin Atlantic. I couldn't figure out their intentions.

My executive team was keen that I sell up and take the money, but my instinct was to run the other way. As I've explained, for a good slice of the upside, I'll generally accept the greater risk. Then Brett called up his supporters and they came round to see me to try to persuade me to hold on and build the company. On the way back to the hotel lift I took Brett aside and said, 'You know, you didn't need the posse: I'm not going to sell.'

Then the fax arrived. And we were back to square one.

Quarter of a billion Australian dollars. There it was, Cheong's offer, in black and white. Brett and I sat there staring at it. This was *twenty-five times* the amount it had cost us to create, less than a year ago. Were we going mad?

I rang up Andy Cumming, our corporate director at Lloyds TSB in London. I told him we had an offer of A$250 million on the table and that we could sell tomorrow, but we wanted to keep hold of the airline. If we turned this lucrative deal down, would the bank still support us?

Andy and many of his bank colleagues have been very helpful allowing us to grow and prosper. They knew the score. Andy said our other projects were safe – we still had their backing.

Then we went back to the sofa and stared some more at the fax.

The next morning we made our decision. We called a major press conference, with dozens of TV cameras and most of the Australian press, at the terminal in Brisbane. There was hush when I stood up.

'Hi, everyone. I've got some good news and some bad news. The good news is that I have this cheque for A$250 million.' I held it up.

(The cheque was a prop, written out on a Qantas Savings Bank cheque belonging to one of the airport managers.) 'And I'm back off to England. Obviously, we've had a fantastic time in Australia. It's sad that we are selling out today – it's an offer we can't refuse.'

Some Virgin Blue girls broke down in tears. I was so startled I forgot my lines. Before I could recover myself an Associated Press reporter rushed out of the hall to file her story. This news would be around the world in a matter of minutes. 'Only joking!' I cried, ripping the cheque up into tiny pieces. I threw them up into the air. 'There is *no way* we would sell out.'

There were cheers and loud hurrahs. The AP reporter heard the commotion, came back and went white. 'I'll lose my job because of that!'

I got down on my hands and knees and kissed her feet.

The night before, as we sat there staring at that fax, Brett and I had become more and more convinced that something was fishy. Singapore Airlines just seemed *too* desperate to get rid of us in Australia and New Zealand. Why would they throw good money after bad, propping up an obviously ailing company like Ansett?

We came to the conclusion that Singapore Airlines had no intention of propping up Ansett. Ansett's only hope was if we could be made to blink, and give up Virgin Blue in return for cash.

The very next day they decided to pull the plug on Ansett, and on 13 September 2001 the company was placed into voluntary administration and the fleet was grounded. Competition from Virgin Blue and the shock of September 11 and the attack on the Twin Towers in New York City knocked the last breath out of them.

More than 16,000 people lost their jobs – the largest single loss of jobs in Australian history. The Ansett collapse became a political issue in the Australian election campaign of 2001. Kim Beazley, the Labor opposition leader, made a promise to keep the airline going and subsidise the jobs. But this brought a challenge from John Howard, the Liberal leader, who said that the free market should dictate and propping up a dying airline wasn't good for Australia. Howard's coalition victory with the National Party put paid to any plans to restart Ansett.

The black irony of September 11 was that many Australians stopped travelling abroad because of fears of terrorism. Instead they turned, en masse, to their own country for holidays in the outbackyard, Cairns and the Gold Coast. As a result, Virgin Blue – with no competition from Ansett – doubled its fleet in six months, then doubled it again, and doubled it again. Its thirty-six aircraft were nearly 100 per cent full, since many chose not to go to Europe or the US.

In terms of productivity, Virgin Blue was streets ahead in the efficiency stakes: while Ansett had carried 10 million passengers at its peak with 16,000 staff, Virgin Blue was employing 4,000 people to carry 15 million.

'Virgin Blue is a lot of media hype.'

'The market is not big enough to sustain Virgin Blue.'

'Virgin Blue doesn't have deep enough pockets to cope.'

'Qantas will employ any options to see off the interloper.'

'They'll be unlikely to survive a year.'

'Claims by Richard Branson that domestic fares are high are misleading.'

This was a range of opinions from senior airline executives quoted in a number of press interviews. We were certainly beginning to make waves in some Qantas back room or other. When I announced we had been given the British rights to fly to Australia (all that was left was for the Australian government to grant us landing rights), a scathing article in the *Australian Financial Review* said that our plans were a 'lot of hot air'.

Enough was enough. In 2003, I wrote a letter to the *Australian*.

> *I'm willing to lay down the following challenge to Geoff Dixon. If
> Virgin Atlantic is flying to Australia within 18 months he'll agree
> to eat humble pie by flying on our inaugural dressed as one of our
> stewardesses serving our customers throughout the flight. If I'm
> not flying to Australia by December next year I'll be prepared to
> do the same on a Qantas plane from London to Australia.*

I enclosed a mock-up picture of Geoff's head on top of a Virgin
stewardess's shapely body.

Geoff's reply was curt. 'We're running an airline – not a circus.'

Qantas shares promptly dropped 3 per cent.

Virgin Atlantic began flying into Australia in December 2004. And
Geoff never did wear the outfit!

Brett is fastidious about his baby. A few weeks before Virgin Blue was
floated on the Australian stock exchange, a group of financial
journalists were waiting to interview him about the numbers. He was
due off the flight from Brisbane to Sydney but there was no show as
the last stragglers came down the exit ramp. An airport staffer was
sent to collect him. He was on the flight, but he was helping
attendants vacuum the aisles, remove the dirty drinks cups and
recross the seat belts to ensure a faster turnaround. He knew that
punctuality was the key to successful business – and flotation.

On Thursday 13 November 2003, Brett and I were partying hard
with a crowd of Virgin Blue people at the Loft cocktail bar in Darling
Harbour. We staggered out at 4 a.m. Three hours later, and under the
harsh lights of a television crew that had followed us throughout the
process, we set off for meetings with bankers and investors.

My meeting with Goldman Sachs a few days later was one of the
most encouraging I have ever had in business. The Virgin Blue
flotation was eleven times oversubscribed. Two hundred and fifty
institutional investors were demanding 3.8 billion shares! Impishly, I

wondered if I should call for Geoff Dixon to raise the white flag on his own business.

On 8 December 2003, the day we floated Virgin Blue on ASX, we had a market capitalisation of A$2.3 billion. Virgin's return on its investment was staggering. But what was even more satisfying for me was seeing Brett, the founding partner, and his team also reaping the rewards of Virgin Blue's success.

Brett's share was A$80 million. Today, he is one of the richest Australians under the age of forty-five, thanks to the millions he made from the flotation. Ask him why he doesn't want to go and retire to a Queensland beach, and he just shakes his head. He can see the opportunities ahead, when Virgin starts flying from Australia to the United States. And besides, he still loves running Virgin Blue.

Maintaining a consistent tone in the face of rapid growth was a key requirement – and here, brand values helped enormously. I think Brett's naturally a Virgin sort of person. Had he never worked with us, his thinking would not be radically different today. But I believe thinking about the Virgin brand enabled him to focus, and to convey values quickly and efficiently to his colleagues and his staff.

The business now employs over 4,200 people – and it is difficult to get around to everybody – but Brett insists on speaking at every induction course to new recruits. At these sessions he is refreshingly honest. He says that a cabin crew member's job can be tiring. If a person has the temperament to smile, stick with it and enjoy it, then that's fine; but he won't throw money at people because they're miserable. He believes it's ludicrous to pay people inflated salaries in order for them to have a bad time in a service job they hate. Look, he says, give it three years or so, then decide. If you like it, stay on – but if you don't then life's too short.

Brett recently recalled to me, 'I was adamant when we started this airline that we would do it from scratch. There was an airline in New Zealand for sale and we didn't want to go near it. I felt we had to start with our own. Our airline wouldn't have been ours if we bought someone else's baggage.' (It's a point discussed earlier: you can't restructure culture. If you've burnt people, if you've killed their enthusiasm or commitment, then changing office spaces or putting a few more dollars in their pocket will not unduly affect the culture that exists.)

At the time of writing this book, the aviation industry is facing global issues that are more challenging than at any time I have known. Virgin Blue and Qantas share prices have fallen and both are having to reduce capacity and look to cut costs to meet our soaring fuel bills. This is the time when a management team really have to prove how strong they are, and show calm leadership and good judgement. I think Virgin Blue was Qantas's wake-up call, and in Geoff they had a talented and capable CEO who has done the job that needed doing. On the other hand, the story of Virgin Blue has been one of bold expansion and great delivery; now, in order to weather these storms, Brett and his team will have to show other qualities, such as protecting your downside and assessing risk.

Now, Virgin Blue is its own, unique proposition. The understanding of the Virgin brand is very strong, and they've taken it and run with it. They've hybridised the Virgin brand with their own national culture to produce something exciting and different – though I have to say success has not made Brett any less cheeky.

On Saturday 29 March 2008, we held a ball for 3,000 people in our massive hangar in Brisbane, a twenty-minute ride from the city centre. Before the big event, I was invited to Brett's home for a VIP reception in the garden. I was a bit precoccupied that afternoon. I had just returned from Makepeace Island, which is being developed as a holiday destination for Virgin Blue staff, family and friends. It's a wonderful tropical island, teeming with wildlife. I had just been given a briefing about a campaign that was hotting up on the island. I was told that Makepeace was the indigenous home of the Queensland tree frog and that this was a protected species. Our plans for the island were endangering the frog and this was causing upset in the local community. I'd been told that there might well be a protest at Brett's VIP party, but that I didn't have to worry because the police would cordon it off. I presumed it was all under control, but the idea that we might have slipped up so badly over a hot ecological matter was concerning. Was I really so out of touch? I'd never even heard of the Queensland tree frog. Neither had anyone around me. Was I getting sound advice?

So there we all were, in Brett's garden, with several major politicians, including Australia's Federal Treasurer Wayne Swan, when, at 4.40 p.m. exactly, Brett took a call on his mobile.

He turned to me and said: 'Do you know anything about this, Richard? There are some protesters heading towards the house with placards and banners.'

I told Brett about the frogs on Makepeace. 'They're Queensland tree frogs,' I said.

Brett whistled through his teeth.

'What?' I said.

'Did you say *Queensland* tree frogs?'

'Yes. What?'

Just at that moment there was a commotion outside on the street and a security guard came bursting through to say that the protesters were heading for the garden. Within minutes, there was a band waving banners and shouting: 'Makepeace not war on the tree frog' and 'Sir Richard – shame on you.'

Brett said: 'Richard, we've got to deal with these protesters and talk to them.'

I just froze.

'Richard, you have to talk to them. It's the *Queensland tree frog* for goodness' sake.'

I couldn't think how to respond. But Brett stepped forward and I realised, with a sinking heart, that I had to give him moral support. I strode up beside him. Locking eyes with me, the protesters turned their protest signs around.

The placards read: '*You've Been Punked, Love Brett.*'

*

In 1973 the economist Ernest Friedrich Schumacher penned a collection of essays under the title 'Small is Beautiful'. It became a credo that was adopted by many as an antidote to the large conglomerates that ruled the business world. E F Schumacher was a great thinker, who made some exact predictions. He pointed to the end of fossil fuels and wrote that the West was consuming too large a proportion of the world's precious natural resources. He believed multinational corporations and heavy industrial conglomerates used up a vast amount of the world's resources yet accomplished little. He was one of the first people to point us in the direction of a sustainable world.

When I read his work again in 1999 I wanted to find a positive direction for the Virgin Group. And I came to the conclusion that there was little purpose in us trying to become the biggest brand in the world. It was much more valuable to become the most respected.

Once I would take a look at any business opportunity where the customer was being poorly served. Now the Virgin Group has more of a geographical focus. Today's priorities for the Virgin Group are transport and tourism, communications and media, financial services, leisure, entertainment and music, health and well-being, and renewable energy and the environment. Not every Virgin business has been a soaraway success. But we've learned along the way. We've learned to improve what was already on offer and to look for areas where the consumer deserved better. We've learned to ride our luck.

We are now a 'branded venture capital' company, and – given the importance of the word 'brand' in that definition – I think now is a good moment to say something about how we arrived at this way of doing things.

In 1989, I asked Will Whitehorn, our former director of communications (now head of Virgin Galactic), to take a look at how companies similar to ours operated. We began to look at different types of business organisation, to see what suited a company such as Virgin. Will's report crystallised our options very neatly, identifying three models of corporate governance we should study further.

America was home to the equity investment option. Big equity investors like Berkshire Hathaway (owned by Warren Buffett, the world's richest man), Blackstone and the Texas Pacific Group took a large share of traditional businesses that had good cash flows, and this proved to be an excellent way of making money for investors, including mutual funds and pensions. The Texas Pacific Group, for example, had stakes in Continental Airlines, Burger King, MGM and the Carlyle Group, one of the world's leading private equity groups.

As a sure-fire way of turning a healthy profit, the equity investment option left us curiously unmoved. It certainly didn't sit easily with the energetic Virgin brand. These groups tend to sit back and simply provide capital. That's not the Virgin way of doing things. We like to get our hands dirty. There were aspects of its organisation that we liked – it could respond quickly to changes in the market, and bail itself out of trouble fast. But it seemed a bit anonymous for our taste, and altogether too concerned for its own well-being.

The second business model Will identified came from South Korea. There, big business is conducted through 'chaebols', which are chiefly responsible for the nation's remarkable economic progress. The *chaebol* is usually controlled by a founding family, and its ownership is centralised. It is, at its heart, an old-fashioned family business – probably a manufacturing company – with subsidiary companies providing it with components. Companies such as Samsung, Hyundai and LG operate a range of businesses, from computer-chip manufacture to laptops, phones, PCs and motor cars. This makes the *chaebol* powerful in certain key industries – computers in particular. However, we saw that its 'family' structure made it difficult for it to raise vital funds at short notice. These companies tended to look after their own; and capital didn't flow so easily between them (an image with which we are all painfully familiar, as we cope with the 2008 global 'credit crunch').

Will's third business model came from Japan. I have admired the Japanese technological revolution ever since I was running Virgin

Records shops. In 1971, Japan was one of the first countries we exported records to, and I went out and launched a joint venture business there. Our Virgin Megastores were first into computer games and consoles with SEGA Nintendo, Atari and Sony PlayStation, all keen supporters of Virgin. And what I learned about the Japanese way of doing business has had a strong impact on us.

Before the Second World War, Japan was controlled by a few major conglomerates under the system of *zaibatsu*. The *zaibatsu* were disbanded by the Allies because they wielded excessive political power, and their machine tools for making armaments and munitions were converted to the manufacture of items such as sewing machines, cameras and motorbikes. From these ploughshared industries, and excellent loans from Japanese banks, the *keiretsu* emerged, and they have since taken world leadership positions in a surprising number of industries.

In 1984, in a *Fortune* listing of the largest 500 non-US industrial corporations, 146 were Japanese. Twenty-eight of the 100 largest commercial banks outside of the US were Japanese – with Japanese banks filling the top four spots. Toyota and Nissan became the third and fourth largest car manufacturers behind General Motors and Ford. Nippon Steel was larger than US Steel. Hitachi and Mitsushita Electric were second and third behind General Electric, and bigger than Philips and Siemens.

When I started in business there were around half a dozen major *keiretsu* in Japan, and I have had business dealings with almost all of them in some way over the last thirty-five years. Where *chaebols* have a centralised ownership, *keiretsu* are held together by cross-shareholdings, and governed by a strong group of professional managers. So, for example, we have a company like Mitsubishi, set up around the Mitsubishi Bank, and working in a host of industries from cars through to brewing, oil, real estate and heavy industry. All of its companies are woven together, yet each is self-contained.

I liked the fact that the *keiretsu* employed a lot of different corporate structures. Indeed, both *chaebols* and *keiretsu* were tempting models to adopt – were it not for the fact that they were so impossibly complicated for us to implement. On the one hand it was hard to see how Virgin could behave as a *chaebol*-like extended family network, given – well – we weren't *really* a family. As people, we certainly tried to behave well and responsibly to each other, but past that point the family metaphor began to break down. It suited neither our flexible way of working, nor the freedom each company enjoyed to pursue its own projects, nor the dizzying rate at which our top people joined, left, rang us up, worked with us again for a bit, vanished again, rang us up . . .

Keiretsu presented us with a different problem. All these cross-shareholdings meant that everyone was working out of each other's back pockets, whether they wanted to or not. It meant we couldn't shed businesses without a lot of pain and, by the same token, our businesses couldn't build up their own head of steam without a lot of interference. Turn us into a *keiretsu,* and I could imagine all 300 companies in the group advising and cautioning each other to death. We'd disappear up our own internal politics in seconds.

We wanted to do something that was like a hands-off *keiretsu* – something with venture capital corporate governance. This is where the American private equity model came in. We realised that, rather than tie ourselves in knots with cross-shareholdings like a *keiretsu*, we could emulate the best of American private equity companies, investing in all our companies like classic Western venture capitalists.

So we were back to the venture capital model again.

For a little while there, it felt as though we were going round in circles – but then it began to dawn on us. What would separate us from all the other venture capitalists and private equity houses out there? *Our brand.* Our worldwide brand name both advantaged our businesses, and bound them together. The solution had been staring us in the face all the time. Indeed, it was already in place and working well. We didn't need cross-holdings, or strong family structures: *we had a flag.*

The bonding power of the Virgin brand has permitted us to take the bold decision to give everyone the opportunity to be entrepreneurs in their own right. It is a flag to which all members of our extended family pay due respect. They enjoy the advantages of doing business under the Virgin umbrella, and in return they agree to protect the integrity of the brand. If they don't, then we can legally withdraw the name. Everybody fights for their own particular Virgin company – and shares in the upside when things go well.

The story of Virgin Active's growth is, in many ways, one of the best examples of Virgin's branded venture capitalism at work.

In 1997, I was approached by Frank Reed and Matthew Bucknall with an idea to set up Virgin health clubs. The pair had just sold their company, LivingWell, to Hilton hotels and they wanted to have another crack at building a health club business with a difference. They felt that together with Virgin they could bring a sense of fun, value for money and quality to a market that was disappointing the customer.

Some of the existing UK health clubs were a little tired, the membership fees too restrictive and the service unfriendly. In a way it was not so dissimilar to the airline industry that we had launched against in 1984.

Frank and Matthew spent two years researching and developing a Virgin product that would stand out from the crowd. The market seemed overcrowded to many and Virgin Active (as the business was called) would have to pass the test with our team.

To their credit they managed it – the large family-friendly clubs hit the spot. In August 1999 we opened the first one in Preston. It was much bigger than the average UK health club and had that sense of fun and value for money which is core to so much of what we do.

The combination of strong and independent management, the brand, great delivery and ambitious staff has been a real recipe for success. In an industry which has had its difficulties, we have continued to grow both in the UK and internationally.

Our big break, for example, was the acquisition of South Africa's Health and Racquet chain, which catapulted the business from a small UK operator to the leading player in South Africa.

Many of our successful businesses have been built from the ground up – employing new people rather than converting existing companies. However, in the case of Virgin Active, we have been able to do both. It is a credit to the management team that we have been able to buy clubs in Spain and the UK, and rebrand them and re-energise staff to do things the Virgin way.

The takeover of Holmes Place in the UK – for so long one of the leading health-club brands – is a great example. Matthew and Patrick McCall saw an opportunity to reinvigorate the business and give it the Virgin treatment. Conscious that we would want to spend money rebranding and updating the clubs, Patrick persuaded the investors in Holmes Place to take shares in Virgin Active and come along with us for the ride.

One of these was Bridgepoint, who had been our partners in the earlier development of Virgin Active and had sold out once but were now happy to reinvest at a higher price. I think they would have been pleased – today the company is one of the top three health-club chains in the world and it is currently expanding in Italy, Spain, Portugal and Dubai.

Virgin Active still retains that spirit of entrepreneurship, independent thinking and commitment that first attracted us, and has built up a strong brand in its own right. To me, it is proof of how if one picks the right management – and gives them autonomy and resources – they will create a world-class business.

We've never let a Virgin company go bankrupt even though we've had one or two companies that we'd like to have seen the back of. Because our reputation is everything, we've always paid off the debts of any company we own that has had problems. And we move on.

We move on. Easy to say: harder to do. And that's why you need honest people around you.

A few blunt ones don't hurt, either. In 1996, Gordon McCallum put my nose right out of joint. I'd asked him for an honest assessment about the Virgin Group. He told me Virgin was fundamentally a parochial British brand and needed to be stronger in other, international markets in order to be truly global. I felt like a schoolboy being handed a 'must try harder' term report.

Today, while we retain our footprint in the UK, we are looking further afield for our opportunities. We've chosen twelve countries which we believe are ripe for development, based on their population, the income of their consumers, the awareness of our brand and the ease of doing business.

So far we've enjoyed success in the United States, Canada, Brazil, France, Italy, Spain, China, India, Japan, Russia, Australia and South Africa. Now, like so many other businesses, we're turning our attention even more to China and India. I'll round off this chapter, then, with a few thoughts about how we hope to leverage the Virgin brand in these culturally complex territories.

For the Virgin Group, expansion into India was always going to be an easier option than China because of our shared culture, the English language and the Indian legal system's mature approach to business. This has all made a massive difference to us.

We took our time in India, making small investments in radio and comics before launching Virgin Mobile with Tata in 2008. Statutory regulations prevent us from being able to use the successful MVNO (Mobile Virtual Network Operators) model – which I'll explain in detail a bit later – so instead we've set up a marketing partnership with one of the country's biggest blue-chip corporations. This is a mouthwatering prospect for Virgin Mobile: Indian phone networks are adding five million new customers a month. This is a massive rising tide.

Our long flirtation with the Indian aviation market didn't turn out quite so successfully. We spent a lot of time talking to Air Deccan, the first of India's emerging low-cost carriers, which had been set up out of a private charter helicopter company in 2003. I met Captain Gopi – G R Gopinath, its founder – and we tried for over a year to take a stake in this growing market. Somehow – and despite the arrival of SpiceJet and Kingfisher and others to compete with Deccan – every time we talked, the price jumped up a bit more. Ultimately we correctly concluded that the industry was expanding too quickly and after some huge losses, Deccan merged with Kingfisher Airlines – a part of the UB Group, owned by the Indian entrepreneur Vijay Mallya. We wished them well and stood aside.

The things that make India an ideal territory for us are the very things that make it difficult. Our impatience with bad service may as well be the national anthem right now, and everybody, but everybody, is seeking to address this national mood. It's hard to be the consumer's champion in a nation of businesses that, rightly or wrongly, claim value for money above all other values. Have we worked out the best way to leverage our brand here? To be honest, I think this will take time.

For me, though, the bigger prize lies to the east. And so it was with no small thrill that I phoned David Baxby. After all, it's not often in life you get to call someone up and say, 'I want you to run China.'

David, who'd been running Virgin Asia-Pacific from Sydney to Shanghai, took it remarkably well. Now that he had anchored our successful businesses in Australia, we wanted him to spearhead our operations in the most populous nation on Earth. Today, we're talking to an exciting new generation of Chinese entrepreneurs. They are intensely keen to retain their Chinese identities and traditions but also to bring in best practices from around the world.

I have been in China several times recently, meeting young business people. The visit that everyone talks about, of course, is the one I made in January 2008, because it coincided with our bid for Northern Rock. It's a pity that the bid overshadowed the substance of our trip, because – unusually for an official mission, a huge amount of very solid work got done.

I'd been invited along to promote goodwill and cement business ties between Britain and China, and I had asked specifically to meet with some of China's entrepreneurs so I could swap notes about their experiences and opportunities.

It was minus ten degrees in Beijing when our flight touched down. I had been asked to say a few words, via an interpreter, about what it was like to be an entrepreneur. Ours was an important visit, diplomatically speaking, and so the size of the audience – several thousand people – was not too much of a surprise. Still, I was surprised and encouraged by the crowd's response: entrepreneurism has been central to Chinese culture for many centuries, and clearly the excesses of China's Cultural Revolution in the 1960s have done little to stifle the Chinese people's belief in themselves as a nation of supremely ambitious shopkeepers.

Indeed, trade and commerce are becoming, once again, a natural part of life there, and the entrepreneurial spirit is much more highly valued in China than it is, say, in Britain. This was very clear when I attended an entrepreneurs' round table in Shanghai.

Novelty explains some of the enthusiasm I encountered. I got talking to Zhang Xin, a fascinating Chinese businesswoman who runs one of the largest real estate businesses in China. She told me that the property boom in China is a continuing opportunity. There are already more than 400 million people who can be vaguely classified as 'middle or professional class' and this category is increasing by 30 to 40 million every year.

Zhang Xin has a passion for art and design and she has won several international awards for her visionary architecture. Born in Beijing in 1965, she moved to Hong Kong at fourteen, came to England and studied at the University of Sussex and then Cambridge. In 1992 she went to work on Wall Street with Goldman Sachs before returning to Beijing to start her own property business in 1995. The rapid rise of small Internet-based companies gave her and her husband an idea for combined living and working spaces. Zhang Xin initiated the concept of SOHO (Small Office Home Office) for young urban professionals and their companies. It's a business now worth billions.

China's own version of Google is an incredible business story, too. On our trip I met Charles Zhang, the CEO of Sohu, the leading Chinese-language Internet business, now listed on NASDAQ in New York. Sohu is a massive branded portal and its related Internet search engine, Sogou.com, has over 10 billion retrieved web pages. Charles told me that Sohu's strong brand had been achieved largely through its online role-playing game Tian Long Ba Bu, which has a massive following among the young Chinese.

For all that, David Baxby and I sensed an atmosphere of anxiety among young business people. The Chinese authorities have opened a door of opportunity for their people, but a tradition of hefty state regulation and interference might yet curtail the record growth of this amazing nation. I hope not.

The catastrophe of the Sichuan earthquake on 12 May 2008 was on a scale to stretch and break China's considerable disaster-relief plans. It was hugely encouraging to see this proud and often secretive nation acknowledging the scale of the plight facing its own people, and welcoming foreign help and support. Managing the Olympics, too, is already proving to the Chinese authorities that they can bend to the rough and tumble of international opinion and still remain true to themselves.

Much has been written about how China's liberalisation of business will lead inevitably to a more liberal political culture. I think that's true, though I suspect it will take a lot longer than the optimists would have us believe. I predict that free speech and open debate will be helped by the development of Chinese brands. Brands, remember, are about meanings. Every brand means something, and nobody can ever really control all the meanings a brand acquires. Brands are ideas.

They are tangles of associations. They are dreams. In the developed world we live in such a brand-rich environment, we take their power for granted. I don't think that we should underestimate the power of the brand in China – as a force for change.

I come from a line of lawyers. My father was a barrister in the English legal system. I was probably the first in a number of generations not to go into law, but I understood the value and importance of protecting a good name. We have nailed Virgin's colours to the masts of many businesses, so every one of them must pull its weight with our customers.

The day-to-day survival of the Virgin brand depends upon all kinds of companies, and if one of our companies spoils your day, then that's the day more than just one Virgin company will suffer. That's the day you write off our TV service and look up another broadband provider. You open your wallet and there, poking out the top, is a Virgin credit card. Well, you're not going to be using that again in a hurry. You reach into your pocket to make your call and there, in your hand, is a Virgin mobile phone. You think to yourself: Was this thing such a great deal, after all . . .?

Whatever your brand stands for, *you have to deliver on the promise. Don't promise what you can't deliver, and deliver everything you promise.* That's the only way you'll ever control your brand. And beware: *brands always mean something.* If you don't define what the brand means, a competitor will. Apple's adverts contrasting a fit, happy, creative Mac with a fat, glum, nerdy PC tell you all you need to know about how that works. Even in the absence of competition, a betrayed brand can wreak a terrible revenge on a careless company. How many brands do you know that mean 'shoddy', 'late' and 'a rip-off'?

You see?

Easy.

And that's why our next chapter is all about delivery.

3

Delivery

Special Delivery

Right now, I'm sitting in my daughter's home in London and the house has been busy all morning with visitors coming in to see me and talk about Virgin. I've already had several meetings with financiers, our bankers and a Swedish television crew making a programme about Britain. I've also taken phone calls from many of our managing directors and business partners. I've asked Nicola, my personal assistant, and other Virgin Management Limited people to fire off a volley of emails. There's been a list of invitations approved for a media launch. And last night, after flying in from Necker Island, I had a late-night supper with the singer Christina Aguilera, who told me how baby Max is doing and her latest music plans. I'm flying off to see the French president later this afternoon. Tomorrow we're heading to Mumbai to meet some Indian business figures from Tata, the industrial group, and then on to Japan where I'm speaking at an investment conference. We never sit around for long — unless we're on holiday. We thrive on ideas, but our day-to-day business is about delivery.

Good delivery depends upon many things. Two of the most important elements are good communication, and attention to detail. Neither of these essentials is difficult to understand or implement, so, naturally, they're often the first things we forget.

In the early days of Virgin Atlantic, I used to write regularly to all our people, telling them what was happening in the business. I'd jot down my thoughts in my notebook, make a few corrections, get someone to sort out my spelling mistakes and send it out to everyone. I thought letter writing was an important way of communicating.

This wasn't so easy as we grew larger, and because of Virgin's success and my subsequent fame, anything I wrote inevitably hit the press as a news story. So it became difficult to pen the unrestrained letters of the early days. Nevertheless, it is important for people running companies to write a regular letter to keep their staff in touch. And a personal letter sent to someone's home is, I think, still very much more appreciated than an email. Be brave: hand out your email address and your phone number. People aren't stupid, they know not to misuse it or badger you – and by doing so, you will be giving the people who work for you a massive psychological boost. In any event, regular communication by the leadership team is a must in any service business. So keep talking and keep explaining.

I now have a team of people who meet once a week to go through every Virgin company, looking at figures, projections and income. They have a list of priorities, and a list of new projects. They make sure that the Virgin Group is running efficiently. This frees me up to dive in and out when necessary. They know if there is something urgent, they can phone me and I can then focus on the things that really need my personal input.

Don't waste your precious time. Phone calls and emails can eat your day. Don't let them. No one will think less of you for getting to the point. Because there are so many calls to make every day, I generally keep them very brief. And a short note to somebody is often quicker than a phone call. As the business has got bigger and spread across the globe, a lot is dealt with by short notes. However, I'm always willing to pick up the phone and talk directly to people if an issue needs resolving that way. There's no question that if you are trying to persuade someone to join you, invest with you, or make some changes, then it's important to speak to them directly and take the time so that they know what they must do. Face-to-face conversations are more efficient, and videoconferencing will always come a poor second to a shared pot of tea.

Recently I had lunch with Raymond Blanc. He's the owner and renowned chef of Le Manoir aux Quat'Saisons in Oxfordshire. The reason Le Manoir is so successful is that Raymond makes sure that every tiny bit of detail is carefully thought through. If you're running an airline, a restaurant or any other kind of company, *it's the attention to detail that really defines great business delivery.*

I'd advise every owner of a company to keep a notebook and jot down the things that need doing. If you're listening to staff or customers, then write down the main points. If you're visiting a factory or touring a new site or partying with your staff, use the notebook. When you're busy with a lot going on around you, if you don't write things down, I doubt you'll be able to remember one out of twenty items the next day.

Let me give you an example. The main reason why staff become frustrated is that the same problems and complaints keep cropping up and never seem to get properly sorted. On a recent Virgin Atlantic flight someone told me that the sugar had run out, not once, but on two or three occasions. Why were we not stocking more sugar? And why were we overstocking vegetarian dishes, so that people who didn't want this had no other option? These weren't major problems, and they were easily fixed, but someone somewhere has to make the call, the very next day, to sort them out. Otherwise we become the no-sugar airline. The healthy-option airline. Worst of all, we're the not-really-listening airline. And there are enough of them out there already.

I carry a notebook everywhere I go. Every blue moon I wax philosophical. But most of my entries are like this one, and these are the sort of dull, dreary, *absolutely essential* entries that everyone should be capable of writing, but so few do: '*Dirty carpets. Fluff. Areas around bow dirty. Equipment: stainless steel, grotty. Choice of menu disappointing – back from Miami, prawns then lobster (as a main course) in Upper Class. Chicken curry very bland. Chicken should be cut in chunks. Rice pretty dry. No Stilton available on cheeseboard.*'

I also noted that the duty-free trolley was going up and down the aisles without making any sales. I looked at the in-flight service report. Sure enough: no sales. Something had to be done either to encourage the passengers or to improve the sales opportunities (more likely, both), or get rid of the trolley altogether and save the weight.

But what's most revealing now – and most useful to you if you really are reading this for business lessons – is this note: '*Staff desperate for someone to listen.*'

Under this I jotted down an idea: '*Make sure flight staff reports are actioned IMMEDIATELY*,' and I'm pleased to say that they now are, and onboard staff get the action and feedback they need.

When we launched our routes to Japan, I knew that we needed Virgin Atlantic to pay particular attention to cultural differences and to the Japanese sense of respect and formality, without spoiling our offering. It's a fine balancing act. On the inaugural flight I added some more thoughts: '*Need slippers in Upper Class, not socks. Need Japanese beers. Only one kind of newspaper from London: English. Need Japanese too. Japanese tea from London, not good. Japanese food from London. Tastes good but must be better presented. Looks like fish and chips. Saucers for Japanese teacups.*'

I think company owners and chairmen should get out from behind their desks and go and sample their own products as often as possible. I do see many bosses doing their rounds speaking to staff, but they never write the details down. They will never, ever get anything sorted. And month by month, year by year, they will suffer the consequences.

*

Imagine trying to do a good job in the teeth of official opposition. Imagine being told constantly to cut corners. Imagine being rewarded for good delivery by having your business taken away from you and redistributed. Imagine winning market share and then being prevented from delivering more of your product.

In short, imagine the British government's railway regulatory system!

Communication and attention to detail can make your business run more smoothly, but saying this doesn't nearly convey their importance. As I think you'll see from the following account, good communications and attention to detail were what enabled us to do business *at all*, in what has to be one of the toughest sectors we've ever entered.

In January 1997, when we took over the first of our two railway franchises, we made a public promise to usher in new trains and lead a 'red revolution' for the travelling public – on the busiest train lines in Europe. It was my personal commitment to deliver on this. It has taken some time. Eventually, we were voted the UK's best train company in January 2008 by the Institute of Customer Service. This, in my opinion, was rather overdue, but gratefully received, nonetheless! Virgin Trains also topped the 'Passenger Focus' National Passenger Survey with a score of 86 per cent for customer satisfaction. And *Travel Week*, a trade magazine, declared Virgin Trains the best railway company, as voted for by the travel trade and travel agents. This string of tributes is principally down to all the Virgin Trains people who work day in, day out, often in fairly arduous conditions. It's also a great accolade for Tony Collins, the CEO of Virgin Trains, who has been a champion for the customer and staff, but a pragmatist about how difficult it is to run a railway.

I'm the kind of person – as most people will know from my ballooning escapades – who is willing to stick my neck out and take risks. When we launched the West Coast Main Line franchise on 9 March 1997, we said we would replace the whole fleet, and improve services and connections. We also promised new diesel Voyager trains on the CrossCountry networks which criss-crossed Britain. But it would take a number of years before we could deliver this. We had inherited the worst part of the system and to start with we had to make do with a lot of 40-year-old rolling stock and clapped-out engines inherited from British Rail. Some of the rolling stock was in a terrible state. My first action as proud owner of a new railway set was to sign a £10 million cheque so that we could get some spare parts to run the trains.

We steam-cleaned them, painted them and tarted them up as best we could. More than that, we kept them running, while promising our passengers a better service in future. It took time and a lot of pain and disruption. And we got a great deal of abuse from people who still didn't like the idea of the railways being deregulated and privatised after half a century of nationalisation.

The 401 miles of the West Coast Main Line from London Euston to Glasgow is one of the world's great railway journeys. As it heads north, the constant twists and turns of its gentle bends make it difficult for a train driver to build up a decent speed. Only tilting trains can counteract the terrain. It's really a misnomer to call it the West Coast Main Line because it touches the coastline only once, briefly, at a small strand near Morecambe Bay. It is an inland route, taking in concrete-encased Birmingham with its landscape of canals, factories and occasional dereliction, busy Midlands towns such as Crewe and Wolverhampton, and Border Uplands. In the 1920s, the opulent steam trains chugged out of King's Cross and Euston at 10 a.m. each day to race to the north. Virgin Trains was ambitious enough to try to re-create some of that lost glamour for the twenty-first century.

We felt we could transform Britain's rail network from the worst in Europe to one of the best. But for the Virgin brand not to be too damaged in the process, we would have to bring the public along with us. Innovation had to be the difference for Virgin Rail.

For the first few months of our franchise we examined all the technological possibilities. In May 1998 I flew out to Italy from

London City airport to the Fiat Ferroviaria site in Turin, which is the train-making arm of Italy's largest private conglomerate. I saw the kind of stylish, well-constructed trains that we needed on the UK's dilapidated system. The innovation of tilting trains was explained to me, along with the complex relationship between tilt, speed and stability. Next day the journey from Turin to Rome was my first on a tilting Pendolino ETR 460. It was fast and smooth as it hit 150mph through the Piedmont countryside. When we returned from that trip I sat down with Will Whitehorn and the rest of the Virgin Trains team. I was wildly impressed, but I kept my head. I said: 'I want these trains to be the best there are – and the safest. I'd like us to look at what's available across Europe and elsewhere.'

As it turned out, I was right to be impressed: the Pendolino proved to be the best electric train anywhere, bar none. Its tilting system allows a skilled driver to control the train at speed with a huge element of safety. The trains can tilt by eight degrees on rail bends – you'll notice it, but it won't spill your coffee. An automatic warning system rings a bell in the driver's cab as he passes each trackside transponder. This sends a message to the driver saying it's safe to tilt, allowing him to increase the train speed from 85mph to 110mph. On straight stretches the permissible speed is 125mph – soon to be 135mph, and we built the trains to be capable of over 140mph, ready for the future if the track is further improved. It is the driver who has the feel of the train and learns its limits – but if the driver ignores any warnings the computer automatically applies the brakes.

We signed a deal worth £1.85 billion – at that time, my greatest ever financial gamble. The bogies of Fiat's Pendolinos would be adapted in Birmingham by GEC-Alsthom for Britain's narrower-gauge railway lines. (Alstom – the merged company dropped the 'h' – took over Fiat's train-making in 2002.)

Stagecoach transport group chairman Brian Souter is one of the UK's leading business figures and a 'transport entrepreneur' through to the bone. He and his sister, Ann Gloag, are a formidable pair: they started out in the bus and coach wars after deregulation before moving into trains. From their base in Perth – with Ann selling the tickets and cleaning the buses, and Brian driving some of the routes, they have transformed the company into one of the UK's corporate success stories. The business was sidetracked when it tried to expand into the United States by buying Coach USA, but through their own determination and drive, Stagecoach bounced back from this setback. As I write this in 2008, Stagecoach is one of the UK's most successful transport companies and Brian is still in the driving seat.

When it was announced I was thinking of a flotation for Virgin Trains, Brian rang me up and said: 'I share your vision for the railway system.' And nine days later we'd done a deal. Stagecoach held 49 per cent of Virgin Trains to couple with its South West Trains, the UK's largest commuter network, and the Isle of Wight's Island Line, a mini-railway company. I admired that kind of decisive action and it cemented a friendship and working relationship that has lasted over a decade. At a time when transport – and railways in particular – was never out of the headlines, we wanted to make a positive statement after years of expectation. It was all about creating a feel-good news event to assure the frazzled travelling public that something was indeed being done.

Brian shared our view that innovation – leading to a better experience – was the best way to encourage more people to go by train. And while he admitted to having reservations about the Pendolino, he said: 'My mother used to say to me that a fool and a bairn should never see a job half done. I think when people eventually see what's being created here they will understand we're really doing our best to improve the railway system.'

In 2003 the Christmas panto season came early. On 4 December I arrived at one of Alstom's vast Birmingham workshops to deliver a massive present.

I was dressed as Santa Claus and sat next to two scantily clad women on a tinsel-bedecked trap pulled by a reindeer. Brian, wearing a Glenalmond school blazer, shorts, an old-fashioned leather satchel over his shoulder and with a blue cap worn at a jaunty angle, was the lucky schoolboy unwrapping his giant train set.

Faced with a gallery of UK media, I called out to Brian asking if he had been a good boy and what did he want for Christmas. 'Some nice, shiny, new trains which go very fast, please.'

I couldn't resist a quip in front of the TV cameras: 'And how about a higher share price?' (The Stagecoach share price was in the doldrums since its mega bus deal with Coach USA. Brian and I have both been through the mill together, so I can get away with jokes like that.)

As the dry ice swirled around, amid sparkling fireworks and the booming strains of the *Mission: Impossible* theme tune, the nose of a new train burst through the satin wrapping. Nationalised British Rail never generated this much excitement. And although it was only the shell of the first Pendolino, shipped from Italy to Bristol and then Birmingham, we were a step nearer.

Virgin West Coast invested £1.2 billion in fifty-three Pendolinos. Each train cost £11.5 million – which we were told by government railway officials was £1.5 million too expensive. The extra safety features I had asked for had increased the price. Passenger numbers began to rise – although they stumbled at times after engineering setbacks on the tracks.

Angel Trains, then a subsidiary of the Royal Bank of Scotland, stepped in to become the train owners; they then leased the rolling stock the way planes have been leased to airlines for many decades. It's a lucrative business because Angel Trains was sold in June 2008 to a consortium led by Babcock & Brown, an Australian infrastructure business, that includes Deutsche Bank and AMP Capital, for £3.6 billion. The train-building work was also a massive boost for Birmingham and kept highly skilled engineering jobs in this industrial heartland.

The new trains give off 76 per cent less carbon dioxide per seat than domestic airlines and are the most emissions-efficient rolling stock in

Europe. They're very reliable. They spend less time in the workshop, more time carrying passengers. Every time the train slows down, the brakes heat up and the regenerative braking system pumps electricity back into the overhead cables – another innovative feature that government transport officials didn't want. With oil at $48 a barrel, they didn't see the point in putting electricity back in the grid. By 2008, with oil prices nearing $150 a barrel, perhaps it's clear even to them that it was a good decision.

The new trains went into service along the West Coast Main Line on Monday 27 September 2004. And on the first day there was a glitch. One that (Sod's Law being what it is) coincided with the announcement in London of Virgin Galactic, the world's first commercial space launch system for both scientific and human space flight. The Royal Scot train leaving Glasgow ground to a halt outside Carlisle. Passengers had to be switched to another train and were two hours late arriving in London. The press put the breakdown and Virgin Galactic stories together and the *Daily Mail* had full-page fun at our expense: *'Euston, we have a problem . . .'* It was an absolutely brilliant headline and it put me in an irritable mood all day.

If I needed comfort, though, I only had to look at the situation by the end of the first week. The news was very encouraging: I wrote in my notebook:

'First week – Pendolinos. 27 September–2 October. 82 per cent punctuality. Promised 72 per cent. Cancellations 4 out of 210 trains run daily. Pendolino tilting in traffic 32, two more than estimated on Monday 27th. Only two trains to fail. Got masses publicity due to space launch. Jack Straw travelled and said PM enjoyed reception – also that he'd had amazing feedback from our staff parties.'

To this I added: *'Delivered exactly what we promised a year ago and general mood of passengers is that it worked well and will steadily improve.'*

In the early days, mind you, we had to weather constant criticism about Virgin's two franchises. Virgin Trains had to take over the worst record for timekeeping in the country. Our West Coast Main Line services achieved a punctuality figure of only 84 per cent in the year to 16 October 1999. And the performance of Virgin CrossCountry, a higgledy-piggledy criss-crossing of routes, was worse, recording a figure of 80 per cent. But this was unfair on our team. We were now operating more services and carrying more passengers on the antiquated track and rolling stock which we had to nurse along until the new trains arrived.

I felt for all of our people. It was demoralising to be constantly criticised. We had worked very hard to get things better and the service had improved. The privatisation of the network brought some real benefits, but it imposed an institutional and political structure that was seriously flawed from the beginning, something which was exposed by the Hatfield accident, after a broken rail went undetected.

The Hatfield rail crash, on 17 October 2000, left four people dead and seventy injured. It was a nadir for the rail industry, and some questioned whether it would ever recover. Railtrack slapped speed restrictions on the whole of the rail network and our passengers suffered misery, delays, late arrivals and cancellations. There were recriminations and blame. I remember long discussions with Stephen Byers, then Secretary of State for Transport, about what needed to be done. Privately I wondered if it would ever be properly sorted. In 2001, following Hatfield, Railtrack, a publicly listed company, went into administration, and the company's shareholders lost their investments. In 2002, the Rail Regulator presented taxpayers with a massive bill for an additional £1.25 billion a year of increased infrastructure costs, largely due to historic underinvestment and Railtrack's loss of control. It was a deep and complex mess.

Since Hatfield, however, the rail industry has slowly begun to turn the corner. The UK government established Network Rail as a not-for-dividend private company to manage the railway infrastructure – that is, the track and the signalling. These changes were implemented in the Railways Act 2005, with the Secretary of State for Transport now responsible for setting the strategy and budget for the railways in England and Wales.

Increasingly, Virgin Rail has developed better partnerships with the government, Network Rail, and suppliers like Alstom and Bombardier, to bring in huge improvements. We've got our trains running every twenty minutes between Manchester and London – the highest frequency for that sort of route anywhere in the world. For business people, trains are now a much better alternative to short-haul flying. Virgin's own delivery has improved, too. In 1997, 13.6 million passengers used the West Coast Main Line. In 2003, this was 14.1 million; 2004, it was 15.1 million; 2005, 18.7 million, and by 2007, it was more than 20 million. Our punctuality was over 90 per cent. What had seemed like Mission Impossible became more than doable. It became surpassable. Network Rail still have big issues to deal with in the way they upgrade the last sections of track and inconvenience the public. But one way or another, 2009 will see another leap in service, speed and punctuality on the West Coast line, which will make it truly a world-class railway. It has been a tough journey but thanks to the leadership of Tony Collins and the support of Stagecoach's top management we have made it through the really tough times.

You must never forget that every change ushers in unforeseen consequences. This applies as much to welcome changes as unwelcome ones. It always tickles me when a spokesperson comes on the television to explain, with an earnest frown, that an ailing company is 'a victim of its own success' – as though it had undergone something rare and freakish and hard-to-credit; some sort of business equivalent of alien abduction.

Success one day does not give you a free lunch every day thereafter. Obviously, you can't plan for the unexpected. All you can really do is never let your guard down. Delivery is not just hard work: it's *endless.*

We had invested more than £2 billion replacing all the trains on our CrossCountry routes with Voyager diesel trains. The trains were popular and extremely reliable. There was a 50 per cent increase in passenger numbers – and suddenly people were finding it difficult to get a seat on the busier routes. We were a victim of our own success!

Altogether more troubling was the thought that our passengers were victims. I received one letter in particular from a couple travelling from Preston to London. They had been planning a treat in London and didn't realise that they now had to book a seat. When they arrived, they found the staff unhelpful. Given the husband was disabled and used a wheelchair, this was pretty terrible of us. I personally sorted this one out, and encouraged my Virgin Rail team to improve. I was concerned that we might have taken our eye off the ball when it came to customer service. I penned a letter to Ashley Stockwell, the brand and customer service guardian for Virgin Group.

> *Dear Ashley,*
> *I am worried about Virgin Trains and the service we are delivering to the customer. We have a board of directors who have understandably got tied down in franchise negotiations and the bigger picture issues. When we first got involved we put people in from Virgin Atlantic who really cared about staff and customers. Somehow, things seem to have slipped. Tony Collins realises this – he told me very frankly yesterday that we had 'lost that customer service'. I'm sure he'll do everything he can to address the problem. Any help your department can give I'm sure would be welcome.*

We got better. Increasingly, we picked up plaudits. By April 2006, when we announced our decision to reapply for the CrossCountry franchise, I was beginning to believe we had achieved something extra special in Britain. Paraphrasing slightly, I used the old Magnus Magnusson line from *Mastermind* to allow us to continue: 'We've started, so we'll finish.'

But there was opposition to our franchise inside the Department of Transport. Before a crucial meeting with officials, I got a phone call from a well-informed transport journalist. He knew the exact time of the meeting and what was going to happen and who would be attending. He was right in every respect. He also told me that the government's endgame was to destroy Virgin's CrossCountry franchise and they were looking for an excuse to stop it. I wrote in my notebook: '*If this guy is right on everything else, is he right on this?*'

We argued that we'd worked hard and that punctuality was the best since we took over, revenues were up 40 per cent and passenger numbers up 50 per cent – and the government were now getting 87p in every £1 of extra revenue.

In my notebook I wrote: '*We've been told that certain elements of the Department of Transport want CrossCountry back so it can be remapped and absorbed by other networks. I hope that's untrue. I'm confident that the Virgin Group's bid will not be bettered by another operator in a competitive tender. I find this all a little bizarre to say the least. But that's the rail business.*'

It certainly was. Having done all the donkey work, taken all the flak and increased passenger numbers by 50 per cent in ten years – Virgin Trains lost the CrossCountry franchise. But that's life in twenty-first century Britain. There are (he says, through gritted teeth) no regrets. And even if there were, in business, as in life, you're better off just moving on. After all, we still had the West Coast Main Line.

Virgin Trains is criticised in some quarters for the supposedly easy money we've racked up in the form of government subsidy. I think those people should consider the time and effort we spent for very little financial return. Out of that subsidy money we had to pay Network Rail for running on their tracks, and as their problems increased, so did our access charges. When we signed off the first deal we never envisaged the increases. So, between 1996 and 2006, we did indeed receive £2 billion in subsidy – and promptly waved it goodbye again, paying £2.4 billion in track access charges, first to Railtrack, then to Network Rail; in other words, back to the UK government. Plus Virgin Trains paid higher charges to Network Rail than any other train operators – this when the subsidy was reduced by half from £526 million to £268 million at the end of March 2006!

Not long ago we put together a proposal to increase the size of each train from nine to eleven carriages so that the business could continue to meet the soaring demand. I explained to Douglas Alexander, then the Secretary of State for Transport, that while we could deliver on our franchise agreement, from February 2012 our passenger numbers would be pushing our current seating capacity to its limit. Our proposal was to increase delivery to ten and eleven cars at optimum time from around 2010. The total investment required would be around £260 million, all to be funded by the private sector. We also proposed additional car parking and smart-card ticketing and in return we would like an extension of our franchise for a couple of years, please. I felt that our track record – excuse the pun – was enough to give us some chance of the government accepting this. But later in the year they rejected our bid to increase the number of cars. At the time of writing this book we are back in discussions over extending the trains again. I hope sense will prevail. But come 2010, if you ever find yourself standing all the way to Birmingham, remember who to thank. It drives me to distraction to think that the increasing popularity of our trains is being threatened by the government's mean-fistedness and lack of vision.

At the same time we are hampered by the poor state of the line which has been undergoing a massive upgrade in the last four years. Our wonderful team – led so ably by Chris Green for many years and now by Tony Collins – has remained focused on delivering a great service in the face of these incredible hurdles. Despite these issues I'm proud to say that Virgin Trains has delivered on its promises – and it hasn't been easy. First and foremost, we knew from the start what it was we wanted to deliver, and we stuck to our guns in the teeth of official discouragement and a negative press. We wanted the best-looking, most comfortable trains because we knew anything less wouldn't wash with a public that had had to put up with a declining service for far too long. Our trains had to be efficient – as green as possible – because we had no idea what would happen to the price of energy, and there was no hint or sign that energy costs were going to come down in the long term. (How right we were!) Finally, we wanted the safest trains possible, because in the travel business, this is the bottom line: people are putting their lives in your hands. Nothing short of an act of God should ever put your customers at risk.

Our proposition, then, was fully considered in the light of our core business values, our medium-term strategic considerations and our long-term feelings about where our industry was headed. However overblown this sounds, this is what you should be doing all the time as you consider how to deliver on your business proposition. Never imagine that you are immune from big events. Make your small decisions in the light of the bigger picture, and you are at least pointing your craft in the right direction to ride out any storm.

Remember, also, that the world is full of people who want to put you right, who want to play the realist to your wide-eyed innocent. Governments are notorious for this sort of thing. Ministers are like mayflies. No sooner do they get to grips with what they're supposed to be doing than they're gone. Keystone of our liberties it may be – in business terms, it's a disaster. In the UK in particular people who have no real tenure over the issues they're handling let long-term considerations fly out the window. It's not that they don't understand them, or even agree with them; it's that they despair of ever getting them past the Treasury quickly enough.

You can spot negative people and stultifying institutions a mile off. Have the courage of your convictions, and ignore them. Instead, gather together people you can trust – get *them* to play devil's advocate; get *them* to point out the problems you may inadvertently be steering towards.

If you're lucky enough to become an agent of change, it's incredibly frustrating when other people fail to grasp your ideas – even worse when they reject them out of hand. But you can see why it happens. Change can be dangerous. Often, the bigger you are, the slower you move, the more dangerous change becomes. Of course governments are afraid of change: they know they'll never be able to get out the way of it quickly enough. Neither can many big companies.

It's no good saying 'Prepare for change' or 'Embrace change' or whatever other cliché the business books are peddling this season. The bald fact is, change, most of the time, is a threat. It's the thing that wants to kill you. And let's face it: one day it *will*.

In business, change always happens more quickly than you want – it steals up on you fast, when you are least prepared. This was certainly true for Virgin Records in the music industry.

For the multinational consumer electronic giants, survival depends on finding the next disruptive technology and getting it into the marketplace. Being the first to do so is admirable. But being the best is what really counts. I've always followed my nose; it's never occurred to me to wait for others to make mistakes, just so I can learn from them. I can't see the fun in it. Beyond that, though, I can't really criticise: the ones in the vanguard are generally the ones who get shot.

During the 1980s and 90s, as the Philipses, Sonys, Panasonics and Hitachis of this world headed down blind alleys with products that failed to bite, the music industry was moving logically and unstoppably towards digital, downloadable music – a process that reached its apogee (at least, from the point of view of where I'm sitting now) in Apple's iPod.

The digital music revolution was heralded by the arrival of the compact disc. The progression from analogue to digital recording was a revolution for the eardrums. In the mid-1970s, the seven-inch single was the gold standard for the pop music industry. All the pop bands (though not all the progressive rockers) wanted a number-one hit in Britain, America and then the rest of the world. To have a number-one hit was to arrive as a band or solo performer.

By the early 1980s our domination of the charts had helped Virgin Records become the world's top independent music company. There was tremendous excitement about seeing a new record breaking into the charts, and the band's virtually compulsory appearance on the BBC's *Top of the Pops* the following Thursday. All this hoopla had a positive effect on the band's album sales; the two went hand in glove.

It's easy to get nostalgic about old formats, but there's no historical justification for it. Since the nineteenth century, most recording technology has turned over on a thirty-year cycle. Thirty years after the wax cylinder carried music to wow the opinion shapers of the 1880s, brittle, shellac 78rpm recording discs revolutionised the listening habits of the masses. After the Second World War, the vinyl LP, the single and the EP (the extended play, containing two or three tracks on each side) made music listening considerably less fraught. Why, you could even send these sturdy, flexible discs through the post!

Those pundits talking now about how digital downloading is killing the major companies should remember that the last time the industry was in meltdown was – surprise, surprise – just less than thirty years ago, in 1982. The economic recession was having a deep impact. At the time, Virgin Retail had over a hundred record stores, in every town across the country – and during weekdays they were deserted.

More people were home-taping off the radio, too, or from a friend who had bought the original LP – a forerunner to the illegal downloading that led to Napster and all the other sites which offered the punters music for free.

The digital revolution had arrived in the recording studio some time before, and computer software was already employed to mix albums and soundtracks. Now, though, digital music was about to take the public by storm.

Dire Straits were the format's first big seller. Vinyl fought a valiant rearguard action, and the aficionados said they still preferred the analogue sound. Many a music snob with a Quad system turned his nose up at Dire Straits on a plastic beer mat. Many, many more went ahead and bought it. Philips, the Dutch electronics giant, predicted at the major Paris music fair that the compact disc would become 'the new world audio standard'.

There was fierce debate in our office between the hi-fi buffs. Could vinyl ever be surpassed by a shallow digital sound system? At the time there was genuine doubt – even today I hear people say that vinyl is much better. An LP's record cover and the sleeve notes, meanwhile, had become a contemporary art form.

But the shiny CD was on the march. It was more convenient, it was easier to use *and* it protected the furniture from your beer glass.

Philips, who had developed the system, announced plans for software to be manufactured and released by PolyGram and sold through record retail outlets, separately from the hardware. The CD also had a competitor in the LaserVision disc which was ready for the spring of 1983. JVC, the Japanese electronics giant, was promoting its VHD system. There were about thirty companies looking at manufacturing special CD players, and I was very keen not to be left behind if this was going to be the new standard.

Only PolyGram and Ariola had made agreements with Philips for the release of products for the new CD system. (At that time, I thought the royalties being demanded by Philips were too high.) Philips began delivering the first CD players in Belgium. They could be attached to a hi-fi system, as a separate, just like the record deck, and were expected to sell for around £300–£400. This was a lot of money for the young record-buying public – and in the early days the CD owner was usually the richest guy in the street.

From launch, around 200 titles would be available, retailing at between £7.50 and £8.50. PolyGram were preparing a disc-pressing plant in Hanover in West Germany, which could produce 500,000 in 1982, and a staggering four million the following year. In June 1982, Sony ran some full-colour adverts in the music press. They showed a full-size twelve-inch LP, alongside a compact disc, depicted in actual size. The advertising campaign was slick and it impressed me: 'Six months from now the industry will expand dramatically.'

The CD was the answer to many a music lover's prayer: no wow, no flutter, no wear, virtually immeasurable distortion, wide dynamic range and no surface noise.

My notebooks are full of the questions I had about the impact on our business and what we should be doing to counter any threats. I wrote: '*What happens to the record collection around the country – do people replace their vinyl with CDs?*'

The arrival of the compact disc was a shot in the arm for our industry but, as with most medicines, in the wrong dose it could quite easily kill the patient. The CD was a game-changing technology – and we had to adapt or die. The arrival of the CD and, later, the DVD would eventually give retail a lease of life, but at first the only way for our business to survive the CD menace was to cut the cost of vinyl. And that's what we did. We needed to start shifting stock and clear the decks for the new. The era of selling vinyl LPs by the truckload was coming to an end.

Meanwhile, in March 1982, Virgin Records shuffled the pricing structure for dealers. Price changes were being forced on all of the industry by high inflation rates in the early years of Mrs Thatcher's government in Britain. We had to put up the price of our chart-topping bands, so *Dare* by Human League was selling for £3.40. We made an 18p increase to £2.92 from £2.74 to dealers for our back catalogue albums. But we reduced a certain number of titles to £1.82 on a purely experimental basis, to see if this could shift material that had been overlooked, such as the Skids and Magazine.

Some of the smaller independent retailers protested. Alan Davison, the vice chairman of RAVRO, the association of record dealers, who ran a small record shop, joked at the time in *Music Week*: 'Trying to think of everything that would be nice for this year, I found the really big thing I would like to see would be for Our Price and Virgin to close down. They can open up again, if they want to, provided they sell records for the right price. Records are a specialist product. Discounting them, like groceries, was the worst thing that ever happened.'

Poor Alan: the only way you can get away with charging high prices in a deflating market is to downsize and specialise. That means you're firefighting and innovating at the same time – a difficult double somersault, and one Alan simply didn't have the will for. He simply put his prices up to the full recommended retail price in order to ensure his business mark-up of 33 per cent. This made no business sense to me. The margin on records and tapes was dropping from 32 per cent in 1978, down to 23 per cent in 1981, and cut-throat discounting had it as tight as 16 per cent. According to the BPI, the notional price of an average LP was £5.22 in 1981 – while the actual price paid by the record buyer was £4.39. Margins were so tight that a record company without hit artists that season was unlikely to weather the storm.

Meanwhile, another new retailing phenomenon was dawning (or looming – it depended on your point of view). In 1980 the British inventor and entrepreneur Clive Sinclair broke the £100 barrier with his Sinclair ZX80 computer. If you were brave you could buy a kit for £79.95 and solder it together yourself. A year later, he brought out the ZX81, and in 1982 he brought out the Sinclair ZX Spectrum. By the middle of 1982, there were nearly 500,000 video-game machines in use in the UK. I was surprised at how rapidly it spread across into our business – and again we had to be prepared for its impact.

One day one of the reps came in to see me. 'Richard, the kids are really getting into this Pac-Man video gaming. Perhaps we should be selling some games, too.'

We started to order computer games directly from Atari – a subsidiary of Warner Communications. The arrival of Pac-Man, a maze-chasing alien who munched up fruit, helped bring in excellent business for years, outselling every other arcade game including the hugely successful Space Invaders, the staple of every single student-union bar in the country. With Tetris, Pac-Man became a starter game for Nintendo's Game Boy, introduced in 1989. In the early 1990s Sega's Game Gear introduced us to Sonic the Hedgehog. Popular games for young people allowed home computer games to lift off, especially in the UK, and introduced a whole generation to computing. The hardware multiplied and diversified at a dizzying rate: the Atari ST, the Commodore 64, the Amiga, the Apple Mac . . . The computer-gaming industry was about to go into overdrive.

Pac-Man was, indisputably, the first computer game icon. We didn't get into our stride until the arrival of Nintendo's Super Mario at Christmas in 1985. It was to become a worthwhile sideline for our stores as they expanded around the UK and into Europe. Software cartridges selling at £15 to £45 offered us a much greater mark-up than music, so computer games and then films – on video, then on DVD – became an increasing part of our range.

The truth is that even from the start our smaller Virgin Records shops made very little money. The stores kept our name in the public eye, and represented our youthful, irreverent brand, but they were unsustainable in the long run. One of my biggest business mistakes – indeed, regrets – was not selling all of our stores sooner.

By 1986, even the Megastores were under threat. Our biggest rivals, HMV, had taken up the cudgels against us and were launching a new store on Oxford Street in June which would stock every record currently available, while Tower Records was opening at a prime site in Piccadilly Circus.

Undeterred, in March we launched our Dublin store, the biggest in the world, at Aston's Quay. We spent £1 million on converting the five-floor 50,000 square foot McBirney's store – and it would be similar to our Megastore on Oxford Street.

The press thought we were mad. Stanley Simmons, a director of Music Makers, pitched into the debate in the Counterpoint section of *Music Week*. 'In my opinion the whole concept of the megastore in UK record retailing is seriously flawed and based on false assumptions.' He pointed out that in the US large retailers were able to negotiate better credit terms and returns that were not available in the UK. And he was right to point an admonishing finger at our fixed overheads – the rent and rates – and our obligation to carry a large amount of stock.

But he was missing the point. Our Dublin store not only stocked specialist classical and jazz, folk and rock music, it also sold music videos, games and computer software. This was where I could see the future of our business. We were now giving the old-fashioned retailers, such as Woolworths, Dixons and Currys, a real run for their money.

Our shop windows and our interiors were dynamic and exciting. If Selfridges could do stunning window design, then we would do it better. When Depeche Mode launched their new album, *Black Celebration*, we had a twelve-foot-high mirror-tiled tower in the window of the Oxford Street shop. It was eye-catching stuff. Inside we began to bring the bands in to perform and play a few songs. They became events in themselves which drove more sales and better publicity.

Our Virgin staff were the key. They were usually music buffs not much older than the customers coming in with their weekly pocket money or cash from part-time jobs. We'd created a cool place to work – and that made it the place to hang out on a Saturday afternoon, too.

Dixons chairman Stanley Kalms was increasingly impressed by what Virgin was able to achieve. We also began discussions with Debenhams to open Virgin outlets in their regional department stores.

The days of the small, please-everybody record shop were numbered, and you can't build a business empire on nostalgia alone. In June 1988 we were approached by WH Smith, and we decided to sell sixty-seven of the smaller shops to them for £23 million, and concentrate on a few

Virgin Megastores, including a new one in Paris on the Champs-Elysées. A larger retail experience had some future. But the glory days of our involvement in the music industry were now behind us.

By 2008, the CD as a retail item was terminally ill. Its zenith had been 1999, when the worldwide market for consumer spending on music had been $17 billion a year. By 2005 that figure had dropped to around $10 billion, with digital downloading emerging strongly. (By 2012, the projected revenues are just over $9 billion, with half of this downloaded via the Internet.) The corporate music industry – some owned by private equity houses – became more interested in selling millions of plastic discs rather than supporting their actual artists and talent.

When we set up Virgin Records we funded the recording sessions, manufactured the product, distributed it to the shops and then marketed the band and the music. We would give loans and advances for touring, for making promotional videos, for equipment, props and lighting. We would also advise and look after the careers of our musicians and handle the accounts and the sales.

Did all this work make us future-proof? Of course not. The value of these services has disappeared, thanks mainly to digital technology, the Internet and the arrival of YouTube and social networking.

Digital downloading is killing music? You could have fooled me. The music scene is changing, but it's certainly not dying. The economics of music production today are far healthier than they ever were in Virgin's heyday as a music company. When we built the Manor recording studio in Oxford (where we gave Mike Oldfield his big opportunity) and the Monster Mobile recording truck, it was a massive undertaking. It cost thousands of pounds each day to rent a professional studio, pay for a top-notch engineer and a producer, plus all the wine you could drink and dope you might smoke. Virgin Records' job was to bankroll this upfront – and take the risks. Now a top-quality album can be made on a decent laptop – and then you can send it as a music file over the Net to a myriad of different places.

The cost of manufacturing and distributing is minimal compared to when Virgin Records was promoting Phil Collins, the Sex Pistols, Human League or even the Stereophonics. To make money, we had to sell LPs and then CDs in large numbers, just to cover the manufacturing, printing, shipping and retail costs and the royalties. That business model no longer exists – gone, I think, for ever. Digital distribution is almost cost-free and it's as cheap per album to distribute a million copies over the Internet as it is to send out fifty by FedEx. Economies of scale don't matter to young emerging bands – although they still matter a great deal to the record companies and their shareholders.

If I was a happening band on the cusp of success today, I wouldn't go through a conventional record company. I'd gather a small team of people around me and release it myself. I would consider getting together and sharing distribution, advertising and marketing with like-minded musicians and marketing people. Promotion is as easy as setting up a page on MySpace, Facebook or other social networking sites. Smaller and newer bands will earn less, because record companies will only be able to promote lesser known bands on the back of major artists. But there will be more new music to choose from, and more people will get themselves heard.

Record companies will survive – but they will have to be much leaner, much closer to my 'small is beautiful' business model. They will have to discover genuine talent. If you want to know what the future of digital download really looks like, think of artists like Brian Eno, the producer of Coldplay's most recent album *Viva la Vida*, David Byrne, of Talking Heads fame and – above all – Radiohead.

In 2007, when the Oxford-based band said that they were going to release their album *In Rainbows* as a pay-what-you-like digital download, they were branded as barmy, throwing away their intellectual musical property. For fifteen years, Thom Yorke and Radiohead have been major-selling rock artists. They were out of a record contract, had their own studio and their own server, and so the costs of distribution were minimal. It was a gamble – but it worked out, and 40 per cent of fans paid an average of £3 each for the album, making the band nearly £1.5 million. Not only that, but they have licensed the music and it went on sale as a CD too. Yorke said that as artists the band had made more money out of downloading than all their other Radiohead albums put together.

This kind of economics is smothering the big labels. Madonna is another artist who has taken control of her music in a recent deal with Live Nation which connects her reputation for fantastic live concerts with the promotion and download of her music by a website.

While recorded music has cycled through different formats and various paths to making money have been explored, music will always be something personal and meaningful, resulting in a deeply emotional connection point for people of all ages. As records have been pressed into vinyl, discs and now ripped online, we at Virgin have been heading to the fields each summer with hundreds of thousands of other fans in an annual communal celebration of music and people.

In 1995 Jackie McQuillan and James Kydd called me. 'Richard, we've got a great idea. It'll be a world first, truly cutting edge and will give Virgin Cola, and naturally (by association) all the other Virgin brands, great music credibility, whether they're in music or not. Oh, and we've met some fantastic, professional people who can help make it happen.'

OK, I was beginning to guess where this was going when James added (tongue in cheek, I have to say): 'Richard, we'll be doing it for the kids,' and Jackie threw in: 'Richard, I swear it'll be fucking huge!' I realised that no matter what this great idea was, they'd talk me in to it.

Within a matter of minutes, after they'd filled me in on the details, I found myself saying: 'If I've got this right – V Festival would be the first ever music festival anywhere in the world to be held on two days, on two sites, on the same weekend by swapping international A-list bands overnight on buses – from one end of Britain to another? What a brilliant idea. I'm in ...' To others, the logistics of this plan might have sounded impossible to pull off – I decided to put my trust in the team and back their gut instincts on this one.

By working with the most experienced concert promoters in the UK – Bob Angus of Metropolis Music, Denis Desmond of MCD Concerts, Simon Moran of SJM Concerts and Stuart Clumpas of DF Concerts – Jackie and James knew they were talking to the best in the business. None of the parties involved had ever produced a festival like V before but they formed a good rapport, and sometimes that's all you need.

The promoters recognised that the Virgin brand could bring something different: a truly punter-focused festival. A brand that believed everything appearing on site should add value to the whole weekend experience – well-lit campsites, directional signage that actually directed you somewhere, longer bars to make sure there were shorter queues and food that people might, for once, want to eat, and the introduction of Virgin Angels to help anyone out if they needed information or assistance. The attention to detail even got down to bringing in ten times the amount of toilet rolls available on site compared to any other festival. I doubt the promoters had ever had such long, or heated, conversations about toilet rolls before, especially not toilet roll printed with the words 'Poopsie and Cack'– a nice little tribute to Virgin Cola's main two competitors!

Jackie and James, in return, respected the expertise of these experienced promoters. After all, they know how to get tens of thousands of people through multiple gates at the same time without riots breaking out, they know about staging, lighting, the temperaments of artists, and how to ensure the safety and security of running a massive music event while at the same time putting on a great show. Although, in true Virgin style, the team insisted on hiring the friendliest security guards in the business, ones who would be helpful and smile. Now that really was a world first!

I am delighted to say the rapport formed thirteen years ago is still as strong as ever. The UK V Festival takes place every summer during the third weekend in August on two beautiful sites, Hylands Park in Chelmsford and Weston Park in Staffordshire. It is one of the largest and most popular in the UK – attracting over 175,000 music fans in 2007 – and plays host to more than a hundred bands. It's an industry favourite, with the live-music business voting V European Festival of the Year for the past seven years at the annual Live Magazine Awards. Good thing I trusted their instincts!

Fast forward to spring 2006 in the US. It's year two in our fight to launch our newest airline, Virgin America, and there is no clear end date in sight.

While the US Department of Transportation took its time making a decision, the design team kept its head down and continued to create a revolutionary new travelling experience for US consumers. But our patience was frayed. We thought we'd have launched a new company by now.

One day that spring, Virgin USA's Dan Porter, who came to Virgin with extensive expertise in technology and music, rang me up and said: 'Richard, Virgin businesses are all inherently social, whether it's health clubs, mobile phones or airlines. So is music. You've been building incredible communities every summer with V Festivals in the UK, so while America waits for the airline to launch, what do you say to throwing the largest music and art festival on the East Coast? Give Americans a taste of the Virgin brand?'

'How quickly can you get it going?' I asked. A big splash could be just the thing, I thought, and it wouldn't have to take as long as starting an airline. I do like live music and believe in the rejuvenating powers of parties. And I certainly enjoyed camping.

'Give us seven months,' Dan said with a gulp.

Now, we'd never put a festival together in the largest music market in the world, and what did the Virgin USA team know about festival logistics, finding the right campsite, locking down the best date and convincing 50,000 people to give it a go? It took the right kind of magic and chemistry to create something like the UK's V Festival. Could it be replicated in America?

The US team decided to launch two festivals, one on the East Coast in the US and one in Canada. Both would be called Virgin Festival – we were lucky enough to have a brand name that didn't sound like a corporation or a cleaning product. We then had to find concert partners who shared our vision; while the festival was a business, it wasn't just something to make money but an extension of the brand and the Virgin lifestyle, so every detail had to be perfect.

Two independent promoters with a strong aesthetic sense and vision joined up: Seth Hurwitz, the last great independent rock promoter in a cut-throat market of giant corporations that were swallowing concert venues and record labels whole; and Andrew Dreskin, promoter and trusted partner who had started Ticketweb with Dan. They felt as strongly as we did about putting on an incredible experience so they didn't hesitate to spend an extra bit of money for the best line-up, the best production, the best food, the best drinks. It was important to stay true to the original values behind setting up V Festival back in 1996 – a truly punter-focused festival. They identified Baltimore as a site in the north-east that was under-penetrated and in close proximity to hundreds of colleges and several key mid-sized to large US cities. Virgin Mobile US joined up as a sponsor and offered their expertise in marketing to a youthful target audience.

Meanwhile, in Toronto, the Virgin Mobile Canada team – including marketing gurus Nathan Rosenberg (recruited from Virgin Mobile Australia to start Virgin Mobile Canada) and Andrew Bridge – began to transform the lush Toronto Island Park into Virgin Festival grounds.

Without a fantastic headliner, there is no festival. In a stroke of luck and genius, the Who decided to tour that summer and Seth signed them up to open for the Red Hot Chili Peppers in Baltimore. It was to be their only mid-Atlantic stop. Once the Who joined us, we knew the festival was going to make a strong first impression.

Dan even convinced my son Sam to get in on the excitement. In June, less than three months before the festival date, Sam kicked off ticket sales at the Union Square Megastore in New York City. He was flanked by a row of lads wearing nothing but socks in a tribute to the Red Hot Chili Peppers. Afterwards, Sam rang Jackie up in the UK and convinced her that he did the media event in nothing more than a sock – thankfully, my son has more modesty than his father and was only winding her up!

I had a busy September that year. On 9 September I helped kick off Toronto's Virgin Festival and then went down to New York to announce during the Clinton Global Initiative that 100 per cent of profits from Virgin Group's transportation interests would be invested in clean energy. Days later, my wife Joan and Sam and I travelled to Baltimore for the US festival. As I walked across the grounds and shook hands with thousands of festival-goers, I was struck by the number of people who thanked me for bringing Virgin and the festival to the US. Many jokily thanked me for saving the Earth but I reminded them that it is just as much their responsibility as it is mine!

While the North America market is very different from the UK market, one thing was clear: we all love a brilliant party. So we responded to each individual market but also gave them signature Virgin touches, most of which were inspired by the UK's V Festival. We wanted to be remembered for unsurpassed production quality, Virgin Angels who helped people in charming and unexpected ways, chill-out areas, delicious food and beverages. We partnered with sub-sponsors who agreed to contribute to the overall consumer experience, not just their logos, and our stages weren't named after athletic shoes or radio stations. Because we took it seriously as a business, people got to enjoy it as a party. In 2007 we launched V Festival Australia (Sydney, Gold Coast, Melbourne and Perth) and the Aussies definitely know how to party!

In an era of digital downloads and headphones that tune out the rest of the world, the live-music experience offers something different, authentic and communal. It provides a rare chance to gather with people to catch favourite acts and also make unexpected discoveries. Little did we know that thirteen years ago when Jackie and James came to me with the idea of starting V Festival in the UK, we would be in the vanguard of new music festivals in North America.

Just as competition is a great thing for airline passengers, competition will be a great thing for music fans. Many new festivals have sprouted up since that summer, and eventually the best will last.

So, the milliner says to his son: 'Don't worry, lad. People will always need hats.'

What he means is: '*I* will always need hats.' Hats are his life, and he is proud of what he does.

Is his attitude a healthy one?

Of course it is. No business lasts for ever, and being true to your life's work carries with it the risk that you may lose your future. This is the deal we make with the world: that we exercise our free will and accept the consequences. (I love ballooning, and it's almost killed me on several occasions.) Every risk is worth taking as long as it's in a good cause, and contributes to a good life.

Of course, if your business involves the investment of other people's money, you are under certain legal and moral obligations. You may have to adapt your business to meet those obligations.

But I have every sympathy – especially in the light of changes in the music business – with those companies who delivered a thing well, with care and pride, long after the thing being delivered had lost its currency. It's a classic case of doing the right thing at the wrong time. Sometimes it's a mistake. Sometimes – and there's not a business book on the shelves will admit this sorry fact – it's not a mistake at all. It's just something dying.

Virgin is not especially aggressive in the marketplace. (We fight hard and long when we have to, but we don't do dirty tricks and we don't go looking for punch-ups.) And heaven knows, Virgin's success is not down to its crystal-clear vision of the future. If it were, you'd be Virgining our company valuations on the Internet rather than Googling them – and our Megastores would have been sold off in the eighties.

Virgin's success is primarily down to the consistent way it's delivered on its brand proposition. Closing the book on Virgin Music *was* pretty painful, whichever way you spin it. But because the central proposition of the Virgin brand is about customer experience, Virgin has overall found it less painful than most to innovate products or services to satisfy changing consumer demands. For us – and we may be unique in this – a change of industry, and a move into a new sector, *does not* entail a wholesale change in our philosophy or life's purpose.

What astonishes people is less our ability to move into new sectors – after all, venture capitalists do this all the time – than the speed with which we deliver. Willingness to change jobs is one thing, but how do we sometimes manage to hit the ground running so fast?

Delivery is never rocket science. When we move from sector to sector, I'd say about 90 per cent of our core delivery strategy comes with us and slots straight in, without adjustment, without fuss, without trouble. Getting to grips with an unfamiliar infrastructure is simply a question of workload – of *mastering detail*. I haven't yet had to be initiated into the mysteries of a cabal, and neither have the people I work with.

However complex the business is, you should be able to boil it down to a proposition that ordinary people can understand. When an industry delivers its proposition in a way that's totally loopy and counter-intuitive, either you've made an elementary mistake and need to go back to your research, or the entire industry is pulling a fast one and is out to rip off the customer. And if that's the case, then you, the wide-eyed innocent, are like the boy who declared that the emperor wasn't wearing any clothes. You are about to change everything.

This can happen. In fact, it happens all the time. In fact, here at Virgin, we could *write a book* on how often this happens.

Welcome – for starters – to the airline industry.

There are a few contenders for Virgin's greatest ever business deal. But the epitome of our spirit was the way we hired a jumbo jet to start up Virgin Atlantic in 1984. Of all our enterprises, it's the classic case of snatching an opportunity when it appears and making it happen. The creation of Virgin Atlantic is the perfect case study of how we have gone about our business since then. Even today, many years on, it shows our pure audacity and it still defies all business-school logic.

I was interested in an airline as a business idea, but it was really my frustration as a frequent flyer that crystallised the idea for me. I was spending more and more of my time in the air and, along with everybody else, I was having a thoroughly horrible time of it. There were no redeeming factors about flying with British Airways, PanAm or TWA. The quality of service was dire and the staff looked bored and morose. Then, at the turn of the eighties, came the straw that broke the camel's back.

Joan and I were supposed to be flying from the Virgin Islands to Puerto Rico, when the scheduled American Airlines flight was cancelled. The terminal was full of stranded passengers. I'd had enough. I called a few charter companies and agreed to charter a plane for $2,000 to Puerto Rico. I borrowed a blackboard, divided the charter cost by the number of people stranded, and wrote down the number. We got everyone to Puerto Rico for $39 a head.

The utter frustration I had been feeling while flying on other people's airlines convinced me that Virgin Atlantic should be a fun airline with a ring of quality and one that got all the little details right from the start. But our big break had to wait till February 1984, when an American lawyer called Randolph Fields came to me with news that there were landing slots available for a British-based carrier from Gatwick airport, outside London, to Newark, New Jersey. Randolph had been hawking the idea of a budget business airline around all the usual airlines, but they were too close to the realities of the market and remembered the harsh lessons of Freddie Laker and Florida-based People's Express – airlines that had both collapsed under pressure from the four transatlantic flyers, British Airways, British Caledonian, PanAm and TWA. The established airlines had conspired to put Freddie out of business by putting pressure on McDonnell Douglas not to supply him with planes; they persuaded the banks not to lend to him when he needed it; and they slashed fares to undercut him. It was a good old-fashioned mugging, and it succeeded. The British public never forgave them, but what did they care?

Randolph had obviously drawn a blank and I must have been on a list of his last-gasp record-label mavericks. In any normal business an unsolicited caller might get through to the chief executive's PA, then be told to drop a letter in (or these days, send an email) to arrange a meeting on another day. Back in 1984, however, we were based on the canal boat and I made a point of answering my own phone. Randolph got straight through to me. He had a very persuasive pitch: he told me there were lucrative landing slots up for grabs but they had to go to a British carrier. Not only this, but nobody else would be able to get in on these slots once they were assigned. It was a genuine opportunity. Was I interested? I asked him to send me a proposal and I took it with me to the country to read over the weekend.

Randolph was proposing a business-class-only airline, but I thought a mix of business and economy would be better so that we could fill the planes at Easter, Christmas and bank holidays. I agreed to put £1 million into the project to get it going. In the meantime, I needed to become an airline expert overnight.

I phoned Freddie Laker and he told me I didn't need to buy a plane – that wasn't the way it was done. He explained that the banks bought the plane in a deal with either Airbus, Boeing, Lockheed or McDonnell Douglas, and then the airlines leased the planes, guaranteeing to pay monthly fees.

I put in a lot of the legwork to find out all I could about starting an airline. We registered the name Virgin Atlantic and submitted our application for the slots. Then I found the Boeing telephone number through international directory enquiries. The actual conversation still makes me laugh. I remember calling Seattle and asking to be put through to the senior vice president for sales. 'Hello, this is Richard Branson from Virgin here and I'm interested in acquiring a second-hand 747,' I said in my politest English accent.

The guy at the other end said: 'What does your company actually do?'

'Well,' I said, 'we put out bands like the Sex Pistols, Boy George and the Rolling Stones.'

'Oh. Really? What did you say your company is called? "Virgin"?'

At the time, worldwide aircraft sales were in the doldrums and Boeing was having problems shifting its fleet of second-hand 747s, with many parked up and decommissioned in the Arizona Desert. So he didn't put the phone down on me. I think perhaps he was intrigued by my chutzpah. He took my details. And he jokingly said at the end of our conversation: 'With a name like Virgin, as long as your airline goes the whole way, we'll consider selling you a plane!'

Boeing sent a salesperson over to meet me. He was a lovely old guy who stayed in a hotel for four months while we tried to get the deal sorted. Boeing finally agreed that if the airline didn't work out, they would take the plane back at the end of the first year.

This meant that we could start our airline knowing that, if I screwed up completely, I had hedged my bets. Looking back, it was one of the best decisions I ever made.

What's the most critical factor in any business decision you'll ever have to make? Basically, it boils down to this question: *If this all crashes, will it bring the whole house tumbling down like a pack of cards?*

One business mantra remains embedded in my brain – *protect the downside*. By having the option of giving Boeing their plane back after a year, Virgin's total exposure was £5 million – half what we were making at Virgin Records. So we were gambling an acceptable six months' loss, for an enormous potential upside. If disaster struck, it would hurt us, but it wouldn't bring the whole pack of cards crashing down. 'Protecting the downside' is one of the very few business tenets that we try to adhere to at Virgin. Yes, there have been occasions when we have broken our own rule, times where I've said, 'Screw it, let's do it,' mortgaged my home and really stuck my neck out. But that's something I don't recommend.

It was soon very clear that there was no way we could launch a new transatlantic airline unless we had working capital of at least £3 million. We had to raise more cash.

While all this was going on, I knew that we needed to run Virgin's other businesses on a more professional footing. So I approached Don Cruickshank about joining as chief executive to sort us out. Don's arrival freed me up from the record business to learn more about the airline industry.

I phoned Freddie Laker (again) and invited him to lunch on my houseboat *Duende* and he told me why he had failed – and what I must do to avoid his mistakes. He warned me that British Airways would become the enemy, that they were ruthless and had destroyed his business.

We had to protect ourselves against currency fluctuations. The fixed instalments for the jumbo were due in US dollars, but sterling's value was plummeting against the dollar. Our customers were paying for tickets with UK pounds, and we had to be careful not to get stung.

We were also responsible for insurance – and here we nearly came unstuck. We could only get insurance when the Civil Aviation Authority in the UK had given us full certification for airworthiness.

So we undertook a test flight, the plane took off – and a flock of birds flew straight into the engine. Which exploded.

A new engine was going to cost us £600,000 – and, naturally, because we'd had to abort the test flight, we weren't insured yet. This nearly brought down the whole of Virgin as it just took us over our overdraft limit. Don and the other directors wanted me to postpone the launch date, but once I was sure everything was safe, I wanted our airline to get going.

In those four months or so to get the airline going, we had to learn every single thing about the airline business, from reservations to ticket sales and whether to sell our tickets through travel agents or to sell them direct. I had to find out about marketing to let people know about our new airline, and to design and colour the plane. At night, I worked on planning the interior designs, selecting fabrics and even discussing the menus and the choice of wines. We had little or no budget for advertising, so I took Freddie's advice. He told me not to be shy, and to use myself to promote the business.

Four months to learn how to deliver an airline. Not easy. But definitely doable. Those business leaders who seek, in interviews and in their writings, to turn their industries into complex puzzles, subtle chess games of one sort or another – these people really, really annoy me. It isn't enough for them that they're good business people: they have to be Confucius. To listen to them, you'd think you must be born into an industry to make any headway in it. And this is rarely true unless you are truffle hunting. A basic understanding of the business, gleaned by immersing yourself in every little detail for months or even weeks, is often enough to get you started. The volume of information you'll need to hack through will be high – so find some friends to help you – but the underlying business model is always fairly simple.

Remember to communicate, and pay attention to detail. You wouldn't believe how far you can get, just by remembering and practising those two rules. But the evidence of their effectiveness is there for all to see, on our Virgin Atlantic flights. And many of our original decisions are still in place. The bar in our business class was unique to Virgin at the time, and it's still there. The ruby-red uniforms were really gorgeous outfits, and they still are. We went for a first-class product but charged a business-class fare – and that remains our philosophy today.

So, on 21 June 1984, we took to the air from Gatwick in *Maiden Voyager*. It was a flight for many friends, family and other well-wishers. Joan and I sat with Holly on our knee throughout the flight. But the airline was very nearly stillborn. The day I returned, Coutts Bank visited my home to say that since we had reached the overdraft limit, they would now start to bounce our cheques. Here we were, one of Britain's most successful private companies, and expected to make £12 million profit, and they were threatening to make the whole Virgin group insolvent because we were just over our £3 million facility. As I said, communication is important – and to that we might now want to add the words, 'especially communication with one's bank!' But honestly, in my view, at that time, Coutts was hopeless. Short of employing a spiritualist and a Ouija board, we were never going to get through to these people. They had no insight at all into our individual projects and subsidiaries. This would have to change. By the end of the week we'd switched banks to Lloyds, who increased our overdraft facility tenfold to £30 million. Don't be afraid of changing your bank if they are unreasonable. Banks are not for life. But don't put it off till the last minute!

Cash flow was exceptionally tight in the early years. Passenger numbers were highest in the high-summer season, yet our costs were fixed throughout the year. But the exciting feeling for everyone at Virgin Atlantic was that people loved flying with us from the very start. We had a sense of humour, which I think is important, and our pilots and cabin crew were all up for the great adventure. My nasty experience with Coutts Bank, meanwhile, had taught me that we needed to have a professional relationship with our bankers – keeping them informed of every move and letting them know precisely our intentions – and we needed corporate managers such as Don Cruickshank to do this for us.

In the fairy tale, when the little boy starts laughing and pointing at the naked emperor, everyone – including the emperor – realises the emperor's mistake, and the little boy is instantly vindicated.

Well, life's not like that. Let me quickly tell you of a couple of occasions when we laughed and pointed at some ludicrous business absurdity – and the emperor's ministers rushed over and promptly smothered us.

On 25 October 2003, Matthew Parris wrote in *The Times*: 'When we were younger we thought ourselves the first generation when everyone would fly faster than the speed of sound. We were to be the last, not the first.'

He was writing about the last commercial flight of Concorde. The BA 002 service from New York touched down at London Heathrow at 16.05 on 24 October 2003, bringing the first supersonic transportation era to a close twenty-seven years and nine months after it began.

British Airways and Air France's decision to ground the fleet was a disgraceful one because it was taken and executed to ensure that nobody else could ever fly the planes again, in some cases by literally cutting off the tips of their wings. It was an insult to Concorde's engineering brilliance. We knew that we could make a go of the service, and Virgin mounted a Save Concorde campaign. But it came to nought, due to British Airways' insistence that no one else could maintain and run the fleet. They hurriedly dismantled the planes and dispersed them to museums around the country – just to make sure. It was a deplorable way to end such a glorious era.

At the post-flight bash British Airways chairman Lord Colin Marshall was keen to show the 300 guests, who had just arrived on the three flights, the live BBC news report of the historic arrivals. To his horror, the soundtrack accompanying the picture turned out to be by John Hutchinson – a former Concorde pilot! John lambasted British Airways for retiring the aircraft while still in its prime, and very generously sang my praises for trying to keep her flying.

Sir Colin disappeared behind the screen – and the sound suddenly cut out, apparently interference from all the TV satellite vans parked nearby . . .

The moral is that it is important to stick to your guns. The public isn't stupid, and I think we've reaped huge rewards for being forthright in the marketplace.

In 1997 I came to share my experience about the lottery business with Thabo Mbeki, who was then the deputy president of South Africa. I thought a national lottery would be an excellent way of raising vital funds for the nation.

A lottery is a licence to print money because there is no competition. There are no risks at all in running a national lottery, and it is also one of the easiest companies in the world to set up. The formula has been tried and tested worldwide. In almost every country and state the lottery is run so that 100 per cent of the profits go to good causes. The country appoints a trustworthy business person with lottery experience and he or she hands the profits straight to the government's charitable arm for distribution to the most important causes in the country – usually for education, health or fighting poverty. What these lotteries don't have is a level of shareholders creaming off the profit between the person running the lottery and the good-cause fund.

I had made two unsuccessful bids for the National Lottery in the UK – in 1994 and 2001 – and to this day it still perplexes me that Camelot, the company that runs the lottery on behalf of the government, and who employed GTech (one of whose directors tried to bribe us during our bid), has been allowed to make so much money at the expense of good causes.

There was not a lot of love lost between me and Camelot in those days. The lottery company once hired Madame Tussaud's, the famous waxwork attraction in London, for a corporate evening. A brother of one of our Virgin Atlantic staff was at the party and found that my wax model had been temporarily removed and put in the broom cupboard for the evening. Actually, I think my effigy took one look at the company it was keeping, and walked.

So I said that if South Africa set its lottery up in the right way, it could be a provider for good. But I was anxious they didn't make the same mistake as Britain. I was seriously concerned that some in the business community were putting pressure on the government to set it up as a profit-making scheme for the business community.

I pointed out that the Conservative government in the UK made that mistake in 1994 and instead of the lottery being something the whole country has been proud of, it is talked about, even among regular ticket buyers, with some contempt. At the time, the opposition Labour Party realised this terrible mistake and pledged to turn the lottery into the people's lottery when Camelot's licence ended.

In 2007, with Labour still in power, Camelot were given the licence for a third time – another political promise broken by a government once in power.

I tried hard to convince Thabo Mbeki and the president not to make the mistake that was made in the UK. But it seems that, in the end, they also fell into the same trap as the UK, and granted the licence to a commercial company, Uthingo Management.

Sometimes you will fail to transform a business because of other people's short-sightedness. Other times, you fail because of other people's greed. It's that simple and that galling. The fight you lost will turn out to be worth it down the line: the public will respect you for it, and show you great loyalty thereafter.

Delivery is the moment where your good intentions meet the real world. Delivery is best approached steadily, and with fortitude. You'll need stamina and patience to deliver well – especially when everybody is out to kill you.

For a long time I have nursed an ambition: to run a profitable airline in America. The most important word in that last sentence is 'profitable'. It was easier said than done, and although the new baby is now doing extremely well, the arrival of Virgin America, our airline in the US, was a slow and painful birth.

The United States of America is littered with the carcasses of British businesses – and rock bands too – that have tried to make it big and then foundered. I wanted Virgin to be different, and Virgin Records USA and Virgin Mobile USA showed what could be done. But airlines – with their huge amount of federal regulation, issues of ownership and industry resistance – are a different ball game. It's a bit like Arsenal playing in the American National Football League.

The first hurdle was the certification process. Under US law, foreigners can own as much as 25 per cent of the voting equity in a US airline and an additional 24 per cent of the non-voting stock. I expected negotiations between the US and the European Union on aviation treaties to loosen this, letting in greater foreign investments and stimulating competition. But it wasn't happening quickly enough, and we had to ensure that at least 51 per cent of the business was owned by Americans.

The arrival of Fred Reid to lead Virgin America, in April 2004, was a boon. Fred, the former president and chief operating officer of Delta Airlines, had a welter of airline experience spanning more than twenty-five years, and he knew his way around Washington, DC. Our legal and political advisers were anxiously pursuing an operating certificate for Virgin America. It was all highly sensitive, and Fred cautioned me and the Virgin people that even the slightest off-hand remark by any of us in any venue official or otherwise could easily trigger a ninety-day delay in certification. It was election year, and our application had unique aspects which made it frighteningly easy for a hostile party to trip us up. And there were plenty of them: Fred told me that every single airline in America was dreading our entry into the market.

After 9/11 and its aftermath, I saw an opportunity to capitalise on the weaknesses of the big US carriers. United Airlines was operating in Chapter 11 bankruptcy protection, and American Airlines and Continental were slashing costs and staff to compete. I've been asked if there are such things as insurmountable problems in business. I think there were for these legacy airlines, with their large payrolls, outmoded practices and ageing fleets of planes. According to *The Economist* in 2007, their own poor management and circumstances beyond their control – oil prices tripling, terror attacks in 2001 and a plummeting dollar – lost them a cumulative $35 billion in the five years to 2005, a mind-blowing amount of money for investors to lose.

We honestly thought that by abiding by the rules of the US government and the Department of Transportation, a timely decision would be made. We did not expect it to drag on and on. Our application turned out to be a lesson in naivety. The US DOT is not accountable to anyone about when it approves applications, and it took its own sweet time. Existing US airlines, although visibly failing to serve the public with decent fares and service, became involved in a spectacular filibustering process to delay and deter us from getting off the ground. We were a visible threat, with our new fuel-efficient aircraft and a genuine focus on the consumer experience. Noticeably absent from all the ganging up were the two airlines we'd surely compete with: JetBlue and Southwest. You would think they had more to lose yet these two healthy and strong airlines didn't jump up and down and cry, 'This isn't fair.'

To meet the DOT's hurdles, the Virgin Group moved heaven and earth, making concessions beyond what was required by US law. Fred Reid reassured the American regulators that our airline was indeed 'Born in the USA'. A tranche of sophisticated investors were on board, and those investors hired Don Carty, a thirty-year industry veteran and former chairman and CEO of both Canadian Pacific and

American Airlines, to lead the board. Virgin had a statutory right to three board directors but we gave up one.

Eventually, in May 2007, we were granted approval – but there was a sting in the tail. Fred was told by the Department of Transportation that since he'd been taken on by me personally (which was not true) – and I was a foreigner – he would not be allowed to run the business.

This was a blow for Fred, and for us: we had to find someone else to lead it. Virgin America should have been ready to launch at the end of 2003. Instead it launched in August 2007. It had taken nearly four years – Virgin Atlantic took four months. During our battle to cut through the Gordian knots of US regulation, six new planes sat idle on the ground for nearly eighteen months. They alone burned $11 million before we made a penny. In its first year, Virgin America has won all sorts of awards, including *Zagat*'s 'best first-class service in America' and 'best domestic airline' in *Travel + Leisure*'s World Best Awards. The airline has stimulated competition among carriers and created thousands of jobs. And as a consumer champion, Virgin is making good on our promise of a better overall experience and better prices whether you fly Virgin America not.

Virgin America's new president and CEO David Cush, formerly of American Airlines, and his team have a unique business model with the kind of flexibility needed to cleverly navigate these turbulent times. They're continuing to deliver a great flying experience to a small but growing number of urban point-to-point centres. Now the battle is to make the airline profitable. At a recent Washington Aviation lunch an American Airlines director said to a colleague that it was ironic that American Airlines had lost one of its best people as a result of its own lobbying on Capitol Hill to get rid of Fred Reid. Some clouds do indeed have silver linings.

All businesses, at least when they start, want to be agents of change. This is not always easy – especially if you're operating on a shoestring in a developing country with poor infrastructure, and where the delivery systems are held together by little more than bribery. In those circumstances, pretty much anything new is a threat to your business.

Equally, it is all very well being cast as an agent of change in an ambitious, developing country – but you can never afford to forget that your arrival is going to hurt people. The welcome changes you're bringing in may well look like threats – and almost certainly *will be* threats – to existing interests. These interests may look rather paltry to you, but they're life and death to some.

Knowing when to tread carefully, and when to put your foot down, is a lesson all businesses must learn, if globalisation is ever to bring about change for the better.

June 2004: I was with my family, playing tennis in our garden in Oxfordshire, when the call came through. I wasn't too surprised to get the summons. For a few years, I had been in discussions with several Nigerian officials about airline services into Africa. Now I was to go to Paris and meet the Nigerian president himself.

Nigeria is a great entrepreneurial nation and there are many excellent business people throughout the country. But it is hampered by poor infrastructure.

Chief Olusegun Obasanjo, now the former president of Nigeria, is a commanding character. A retired army general who has served his country, he is a towering presence throughout Africa. What I liked about President Obasanjo was that he came across to me (then) as a very honourable man. He liked me, and I him. That's the way it is in business. The president was very open and honest about the problems of the past. He was now pursuing a programme of privatisation. The airline industries, however, posed serious difficulties, particularly regarding regulation. In the past, the president acknowledged, there had been all kinds of shady deals and lobbying done between the airlines and the aviation suppliers. He wanted a much fairer and transparent system. (Later, in my notebook I wrote: *'In all my dealings with him and his cabinet, never a hint of corruption. A desire to cut through red tape and get things done.*') I agreed, saying that we weren't interested in being involved with anything that meant backhanders or 'special' payments. If he wanted us to help, then we would work together on a basis of trust.

The airline industry across parts of Africa has an atrocious record on safety – planes crash quite regularly, particularly in Sudan and Nigeria. I wanted to use our expertise to make a difference. But I was also very mindful of affronting people's sensibilities – a Westerner criticising a developing nation even as it tries to turn things around. My experiences with Virgin Nigeria were to throw these tensions into sharp relief, as we struggled to attain world-class excellence in an underdeveloped and undercapitalised industry.

I had told the president that my vision was the creation of 'a world-class airline with a spirit of Africa and Nigeria at the hub'. It was certainly something that Obasanjo thought would give Nigeria a renewed sense of stature. But we had to set about a serious issue: the African air traffic control system was in need of overhaul and investment, its operators were in dire need of retraining – and Nigeria had one of the bleakest aviation track records in the world.

In early September 2004, I was in Nigeria's capital, Abuja, for another meeting with the president. It was nearly 1 a.m., and a long queue of Nigerians were waiting patiently in the corridor of one of the city's best hotels. Fortunately I was able to jump the queue, as government advisers whisked me to his top-floor suite.

He put his hand on my shoulder and said: 'I like you, Richard.'

'Thanks, Mr President,' I said, rather bowled over by such a welcome. 'Erm, what is it about me that you like?'

'I like the fact that you never wear a tie. I hate those stuffy English gentlemen with their ties.'

Our talks went extremely well and I was able to say that he could be assured of Virgin's commitment to his country. We shook hands on the deal, and the next day we launched a new airline for Africa.

I knew the president admired our flagship, Virgin Atlantic. Though launched as a cut-price airline, its success was also based on giving the business traveller the best customer service in the world. We'd offered our business travellers what first-class passengers on other airlines didn't get. We had pioneered comfortable reclining seats, flat beds, lounges with hairstylists and masseuses, and a motorcycle and limo home-pickup service.

In economy, Virgin Atlantic was the first to provide personal video screens in every seat-back, so that the traveller could choose the films and television shows he or she wanted to watch.

Nigerian Airways had been the nation's flag carrier from 1965 until 2002, but it had been overrun with bureaucracy and riddled with corruption. During the summer of 2004, the Nigerian federal government proposed a new flag carrier as part of its privatisation process. They wanted Virgin's support. On Tuesday 28 September 2004 – the same week we were making an announcement about Virgin Galactic – I flew from London to Abuja to join President Obasanjo once again and the Minister of Aviation, Mallan Isa Yuguda, to sign a Memorandum of Mutual Understanding, which formally established Virgin Nigeria as a new flag carrier.

The airline was created with a $50 million investment, the shares split between the Nigerian investors, with 51 per cent, and Virgin Atlantic, with 49 per cent. The aim was to widen the offering in time on the Nigerian stock exchange. It was set in stone that the home base would be Murtala Muhammed International Airport (MMIA) in Lagos, flying to London, Abuja, Kano and Port Harcourt, then to Abidjan, Accra and Dakar. Although we'd be a minority partner in this new airline, I wanted us to bring all our expertise to help our Nigerian partners create the best airline, not just in Africa – but in the world.

We brought in Simon Harford, who had worked with Barbara Cassani on setting up British Airways' low-cost airline, Go, to be the CEO, and he set about his task with alacrity. He signed up KPMG and Philips Consulting to handle recruitment – a key area for us. We were swamped with applications – nearly 25,000 wanted to join the airline.

Virgin Nigeria was to be built from scratch: a modern airline with excellent service. We believed the business would create several thousand jobs within five years and, indirectly, a further 200,000 jobs.

We set about building a best-in-class terminal for Virgin Nigeria at MMIA, and commissioned EDS to deliver us an integrated airline reservations, ticketing and baggage system that was as good as anything else in the world. We signed a deal to lease the first of our Airbus A320s, with sixteen business-class seats, for the domestic routes.

Meanwhile, Simon and his team were working to finalise approvals from the Nigerian Civil Aviation Authority. On 13 June 2005, tickets went on sale – via phone, travel agents and the Internet – for our inaugural flight from Lagos to London Heathrow, arriving at Terminal 3. The tickets were sold out within a few days. We aimed to fly weekly at first and then three times a week operating an Airbus A340-300, with 187 economy, 28 premium economy and 40 business-class seats.

Our maiden flight left Lagos for London on Tuesday 28 June. The aviation minister, Isa Yaguda, presented the first group of trained cabin crew with their 'wings to fly'.

In the following days the domestic services would be launched too. The initial feedback was tremendous. One regular flyer, Dan Ekpe, said the sight of Virgin Nigeria's aircraft on the tarmac in London had filled him with 'a sense of pride' that a Nigerian carrier was now doing a great job.

In the first ten months, we flew 500,000 passengers on our six planes, two Airbus 340-300s, an A320-200 and three Boeing 737-300s.

On 11 July 2005, President Obasanjo sent Virgin a note to thank us for our commitment: 'I believe that your role in the aviation sector will bring innovation, competition, new technology and, of course, a lot of satisfaction to the Nigerian public.'

He then went on to remind me that there was a need to 'Nigerianise' the staff at all levels in order to anchor the future of the airline on indigenous capacity from management through to technical and cabin crew. 'I know that you have put a quality training facility and programme in place. It is my expectation that you will use these facilities to train Nigerians in all critical areas of airline management and operations.'

We did indeed. We put a lot of time and effort into training and recruiting staff for the airline. We set up a technical partnership with the Nigerian College of Aviation Technology to train new pilots who would then be sent away to get experience on short-haul airlines. We also set up apprenticeships, and offered automatic employment to those trainee engineers who successfully completed their courses.

Within the first year we were able to expand services to Dubai, as well as increasing the internal domestic routes from Lagos to Abuja, Port Harcourt and Kano, as well as Lagos to Johannesburg.

In November, having taken the airline through its momentous launch – a remarkable job in such a short time – Simon Harford decided it was time for someone else to take the reins; he announced that he was moving on. His job was taken up by Conrad Clifford, who had come with me and Simon on my first trip to Nigeria in 1996. It was a challenging time to be taking over, but Conrad, who had set up Virgin Atlantic's operations in Nigeria, was ready to take the airline to its next stage of expansion.

However, I can't deny that I had some concerns about the way things were going.

For the existing Nigerian airlines there were serious problems. One was bankrupt, and while it had enough cash to cover the cost of crews, landing and navigational fees, fuel and insurance, there was no money left for reinvestment and maintenance. Another had only one serviceable plane. The remainder of its fleet was grounded because they could not fund maintenance. This was a simply atrocious situation.

The Federal Airports Authority of Nigeria still required a lot of help to make things work more smoothly. The feedback I received told me that outside Virgin Nigeria, things were being very badly run. It was going to take time to create a superb new airline in Africa. Our competitors in Nigeria still had planes falling out of the sky and customers plummeting to their deaths.

On 22 October 2005, a 25-year-old Bellview Airlines Boeing 737 took off from Lagos with six crew and 111 passengers on board. After passing through 13,000 feet, the plane stalled, tipped and nosedived into the ground. Although the aircraft came down nineteen miles north of Lagos, it took the rescue teams nine hours to locate the wreckage. The plane had an old search-and-rescue system which hampered search efforts.

On 10 December, a Sosoliso Airlines DC10 from Abuja crashed on landing at Port Harcourt, killing 109 people. Among those who died were seventy-one students of Loyola Jesuit College in Abuja who were returning home for their Christmas holiday.

A few months later, again at Port Harcourt, an Air France jet was badly damaged after crashing into a herd of cows. Thankfully, this time, no one was hurt.

Then, on 18 September 2006, a Dornier 228 military plane crashed killing fourteen officers, including ten generals. In another Nigerian crash, a number of senior politicians were killed.

Delivering the Virgin brand in Africa is important – it must stand for the same values as in other parts of the world: integrity, safety and a commitment to customer service. Maintaining the highest standards of safety is something that can never be compromised, and over the years several international transportation groups have been forced to pull out of Africa because the cut-throat local competition chooses to ignore the regulations.

Working in the Nigerian marketplace was becoming increasingly tough. I and my team in Virgin Nigeria were growing increasingly frustrated. We were striving so hard to build a safe, high-quality airline, but we found ourselves thwarted at every turn. We were incurring all the costs of putting together a quality operation from scratch, but in a market that put safety and quality last. We were, in the end, just an airline: we couldn't hope single-handedly to transform the industry's entire infrastructure. We needed help.

I appealed to the president to ensure that companies that were not prepared to operate to the correct standards or who cut corners were dealt with rapidly. If necessary, he should take steps to remove their Air Operator's Certificates. It was simple: unworthy aircraft should be fixed – or scrapped.

Not long after, a directive arrived, forcibly ejecting Virgin Nigeria from its operational base at Lagos Terminal 1 (home of Virgin Atlantic's Nigerian operation), and relocating it at Terminal 2.

We wanted to keep all of our operations in one terminal – to create a hub, rather than be split across two terminals – and this was the binding contract we'd entered into with the government. Conrad and his team were trying to create an airline that could effectively compete on the world stage. The airline had grown dramatically since 2005, operating thirty flights per day with an excellent safety record. Splitting the airline would increase costs considerably.

We prepared to challenge the directive in the courts – and just hours before the hearing, agents who appeared to have the approval of the Federal Ministry of Transportation and the Federal Airports Authority of Nigeria came in the night like mafiosi with sledgehammers and demolished our business-class lounge.

I had to write to President Yar'Adua, Obasanjo's successor, asking him to intervene personally in this dispute. I knew that Nigerians wanted an international and domestic airline that they could be proud of – and we'd worked hard to deliver this. What we needed now was some common sense and cool heads to ensure that disputes never again escalated in this way.

Fortunately, the president took on board what I said in my letter, and as this book is going to print the issue appears to have been resolved.

*

Out of recession, new ideas and new businesses often grow. But how do you deliver new products to a market that's barely staggered free of the emergency room? How do you get people who've spent the last months or even years firefighting to think strategically? This was one of the challenges facing me as I set out to create mobile networks across the world.

Since 1995, I had been harrying our Virgin management team in London to find a way into the growing market for mobile phones. In the last fifteen years, the mobile has become the personal possession that has most changed the way we live and work across the globe. In 1998 more mobile phones were sold worldwide than cars and personal computers combined. But the early dominance of the giant mobile phone companies was not doing the consumer any favours. I was increasingly frustrated and keen to get involved, but we had neither the firepower nor the infrastructure. What we had was the Virgin brand and a service ethos.

Following Gordon McCallum's arrival, we focused on mobile phones as the sector meriting our greatest attention. One of the downsides was that Virgin Radio, our FM radio licence, was doing well, selling advertising slots to the major phone companies, and the management were trying to discourage me from anything that might jeopardise their revenue. The competitive mobile companies were spending huge amounts and there was a fear – unfounded, in my view – that we might lose their custom.

Gordon McCallum, Stephen Murphy and the team identified a report from Goldman Sachs which they thought might whet my appetite. It was all about MVNOs, and as you can probably imagine, it wasn't exactly bedtime reading.

An MVNO is a *mobile virtual network operator*. It's a phone company, but a phone company without any of the usual telecoms paraphernalia. No telephone exchanges, no phone masts, no networks, wires, switches or cables under the ground. Instead, an MVNO rents time and bandwidth on another carrier's system.

I'm always scouring around for a bargain. And you can usually track them down where someone has produced too much of something and isn't selling enough even to cover their costs. This was happening all over the telecoms industry. The big mobile phone operators had paid vast sums upfront for their mobile infrastructures – now they needed to pull in revenue, and so were keen to lease time to others.

Our first call was to British Telecom, the UK's national phone company, employing tens of thousands of people. Since they had been privatised, BT had been forced by European Union regulations to allow other phone and Internet service providers to piggyback on its massive, fixed-line network. Setting up our own stand-alone telecoms company didn't appeal to us. During our talks I met Tom Alexander, a former professional go-kart racer, who was working with BT Cellnet as deputy commercial director. My instincts about people are usually pretty sharp, and I liked Tom. He shared my passion for business. (He later told me his father had been an inventor in the horticultural industry, and that this had inspired his entrepreneurial streak.)

We thought BT Cellnet would make a good partner, so Virgin made an offer. We started fleshing out how Cellnet as a 'consumer-focused, youth-oriented mobile business' might work with us – and we were also keen to work with BT to secure a third-generation (3G) mobile phone licence. Competition for these five licences on offer in the UK was proving so fierce BT Cellnet had to abandon discussions with Virgin to concentrate on their bid (and, as we subsequently discovered, on one of the most successful rebrands I can think of, to O2, with a much more youth-focused orientation that competes head-on with Virgin Mobile!). Nevertheless, I called Tom. 'Why don't you come over and have a chat about setting up a new company?'

Tom came over that same day to my house in Oxfordshire and we sat with a notebook and pen and plotted how we might run an MVNO.

Gordon and I managed to persuade Tom to jump ship, bringing with him his colleague Joe Steel, then in his early thirties and a mobile phone whizz. Meantime, we began looking for another partner, now that BT Cellnet had pulled out to pursue its bid for a 3G licence. One2One was a company operating in the south-east of England, in the area contained by the M25 orbital motorway. The company was a joint venture between Cable & Wireless and US group MediaOne, and they were keen to talk to us. One2One's strategy of free weekend and evening calls had left it with a network that hardly anyone used during the day. I was sure that Virgin could fill their dead air.

We signed a deal on 1 August 1999, announcing the plan to launch Virgin Mobile in November. Together we were committing over £180 million to the joint venture, using our high street chain of Virgin Megastores and V Shops as our retail channel. But a few weeks later, Cable & Wireless announced it was selling One2One. Deutsche Telekom swooped to buy and it looked as though Virgin Mobile was dead in the water. I decided to intervene. I went to see Deutsche Telekom boss Ron Sommer to smooth the position. To their credit, the Germans got up to speed with our plans incredibly quickly. And to our delight, they liked what they saw: they agreed to proceed and signed off the joint venture, with One2One now becoming T-Mobile.

The Virgin Group and T-Mobile each invested £40 million, giving us £80 million. And we started negotiations with Royal Bank of Scotland and JP Morgan for extra bank debt of £100 million. It was one of the UK's biggest ever start-ups, employing more than 500 people with plans for another 500 jobs within two years. City analysts Investec Henderson Crosthwaite Securities valued the business at £1.36 billion – and we'd yet to make a penny! We had the seed money. We had the confidence of the analysts. Now we needed to prove ourselves. Fast.

If you are a late entrant to a market, you need to be radically different to win over customers. First-mover advantage is often cited in business as giving the early players the edge, but there are plenty of occasions when this isn't the case. In Virgin's favour is the power of the brand, and its arrival into a market can cause some shock waves. This was what we hoped to do with the mobile phone market.

While Tom and Joe were whizzes in the telecoms field, they required an informal lesson in the Virgin brand. The best person to deliver this was James Kydd, who had been working on the launch of Virgin Cola. James was an advertising executive who had known Will Whitehorn since their beer-drinking days in the student union at Aberdeen University, and he had worked in a number of high-profile consumer brand companies. Like so many people who now work for Virgin, he arrived in 1993 to help the airline for three months and ended up staying. We'd had a woeful business-class campaign and I wanted to scrap it. James fixed it and thought it would be fun to hang around Virgin for a while, so we gave him one hell of challenge: the marketing of Virgin Cola and Virgin Vodka. Taking on Coke was, as I'll discuss later, one of our more ambitious business adventures. In 1998, I asked him to join the team on the Virgin Mobile project as brand director.

Meanwhile, the major mobile phone companies were making the consumer's life complicated – deliberately. Across Europe, the consumer demand for mobile phones was shooting into the sky – yet the cost of the latest stylish Nokia, Ericsson, Siemens or Motorola was often prohibitive. So the phone companies began tying the unsuspecting consumer into two- and three-year-long contracts. 'Confusion marketing' was the spurious tag. A customer would sign up and pay for 200 minutes of voice and 100 text messages, but if they used more than this they were charged more per minute not less, as you might expect for being a good customer. This was barmy logic. Of course it was: it was designed to fool people. The industry was deliberately shrouding itself in complexity to fleece people.

James Kydd and Will Whitehorn attended a day-long powwow at a Hertfordshire hotel to discuss the way ahead with a dozen One2One people, including Alan Gow, the finance director, and Tim Samples, the managing director. The discussion was about how the Virgin brand might be effectively applied to the mobile phone market. There were plenty of mobile phone specialists there who could recite the technical spec, but they weren't people who understood our brand. I heard later that James and Will became a little aerated when they tried to defend Virgin Mobile as a consumer-led mobile phone product.

For Virgin, a recurring problem has been that some people who have tried to do business with us think they have bought a label to stick on the front of a product – that 'Virgin' is only a marketing tagline. On the contrary, Virgin has to be the consumer's champion, rather than just a bold red logo. It has been a difficult job over the years, explaining the commercial benefit of this approach – but I think the success of Virgin Mobile has proved beyond a shadow of a doubt that it works. We started from the basic premise: if you rip off the consumer, then you will destroy the integrity of the brand. It's as simple as that.

So we would not follow the 'confusion marketing' of the other guys. I wanted the whole mobile business to be simple enough that even I could understand what I was being charged. It's a basic business message. If the directors can't get their head around the pricing structure of anything, then how on earth is the consumer going to work it out? And we would move into the prepay market so that more young people and those on lower incomes could join the mobile phone revolution.

We needed to keep the tariffs simple. I wrote in my notebook: '*Let people know exactly what they are paying for – and reward those who stay with us. James said think tins of beans! (The more beans they buy the cheaper the price.)*'

James told me later that all the phone people looked on in horror when it was suggested that we make life easy for people. It wasn't what our telecoms partners wanted at first. They wanted to continue with the established charging structure. Joe Steel had experience of this kind of pricing plan – so we asked him to turn it on its head. He got it straight away. We looked at discounting – which had to be a central part of our offering – and rewards for loyalty. If your whole family bought mobile phones it would be cheaper; if it was a Virgin to Virgin phone call it would be cheaper. So there was a distinct reason to buy Virgin. We wanted people to come into Virgin Megastores to buy their phones and purchase their prepaid vouchers for airtime, and we signed up a huge number of places – filling stations, high street chains, local corner shops, even nightclubs – where people could top up their mobile phones.

For the launch we set a simple tariff: 15p for the first ten minutes, then 10p for the next ten and then 5p after this. Later, I wanted to make this even simpler. We settled on 15p for the first five minutes and 5p after that. There would be no confusion about peak or off-peak, local or national calls. Calls to other mobile networks would be charged at a flat rate of 35p per minute. Customers would pay £12.50 for a one-off service pack, including a SIM card, phone number and £10 of free airtime. And they would be able to buy their own phone, choosing from seven models priced between £70 and £380.

Once all this was set in stone I had faith that the team we had put together would be able to run and deliver a great business. I wasn't let down – each one of the Virgin Mobile team could feature in a business-school case study of how to build great collaborative business teams. Graeme Hutchinson, who played with a heavy metal rock band that made two albums, was our head of sales. Andrew Ralston in the customer services office worked exceptionally hard to ensure consistency across our call centre. Steven Day, the former *Daily Express* journalist, joined as director of communications and did a brilliant job of keeping us in the news, as well as helping with investor relations.

Tom, Joe and the team had a real sense of autonomy at Virgin Mobile. I didn't need to be involved day-to-day, but I was sent regular information and figures, which I looked at each night. From the off, the business acted like a listed company – and that's how all start-ups should try to behave. I loved going to the call centre in Trowbridge in Wiltshire to meet the exuberant staff and join in the parties – they knew how to let their hair down and I was exceptionally proud of them all – and delighted for their success. The young Trowbridge staff would turn out in force when I came to visit and they all volunteered to be Virgin Angels at the V Festivals, helping people put up their tents and handing out goodie bags. One of our parties got a little out of hand and the local paper declared on its front page that it had become an orgy, in which drunk young people coupled indiscriminately in the nightclub car park. Good luck to them, I thought: since outside it was minus ten degrees with a foot of snow. Accurate or not, this nonsense was better than a full-page recruitment advert – the following week we were inundated with people wanting to work at Virgin Mobile!

The launch idea was a great caper too: extremely saucy, it made the headlines in all the major UK newspapers. On 11 November 1999, I appeared with seven very attractive women – all naked, except for some strategically placed orange cushions – announcing Virgin Mobile in a giant see-through mobile phone in Trafalgar Square, in the centre of London. Our slogan was: 'What you see is what you get.' I said the confusing range of offers and tariffs out there was just there to fool people, and that if everyone in the UK with a mobile switched to Virgin, they would save a combined £1.6 billion per year.

The Metropolitan Police turned up to find out if our lovely ladies really were stripped bare. We made a swift exit.

I had no idea, back then, how successful this business would become.

On 21 February 2001, I was in Cannes at the 3GSM World Congress, and I announced our intention of making Virgin Mobile the first global MVNO, with non-stop plans to serve ten countries across five continents in the coming years. I informed the delegates about our partnership with Singapore Telecommunications which would result in the launch of Virgin Mobile Asia that summer, and said that partnership plans for Virgin Mobile USA would be announced imminently.

I said Europe, Africa, China, India, Indonesia, Hong Kong, Taiwan, Vietnam and elsewhere throughout South-East Asia and the Pacific

Rim were all ripe for MVNOs. I felt I had to explain how it all made sense. 'I believe no self-respecting GSM or future UMTS network could afford to be without an MVNO.' (There were so many acronyms in this business, I'd had to spend the morning rote-learning them. For the record, GSM stands for Groupe Spécial Mobile – the most popular world standard for mobile networks. UMTS – Universal Mobile Telephone System – is its successor.)

It was easy to see why you might want to set up an MVNO. The start-up costs are tiny compared to buying an existing mobile business, and practically non-existent when compared to the cost of building a new network. But what were the benefits for existing network operators?

MVNOs are great at cutting network churn. If a customer is going to leave an operator isn't it better that they go to the MVNO partner than to a rival? Then at least they are still on the network and there's a half-share of ongoing revenues. The MVNO has its brand and the network has its own brand, and different brands attract different people. Two good brands together will invariably attract more custom than one good brand on its own. So, I argued, networks should think of MVNOs as a kind of insurance policy. Collaborating with an MVNO spreads the risks of the business. The 3G standard had made a lot of extra services possible – from on-the-go email to video messaging – but no one really knew how best to exploit, package or sell these services. 'So,' I argued, 'an MVNO with a different strategy on the same network increases the likelihood of success, while stimulating traffic and revenues.'

It wasn't the wittiest presentation I had ever given and it wasn't the glitziest. But my audience was certainly paying attention. The market was in a quandary, and people were anxious to find 3G business models that would work.

The original mobile networks were built mainly for ordinary voice telephony, and assumed transmission rates that these days seem quite slow. At the end of the 1990s, the International Telecommunication

Union created a new set of standards called 3G, so that network operators could offer users a range of more advanced services, including video calls and high-speed Internet access. Because 3G networks each use a much narrower band of the radio spectrum than the old networks, there was now room on the spectrum for newcomers to come and try their hand at the mobile telecoms business. At least, that was the theory.

What actually happened was rather different. In Germany and in the UK, for example, the governments' auctions of 3G licences impoverished the very markets they were supposed to encourage. In the UK, the auction effectively imposed a crippling tax on mobile phone operators. It all helped Gordon Brown and Tony Blair and their New Labour project. The money heading for the UK government's coffers was an unbelievable £22 billion, which was a lot of schools and hospitals. To that extent you could see why they were tempted into taking advantage. But it backfired in a way, as the auction winners spent so much on their licences that they ended up really dragging their feet building their networks and developing the very services that the government wanted to promote! We were concerned that T-Mobile might not give us access to 3G, so we wanted to bid ourselves.

Our consortium decided to stick at £1.5 billion, and when bidding for licences began, we were decisively outgunned by silly money. On 5 April 2000 we pulled out of the bidding. At the end of April, the winners were announced: TIW, the Canadian Telecoms company in which Hutchinson Whampoa, better known for 3, have a stake, paid £4.3 billion; BT, One2One and Orange, around £4 billion; Vodafone paid a swingeing £5.9 billion!

We had had a lucky escape by sticking to our principles and only bidding what we thought the licence was worth, not allowing ourselves to get carried away by the open gambling nature of the process itself.

*

In February 2001, as I was speaking at Cannes, describing what I believed was the future for mobile telecommunications – even as I was juggling, or trying to juggle, all those unlovely capital letters, like something out of Dr Seuss – Virgin Mobile's plans were gathering pace in the United States.

In America, the problem with the mobile market wasn't so much that the government had sucked the blood out of it, but more that everyone was reeling from the sheer cost of creating the infrastructure you need to take full advantage of the 3G standard. In the wake of deregulation, companies had piled billions of dollars into new communications gear to deliver everything from telephone services to viable TV networks to high-speed Internet capacity. The capital spending on infrastructure was massive – more than $100 billion in 2000. Dozens of telecoms start-ups set in place during the previous few years began running out of money and folding. Between June and September 2000, the telecoms giants in the US also began to melt down. *Business Week* in September talked about an industry downturn as the Big Three local phone companies – Verizon Communications, BellSouth and SBC Communications – watched their shares slide.

Annual revenues – increasing at a respectable 10.5 per cent a year – were simply not keeping pace with the cost of these soaring capital projects. Investors were getting their fingers burned. This was what made Virgin Mobile's MVNO such an intriguing option for our new partners, Sprint.

The problem was, Sprint was hurting just as much as everybody else. They were spending more and more time firefighting, less and less time thinking strategically. Shaken by a bad set of quarterly results, Sprint began to lose their enthusiasm for our innovative scheme. Things began to look dodgy and after nearly a year and a half of discussions and investment there was pressure from the finance team to shut it all down. Charles Levine, the president of Sprint PCS, the wireless division of the US telecoms giant, wanted to go ahead, but he was facing strong opposition. It was time for a last-gasp effort. Gordon encouraged me to phone Sprint's group president, Ron LeMay, and the chairman and chief executive, Bill Esrey.

I said it wouldn't cost them a lot.

No response.

I said it would make money for them in a new category.

Nothing.

I wheeled out the big guns. I told them we could transform their stuffy image.

Nothing.

'Look,' I said, fairly desperate by this time, 'you need a brand like Virgin. Right now you're the phone company of choice for . . . for *young Republicans.*'

And Bill changed his mind.

We were on.

In June 2000 *Red Herring*, the business technology magazine, listed the '100 Most Important Companies in the World' and their branding. Virgin didn't make the list. *Forbes* magazine spent time following me for a cover story in July 2000 and its writer Melanie Wells concluded that our brand was stretched too thinly across too many businesses. Gordon McCallum had told me to my face that Virgin was still 'a British brand'.

We needed to be more focused and show we could deliver an outstanding product to tough international markets. We needed to prove ourselves in the right place. And that place was the United States.

In October 2001, Sprint and the Virgin Group officially announced our joint venture – a Virgin-branded MVNO running on Sprint's PCS digital system. Our aim was to target fifteen- to thirty-year-old consumers in the United States.

Our eyes and ears in America was Frances Farrow. I'd asked her to join the board of Virgin Atlantic back in 1993 and she was a thoughtful and incisive person. She was now CEO of Virgin USA, the headquarters of the Virgin Group in North America, responsible for expanding the Virgin brand, developing new business and managing investments in the region.

Conventional wisdom had it that the prepaid market simply wouldn't work in the United States. Prepay phones effectively guarantee anonymity, and people told me that the only people wanting phones like this were the three Ps market: pimps, pushers and prostitutes! We were less than charmed by that argument. We said that it was fundamentally wrong; that the prepay phone was an attractive category for younger people who didn't want to lumber themselves with niggling financial commitments.

We were reminded of an extremely smart guy called Dan Schulman, the CEO of Priceline.com, one of the most recognised brands on the Internet. Dan, who had previously been president of AT&T's consumer markets, was just then bringing Priceline.com into profit. We had already been talking to him about Virgin Atlantic flights on his price comparison site; now we began talking about the future of mobile phones. On 15 June 2001, we were able to confirm the rumours – and we launched Virgin Mobile in the USA.

In the UK, we had now signed up our one millionth customer. In just nineteen months we had established a record as the fastest growing mobile business Britain had ever seen. (It had taken Orange more than three years to hit a million customers, One2One in excess of four years, Vodafone more than eight years and Cellnet almost a decade!)

We were already rolling out Virgin Mobile Australia to a market that was gasping for innovation; Virgin Mobile Canada, France and South Africa would follow once we had perfected the business model. In a Memorandum of Understanding with Sprint, we said our intention was to launch a Virgin Mobile-branded joint venture company in the USA.

Sprint would be hosting the first MVNO in the US. This gave us a head start; but I knew that others would be watching with interest, and it wasn't long before Disney tried – and failed – to do their own MVNO deal. We soon needed a larger injection of capital. We needed a bigger corporate hitter. We asked the executive headhunters Heidrick & Struggles to scour the market and they coincidentally suggested Dan Schulman who moved to us from Priceline.com in May 2001.

Complex as this account has been, I hope it's clear by now that you don't necessarily need an accounting or a legal brain to run a successful business. Our approach has come by asking questions.

What if we create a product and it's the best in the world – will there be a market for it? The answer to this isn't as obvious as it looks at first. If quality always won out in the marketplace, the Betamax videotape format would have trounced VHS and there would be more Apples than PCs.

If, on the other hand, I asked you: 'Do people want to fly with the best airline in the world?' Without any figures or numbers, your answer would be 'Yes'.

When you're first thinking through an idea, it's important not to get bogged down in complexity. Thinking simply and clearly is hard to do. It takes concentration and practice and self-discipline. Reducing those initial reports on the MVNO model to a simple business proposition took work. It also, dare I say it, took a pinch of courage on the part of Virgin risking its brand and on the part of those who left cosy jobs to make the vision a reality.

It's easy to be hoodwinked by technical-sounding detail, and to parrot it at others, and to feel important in doing so. It's hard to ask the naive question. Nobody wants to look silly.

But I would say you can never go too far wrong by thinking like a customer who's new to the business. Why do these mobile charges make no sense? Because they make no sense, that's why! Because they are there to fool you! It staggers me to this day that, when we entered this lucrative and exciting young market, we were the only one in the crowd pointing and laughing as the emperors of the phone industry strode by.

It's easy – too easy, in fact – to relinquish your responsibility for your idea to experts. This is almost always a mistake, because experts are only experts in their field. They're not experts in your idea. At this stage, the only person qualified to assess your idea is you.

Your initial business ideas may lack detail. That's fine – but it doesn't give experts anything to work with. Ask them for their opinion, and they'll give you something back that's generic, predictable and fairly useless. I know that if I present an unready idea to experts such as Ernst & Young or McKinsey, they will advise me how much money I stand to lose. If, on the other hand, I go to PricewaterhouseCoopers or KPMG with the same idea, they could well tell me how much I'm going to make. In neither case do I learn anything useful about my idea.

You need to flesh out your own ideas. You need to do your own research. You need to take responsibility for how you plan to turn an idea into action. That way, when you approach the experts – the accountants, the legal brains – they have something to get their teeth into.

Virgin's move into the finance sector astonished many, and still raises an incredulous eyebrow among some politicians and heads of industry. Finance, surely, is sacrosanct: an impossibly arcane and rarefied practice – the province of experts?

Our success in the financial sector has come from asking very clear questions of ourselves, and then (and only then) surrounding ourselves with experts who are demons at cutting through the verbiage to the relevant details. An expert who makes things more complicated isn't doing their job right – and frankly, this is probably your fault. An expert should make things simpler. An expert should give you twenty-twenty vision. Given the right tools to do her job, she is a marvel to behold.

Enter Jayne-Anne Gadhia.

Jayne-Anne qualified as a chartered accountant with Ernst & Young and went to work with Norwich Union, the insurance and pensions giant. She became one of their rising stars, working in unit trusts and PEPs, a tax-efficient personal savings product. Now she was looking for her next move.

One day in 1994 she took the train to London, in time for lunch with Alastair Gornall, a PR agent who ran Consolidated Communications. On the train, she flicked through a copy of *Hello!*. There was an article and colour photographs featuring a bearded and grinning Richard Branson talking about the Virgin Group.

'I read that article and I thought, Gosh, it's so different from Norwich Union; it must be fantastic to work for a guy like that,' she later told me.

She mentioned the article to Alastair. Alastair was a friend of Rowan Gormley, who had just joined Virgin and was the brains behind a joint venture project between Norwich Union and Virgin. It was called Virgin Direct.

Jayne-Anne came to see me for a meeting at Holland Park. There was a lot of commotion because we'd just set up Virgin Cola. She recalls ringing the doorbell at Holland Park and having to find her own way around. She wandered up the stairs and found me working in one of the bedrooms. I led her into the snooker room where her boss Philip Scott had brought along all the papers to review. We worked on the plans to launch Virgin Direct in the snooker room, then we went back downstairs. Philip had a quick gin and tonic and left to catch his train.

I shook my head and said to Jayne-Anne: 'How life moves. One day we're dealing with the Sex Pistols, the next day we're dealing with pensions.' I pointed to the chair Philip had been sitting in. 'Sid Vicious was sitting there not so long ago.'

'Really?'

'Yeah. You see that corner there?'

'Yes?'

'That's where he threw up.'

We signed the deal to set up Virgin Direct on 19 December 1994, with Norwich Union and Virgin both putting in £2 million.

We worked hard to get the deal done, the business launched and all the regulatory approvals in place, but we still managed to have some proper fun. I think that's what Jayne-Anne liked about Virgin.

Virgin Direct in December 1994 was a new player because it was one of the first financial service companies to sell products over the telephone. Jayne-Anne said to me that approval from LAUTRO (the Life Assurance and Unit Trust Regulatory Organisation) and IMRO (the Investment Management Regulatory Organisation) would take months and months. I thought at first she was talking about her Italian cousins. I said: 'I can't understand this, Jayne-Anne. This is a relatively small company – we launched an airline in ninety days.'

But we pushed on and the combination of Norwich Union, Jayne-Anne and Virgin gave us enough clout to get the job done on time.

We needed a new computer system and we approached the big players. IBM estimated it would cost £7 million and would take many months to build. We didn't have that kind of money and we didn't have that amount of time. So one of Jayne-Anne's colleagues, Kevin Revell, and a computing friend, set up the first system for Virgin Direct in his attic in Norwich. In all, it cost us £17,000. On Sunday 5 March 1995, Virgin Direct was launched on that system, with sixty people taking the telephone calls at Discovery House, Whiting Road, which is still the office of Virgin Money. I went up to Norwich for the launch. The office looked pristine, it sported the new signage, and all the computers were working. The boss, Rowan Gormley, wasn't there as he was due to appear on the BBC's *Money Programme* to explain our arrival on the marketplace. So I took the lead: I jumped on a desk and shook open a bottle of bubbly – like they do on the Formula One rostrum. It fizzed up brilliantly into the air, over all the cheering staff and over four of the PCs. The computers started fizzling. Then they blew up.

It was clear from day one that the Virgin brand was going to succeed in financial services. The staff were brilliant and worked their socks off. The £17,000 attic computer system became the prototype as we launched life insurance and pensions too.

Norwich Union didn't have the appetite for building a bigger business, but Virgin Direct needed the capital to grow. So in 1997 Norwich Union sold its 50 per cent stake in Virgin Direct to AMP, the Australian life assurance business and owner of Pearl Assurance. AMP and Virgin became fifty–fifty joint venture partners. In November 1996 I wrote to George Turnbull of AMP, proposing 'a business plan to launch a basic mortgage first (together with a card) followed by a mass-market card'.

The question was: how? Almost all of the UK's high street branches had approached me to talk about banking and financial services. They wanted to shelter under the umbrella of the Virgin brand. As simple as that. But Virgin wanted to do much more than stick their logo on someone else's product. Then, in 1997, I was contacted by the Royal Bank of Scotland, at the time being run by George Mathewson and Fred Goodwin. Finally, here was a company that wanted to innovate.

The idea around the Virgin One account was revolutionary and simple – even I could get my head around it. It had originated in Australia where it was increasingly popular. It was about putting all of a customer's products together. At the end of each evening your net balance is charged interest. Most people have a separate mortgage, current account and savings, and you're paying interest on the whole mortgage. If you roll everything together, you'd have a lower negative balance and you could pay off your home loan more quickly.

George Mathewson, a shrewd and canny Scot, went to see Jayne-Anne Gadhia in Norwich. He was enthusiastic but, at the same time, seemed reluctant to make a fuss about this great product.

'You don't seem to want to shout about this,' Jayne-Anne observed.

He replied that if it were successful, he would take half the profits; if not, nobody would know he had anything to do with it.

But in fact George and his team were brilliant and our relationship is a long one that has lasted to this day (he advised us on our bid for Northern Rock). He said to the Virgin One team that he wanted us to build a business around what worked for customers. He admitted that if RBS could have done it themselves as a mainstream bank they would have, but they liked Virgin's culture of innovation and our history of delivering on our promises. In October 1997, the Virgin One account was launched internally to Virgin Group staff, and then rolled out in 1998. I admit it was a difficult start because the UK public weren't used to the idea of putting all their eggs in one basket, however safe it might be. By October 1998, we had opened 2,000 Virgin One accounts. The following year we opened 9,000, and 15,000 the year after that. We were up and running.

The dinner-party brigade became our best promoters. Doctors, lawyers and professional people were converting to its merits; they told their friends, and the idea began to spread through recommendation. We heard that people would take their Virgin One cards out at meals with friends and sell the idea. In business terms, this is pure gold. You can't buy this kind of advocacy. In Norwich, Virgin One recruited people who wanted to help the customer and make a difference – it was a huge part of the training. There were no stifling scripts to follow, or average talk-times to listen to. We just answered the questions. We hired people who believed – like we did – that Virgin was on a revolutionary crusade to change banking in the UK. One theme was 'uncommon people' – that those who worked with us and our customers were special because they were 'uncommon people'. We had baseball caps, T-shirts and jackets made for 1,500 staff and for customers, to trumpet our attitude of going the extra mile.

In 2001, RBS could see this was a great business. They decided they wanted to buy 100 per cent of Virgin One. They already had 50 per cent, but the remaining part was held by Virgin Direct, which was a fifty–fifty joint venture between Virgin and AMP. I owned a quarter of this and there was a lot of discussion about the shareholding. I had lunch with Fred Goodwin and Fred was quite clear with me: he didn't have a huge amount of time for AMP.

I wrote in one of my notebooks: '*Fred Goodwin. "Don't want to come into three-way venture. Try to buy out other 50 per cent of Virgin One. Come up with basis to take out 50 per cent. Somehow chemistry: us and AMP don't get on. Have relationship with CGNU."*'

On a nearby page I added: '*A game of Monopoly. I used to enjoy playing Monopoly as a child. Recently I began to realise that I've never stopped. Mortgaging my hotels to keep Euston Station. Mortgaging my houses to acquire the Utilities. Borrowing from the bank to pay for everything! Selling everything to pay the bank!*'

We eventually sorted out a deal with AMP. Once it was announced I phoned Jayne-Anne.

'I'm really sorry.'

'About what?'

'About losing you. I'm phoning to say how sad I am today.'

'Sorry? Why?' she said. 'I've just got a very decent cheque and so have my team.'

'Well, I feel as if I'm selling you and the guys along with all of the furniture. I've signed a clause with the Royal Bank saying we can't go into mortgages in the UK for the next two years. Look: if you don't like corporate life in two years' time, come back to us.'

Two years to the day later, I phoned. 'Are you happy?'

My call had surprised her, and pleased her, but – yes – she was happy. She was doing extremely well with Sir Fred, helping develop the One account, and the First Active account. She was now responsible for all of RBS's consumer finance in the direct market – and later the whole mortgage business in the UK. She was such a fit and capable person: it occurred to me that she should be running a bank.

She kept in touch and on 19 December 2006 – the anniversary of launching Virgin Direct – she left RBS, departing on good terms. We were keen to get her back to Virgin to take hold of our money business. Luckily Gordon managed to persuade her to return after a short rest, and she rejoined in March 2007. I phoned her from Necker: 'Jayne-Anne – welcome home.'

By then Virgin Direct had evolved into Virgin Money – a joint venture model offering products with several different partners, whilst the business is owned by our group. Virgin Money undertakes the marketing and designs the products – credit cards, savings and investments, life and general insurance – while our partners provide the rest. (Bank of America operate our credit cards, which means the cards are on Bank of America's balance sheets, not Virgin's!) But (possibly fortunately given the unfurling of the mortgage crisis) we hadn't been able to get back into the mortgage business since selling the One account. I asked Jayne-Anne and the team she brought with her to re-establish the One account on another level to fill the gap left by all the struggling mortgage lenders. It was this springboard that gave us the ability to make a proposal for Northern Rock – which I'll talk about in the next section.

In this chapter I've tried to demonstrate how Virgin has delivered on some of its best ideas. I've tried to illustrate the importance of good communications and attention to detail. I've stressed how vital it is to think clearly, reducing a business to its essentials. Do not underestimate the effort required to do this. It is very hard to look outside your own industry, and think the way a customer thinks, particularly if, as is likely, your life's efforts are devoted to one operation, in one sector.

Virgin's brand values of informality and plain speaking are incredibly useful to us in our day-to-day delivery of business, because they keep us grounded. They stop us from losing touch. They prevent us from ever, in our wildest nightmares, contemplating anything as self-defeating as 'confusion marketing'.

Remember: complexity is your enemy. Any fool can make something complicated. It is hard to make something simple. Use experts wisely. Direct them. Give them work to do. They're not there to hold your hand. Ignore flak. Remember, everyone has an agenda, so the advice you receive from outside your trusted circle is not just to benefit you. Almost all of it will be well meant, but even the best of such advice needs interpreting.

Keep a cool head. You're in business to deliver change, and if you succeed, the chances that no one will get hurt are virtually zero. This is the rough and tumble of business. Be sportsmanlike, play to win, and stay friends with people wherever possible. If you do fall out with someone, ring them a year later and take them out to dinner. Befriend your enemies.

Engage your emotions at work. Your instincts and emotions are there to help you. They are there to make things easier. For me, business is a 'gut feeling', and if it ever ceased to be so, I think I would give it up tomorrow. By 'gut feeling', I mean that I believe I've developed a natural aptitude, tempered by huge amounts of experience, that tends to point me in the right direction rather than the wrong one. As a result, it also gives me the confidence to make better decisions.

My plans acquire detail as I test them against questions that on the face of it are really quite simple – and more to do with emotions than figures. If we create the best health club in town, will existing gym users go to all the bother of transferring their membership to us? If the answer is 'Yes', then we will give it a go and see if it works.

This is the point where being a well-funded company puts you at a tremendous advantage. Big businesses can afford to do this sort of thing. The good news for small businesses is that the big ones rarely bother to use their advantage to its maximum. Why? Because they've forgotten how to think like entrepreneurs. Worse still: many of them have forgotten how entrepreneurs feel.

4

Learning from
Mistakes
and Setbacks

Damage Report

In 1969 I made the biggest mistake of my life. It was an event referred to as recently as late 2007 by the Liberal Democrat MP Vince Cable in the House of Commons during Virgin Money's bid for the Northern Rock bank. He said, when speaking under UK parliamentary privilege, that I was not a fit person to run a bank. In the UK, nearly forty years after a lapse in judgement, I was still being pilloried.

I was nineteen years old and driving a shipment of records to Belgium when I stumbled on the fact that records bought in Great Britain that were intended for export were not subject to purchase tax. So I bought the records I needed, pretended they were for export, and then sold them to British customers. The whole ploy involved driving four Transit vans loaded with records to Dover, taking them to France, then returning on the next ferry with the records still on board. It was not only illegal, it was really pretty stupid. In May 1969, I was caught red-handed by HM Customs & Excise, put in a cell overnight and charged under Section 301 of the

Customs & Excise Act 1952. It nearly killed off my entrepreneurial dreams; thankfully it didn't – but it did teach me a hard lesson about never doing anything illegal or unethical ever again. I hadn't fully appreciated the seriousness of what we were doing or the potential damage it could do to my reputation. It was my mum and dad who bailed me out, putting up their home as security. In the end, customs agreed not to press charges as long as I paid back three times the tax that had not been paid – around £60,000 – and I was spared a criminal record. What I didn't know at the time was that the big record retailers were pulling the same stunt in a more systematic way, and they too soon ran into the same problem.

After this shock, all the staff got together and we agreed to work night and day to settle our debts, expanding the company as fast as we possibly could in order to pay off these debts and to avoid me going to court.

It took us three years. But I learned a very important lesson: *never do anything that means you can't sleep at night.*

One thing is certain in business. You and everyone around you will make mistakes. When you are pushing the boundaries, this is inevitable – and it's important to realise this. Even when things are running well, there is always the prospect of a new reality around the corner. Suddenly, all the good decisions you made last week are doing you untold damage. Where on earth did you go wrong?

At Virgin, we have always been prepared to face the facts – however unpalatable they might be. Failure usually occurs when leaders avoid the reality of business. You have to trust the people around you to learn from their mistakes. Blame and recriminations are pointless.

In business, as in life, there will always be external risk factors that are beyond your control. Oil prices triple. A terrorist blows himself up in a shopping mall. Hurricanes level entire cities. Currency fluctuations leave behind trails of bankruptcies.

But you can take measures to mitigate and manage business risks. Then, if disaster strikes, at least your attention won't be split every which way by other worries. *Always,* always, *have a disaster protocol in place.* Because if something truly horrific occurs, a lot of frightened people are going to come to you looking for answers.

On 23 February 2007, at around 8.15 p.m., one of our new Pendolino tilting trains – travelling at 100mph – jumped over a set of points in Cumbria in the north-west of England, on a remote and scenic part of the West Coast Main Line.

On board was Margaret Masson, an elderly lady travelling back to her home in Cardonald, near Glasgow. Margaret – her family and friends called her Peggy – was thrown around in the coach as the train slid along the railbed and then careened down a steep embankment.

For ten years, Virgin Trains had been safely carrying millions of passengers all over the UK. Virgin Atlantic, meanwhile, had flown millions of customers around the globe without injury. That night, life changed in our business. We had our first casualties. Margaret Masson was dead. Several other people were seriously hurt.

Zermatt, Switzerland. My family and I came off the slopes after a brilliant day's skiing. There had been a welcome dump of snow and everyone agreed it had been a perfect day. In the evening, exhausted, we all sat down together to watch a film in the local cinema, when I felt eight or nine gentle buzzes on my mobile phone. I went outside. The text message said there had been a rail accident and that it was Code Black, indicating that it was serious. I phoned our then director of communications, Will Whitehorn (now president of Virgin Galactic), who sits on the board of Virgin Trains. The call went to voicemail – an unusual event for a person who is always in touch with me. I called Will's wife, Lou, on her mobile and she reminded me that it was his birthday; for the first time in a year, he had actually switched his phone off. I phoned Tony Collins, the managing director of Virgin Trains, and the man responsible for building the Pendolino trains.

'I'm afraid it's a serious derailment. The train's gone down a ravine and the police are trying to get to the passengers. We should prepare ourselves for the worst.'

'I'll be there in a few hours,' I said. 'Can you meet me?'

'I'll pick you up when you get in. Just let me know your arrival time.'

I couldn't get a helicopter because the snow I had just been skiing over and having such fun on was still falling, shutting down much of Switzerland. The airports at Sion and Geneva were both out of action. The best I could manage was to drive to Zurich, which was five hours away. I hired a car and drove through the night. I got the first flight out of Zurich at 6.30 a.m. The flight went to Manchester and I met up with Tony Collins and with Will, who had flown in from Heathrow. They briefed me on the latest situation, and then we caught the BBC morning news. The reports said the train was intact, and that this had contributed to the large number of survivors. That was heartening: Pendolino No. 390033, *City of Glasgow*, like all our new trains, had been deliberately built like a tank. An interim accident report, later confirmed, suggested that a track failure was responsible for the accident. This news, too, reshaped our task and made it somewhat easier, because we could be fairly certain by then that nothing Virgin Trains had done or failed to do had contributed to the incident.

As we headed to the Royal Preston Hospital in Lancashire, however, we still had little idea of the scale of the accident. The hospital registrar there said the emergency services had been gearing up for over 100 casualties when they first heard the news. Because the Pendolino carriages coped well, only twenty-four people needed to be taken to hospital – still, the scale of the medical preparations we saw was daunting.

We went up to Grayrigg, to visit the crash site. It was as if a massive Hornby model railway set had been picked up by a spoilt giant and dashed to the ground. With a jolt I recalled how much I'd had to argue with the Department of Transport – which provides large subsidies for the railway system – to allow us to increase the safety specifications of our trains. If this had happened to any of our old BR rolling stock, the injuries and the mortalities would have been horrendous. As it was, the carriages had held together. Even the windows were intact.

It was while I was surveying the devastation that I was first told about the bravery of one man. Since that time, whenever I think of the courage of our test pilots, or my friend the explorer Steve Fossett, who's sadly lost to us now, or the ballooning guru Per Lindstrand, I also consider the resolve it must have taken to deal with 400 tonnes of derailed train. The actions of the train driver Iain Black, a former policeman, were incredible. Once the train had derailed, its own momentum propelled it a further 600 metres along the railbed. Iain battled to slow the train down on the stones. He stayed in his seat for a quarter-mile, trying to control the train. He didn't protect himself by running back from his cab. Instead, he did everything he could to save his passengers, and in the process he sustained serious injuries to his neck. It was his selfless action that averted more casualties. In my book, he is a true hero.

We stared numbly at the wreckage for a while, then returned to the hospital.

I met Margaret Masson's family in the hospital mortuary, of all places. They were clearly devastated. I offered them my condolences. We found ourselves hugging each other.

The next minute – or that's how it seemed – I was facing television cameras and a press pack hungry for answers. I thought I was going to choke up. I came very close, but held it together and stuck to the facts as we knew them on the day.

At the time I couldn't say much. Again, I offered my condolences to Peggy's family. I also expressed my gratitude to Iain, who lay in another hospital nearby with injuries that would keep him off work for many months. Our other on-board staff – Karen Taylor, Derek Stewart and Gordon Burns – had all behaved in an exemplary fashion, and well beyond the call of duty, ignoring their own minor injuries in order to lead customers safely from the train.

After that, if I wanted to help people – the police, emergency and hospital workers, the mountain rescue volunteers, railway colleagues from Virgin, Network Rail and other companies – the best thing I could do was to keep out of their way. I left feeling unsatisfied: was there really no more that I could do? There didn't seem to be, but I comforted myself with the thought that at least I'd been there.

It is a boss's duty to get to the scene as quickly as humanly possible. If you delay showing your face in public after something like this, recriminations, anger and blame set in. This will be bad enough for you; imagine what all that confusion and worry does to the people who've been affected by the incident. In my view, if the press are demanding early answers for good and just reasons – and that was very much the case here – it is imperative for business executives to be prepared to face the media at the first opportunity. Every senior executive should be capable, if push comes to shove, of becoming a visible company spokesperson. I remember, after a serious plane crash at Kegworth in January 1989, Sir Michael Bishop, who was CEO of the airline British Midland, spoke to the media straight away with great clarity and care.

When Virgin Trains was putting its own emergency procedures in place, we analysed a number of serious rail incidents, and had been consistently appalled by the amount of time it took before anyone stood up and said: 'Speak to me about this'. And we were daunted at how fast confusion and blame set in as people waited for any kind of statement from anybody about what had happened and why.

So our disaster-planning scenarios have three main aims: to get to the scene fast; to be efficient in dealing with the passengers, staff and media; and to be honest about what is happening. The other lesson to come home was that the tremendous planning and refusal to skimp on costs on building the Pendolino to the very highest standards in the world really paid off and saved the lives of people who would not be here today if they had been travelling in the old trains we replaced.

*

You can't protect yourself against the unexpected, so you need to keep your house in as good an order as you can. If disaster strikes, you don't want to find yourself doing twelve things at once and misprioritising them in public. It's vital, therefore, that you take control of your internal business risks – the ones you *can* influence.

I've failed to follow my own advice here on a couple of occasions – and I've always regretted it. For instance, I'm not always good at cutting my losses. I should have faced up to the realities of the market and sold off Virgin Megastores years before we did. My decision to overrule my colleagues and hold on to them for too long cost us a lot of money, only balanced by the fact that the chain's very existence and brand was the distributing channel and bedrock of the early success of Virgin Mobile.

I don't think that a chairman need fall on his sword if someone messes up in the company. Chairmen must learn from the incident and try to make sure that particular mistakes are never repeated. An apology on behalf of the company – perhaps in a public forum, sometimes in person to the individual who has been messed up – is an appropriate starting point. I know business books that say you should never admit to failure, but I would not tolerate such an attitude among my people. I see nothing wrong with admitting a genuine mistake.

An entrepreneur has to make the tough calls. Some say it requires a ruthless streak. I don't agree. I don't think I'm ruthless, although I have been portrayed that way by a few people who don't really know me and have never met me. There are some things in my business life that I regret – and I have made mistakes about people. One of my faults is that I have often been so focused on a business project or an idea that I have been unable to appreciate what was going on in someone's life right in front of my nose. I've tried to learn from this, taking extra time to listen. Actually, I think it is counterproductive to be ruthless. *You've got to treat people as you would yourself, or better.*

Let's be clear about the manager's responsibilities here. There's an idea abroad that people no longer resign when they should. To hear some people spin it, you would think resignation is the only effective action the manager of a troubled company can take. This is patent rubbish. And for the record, there never was a time in business or political history when talented people resigned over trifles, or out of some notion of honour. It's a myth.

If something catastrophic happens to a company, and the chairman actually appointed that person who caused this systemic failure of the business, then the chairman certainly needs to consider his or her position. If a major bank does not have the security systems in place to protect itself from a rogue trader, and that trader does immense damage to the company, then, yes, the chairman or chief executive should probably consider resigning their position. They are ultimately responsible.

In most other cases, managers should stay where they are and sort their messes out. It's what they're paid for, after all. Most importantly, someone should apologise for the mess happening in the first place.

You definitely should get the best people around you when confronted with a serious problem. Don't try to deal with it all by yourself. Don't be afraid to seek help and advice. If someone else is better than you at dealing with it, then for goodness' sake delegate it. And equally for goodness' sake, don't jump down their throats if they fail.

My management team reckon 2003 wasn't exactly a vintage year. That was the year Apple's first iPod personal music player was emerging. We had a couple of very bright people from Palm who came over with their own funky version of the MP3 and a range of accessories. The analysis didn't truly stack up according to the management team but I insisted we push on with it: our very own MP3 player, Virgin Pulse! We had to make some heroic assumptions about how to scale up because we were buying the devices from China and Taiwan. We spent $20 million on designing and bringing it to market – and our products were critically acclaimed in the United States – but it didn't have the simplicity of the iPod and the cost of manufacturing just throttled us out of the marketplace. Apple had taken a leaf from Texas Instruments, the pocket-calculator experts who dominated their market for many years. If you drive down the retail price fast enough when you are the dominant player, you never allow anyone else to catch up because they can't make enough money. It requires the dominant player to be brave, because it can mean cannibalising your existing sales by dropping the retail price. That's what happened when iPod introduced the cheaper and smaller iPod nano – it slammed the door on anyone else trying to build significant market share beneath them. The Virgin Pulse bombed and we had to write off $20 million.

It's often hard when you're focusing on the day-to-day in business to admit that what you thought was right becomes wrong. For example, we put a truly innovative upper-class seat on Virgin Atlantic's planes in 2000. However, we took too long to develop them and did not keep the project secret enough. British Airways got wind of what we were up to (and even got hold of our plans) and out-innovated us with a better seat. Customer feedback was swift and brutal. People were voting with their credit cards and travelling with other airlines – and our airline began to suffer. We could have kept the seats until they depreciated, but we decided the mistake was just too ghastly to live with. We cut our losses and dumped them. The cost to us? £100 million. The benefit to us? We now have the best business-class flat beds in the world, designed by our own team, and we have created a product our rivals cannot match. We have easily recouped our losses with this decision.

It's embarrassing to admit this stuff, and I think it's a fear of embarrassment that discourages many chairmen and bosses from doing their jobs properly. It's all very well sitting there wondering why your business is disappearing, but it's only by getting out from behind your desk and sampling the products that you will ever see what's going wrong. When you have found out what is going wrong, the next step is to get the team involved to fix it rather than fire them. That way, you can keep your team together and close the door on rivals who might benefit from your mistakes by hiring the very people who have just learned the lesson the hard way.

Starting a soft-drinks war with Coca-Cola was crazy. It was one of our highest profile business mistakes, though it was also one of the things that raised the profile of the Virgin name in America. Launching Virgin Cola in 1994, we were having fun and revelling in underdog bravado, so pleased to be snapping at the heels of the biggest dog in town. Taking on Coke taught us two things: how to make a great cola with a different taste; and how to antagonise a global business that brought in $28 billion in 2007, with profits of $5 billion.

It was only several years later that I learned how Coca-Cola eventually set up a SWAT team to ensure that Virgin Cola never got a proper foothold in the soft-drinks market. Yes, we somehow contrived to blind ourselves completely to the power and the influence of a global brand that epitomises the strength and reach of American capitalism.

Here's how we did it – and, whatever you do, don't try this at home.

The Virgin Trading Company, a wholly owned Virgin subsidiary, was our beverage start-up division. Virgin Spirits, a joint venture with Scottish whisky distiller William Grant, had been established to market and distribute Virgin Vodka. You can still enjoy a bottle of Virgin Vodka – it's available on Virgin Atlantic flights, along with our special Glenfiddich Scotch whisky.

The Virgin Cola Company was a joint venture with the Canadian soft-drink company Cott Corporation, the world's largest supplier of retailer own-brand soda drinks. Cott bottled own-brand products for such chains as A&P, Loblaw's and Safeway in Canada and Albertson's, K Mart, Safeway, 7-Eleven and Wal-Mart stores in the United States. Virgin Cola was introduced in the UK in 1994 and we originally achieved success in the pub and restaurant trade. I was convinced by the late Gerry Pencer, the chief executive of Cott Corporation, that we were in a position to make a strong bid for a portion of the global market. After all, Cott had customers in Australia, Britain, Hong Kong, Israel and Japan, and these were key markets for us. But Cott baulked at taking on Coke directly. We should have listened.

We knew there was a lot going on behind the scenes. One of Tesco's main buying team, John Gildersleeve, a senior director who was a non-executive of several companies, had indicated that they would take one million cases of Virgin Cola. The next we heard, he had told Simon Lester at Cott that they wouldn't be supporting us after all. This was three weeks before the launch – and the invitations had gone out for the event at Planet Hollywood in London.

I phoned John to ask why the change of heart. He said: 'It was a very fine decision – the door's not completely closed.' He knew I wanted to make a press announcement, and he knew I needed the confidence of having a major retailer on board. 'But we have two concerns. First, there are some commercial considerations. They can be resolved. But second, there's this whole question of the brand positioning and what it might do for us.'

He explained to me that a solus arrangement – an exclusive deal with Tesco – is a two-edged sword. He said Tesco would be identified with the product whether it was good or bad. If I got fed up with it in three months' time, it would reflect on Tesco – good or bad. He said when Sainsbury's launched their own Classic Cola, Tesco adopted a position that they would only sell 'The Real Thing'.

John said that he was worried that we might be a bit inflammatory in the way we attacked Coca-Cola. He pointed out that Coke had been very good customers for Tesco and the last thing he wanted was

Coke being taken out of his stores. This was an honest opinion that I respected. I could see Tesco's position, but it was very important for Virgin Cola to be on the supermarket shelves – preferably on offer at the end of the aisles.

I explained that every company we start, we stick with; that we wanted to give the public more choice; and our campaign was focused on defending our position and explaining why we were better – we weren't interested in merely slagging off a competitor. I told him this applied to all our campaigns – even to Virgin Atlantic's battle with British Airways. I pointed out our reputation among consumers was very good. (A NOP market research survey in a recent edition of *PR Week* was conveniently to hand to back this up!) Both David Sainsbury of Sainsbury's and Archie Norman at ASDA had also told me they would stock Virgin Cola.

The next day John came to see me in person. As a consequence of the call and our meeting, Tesco changed its mind and decided to stock our cola. It was a wonderful boost for us. In December, sales of cola went up 36 per cent in Tesco stores – and 75 per cent of these were sales of Virgin Cola.

Then Coke started to make life more difficult for us.

I was in a Virgin Trains meeting when one of the former British Rail executives told me he had been on a management away-day at an assault course, and he had met some Coca-Cola managers. He'd asked them what they were doing on the assault course. They replied: 'We're getting ready for action with Virgin Cola.'

I thought the story was over the top at the time, but with hindsight I can see that, once Coke had woken up, of course they had read the launch of Virgin Cola as a declaration of war.

Coke's commandos went into action. Coca-Cola's secret recipe is a syrup essence shipped to hundreds of independent bottlers around the world and they are responsible for producing, packaging, distributing and merchandising. Coke visited every bottling business and said they didn't want Virgin Cola to be produced by their bottlers. It wasn't simply the cola – the bottlers also depended on their livelihoods for the other soft drinks in the Coke portfolio, such as Sprite, Fanta, Diet Coke and Minute Maid: all highly lucrative business for the bottlers.

In 1998, we acquired Cott's share of the business and relaunched Virgin Cola with a further $25 million investment. Our goal: to take on Coke on their home territory. Coke wanted war. So we drove a British tank into Times Square in New York and fired a mock round at the Coca-Cola sign (we'd secretly had it wired up the night before by a pyrotechnical team and it looked like it had gone up in smoke) before ploughing through a massive wall of cola tins. Sightseers ran wailing from the square and we nearly ended up in jail.

In Britain, Virgin Cola was flying off the shelves. In France, we were closing in on Pepsi, doing well in Belgium and Switzerland and negotiating a franchise in Japan and Italy. We thought we might be able to pull it off.

In 2004, I was invited to meet my new corporate bank boss, Diana Brightmore-Armour, a very bright woman working in London for Lloyds TSB. We were enjoying a fun evening when she revealed to me: 'Richard, you don't know this, but I was working for Coca-Cola in Atlanta when you launched Virgin Cola – I knew what an impact you would have so I persuaded the senior management to set up a SWAT team to ensure that Virgin Cola failed.'

I was quite amazed. In 1997, we knew that Coca-Cola were keen to drive us out of business but we didn't realise to what extreme.

'I was at a senior executive meeting when it was reported that you were preparing to launch the cola into America. Most people at the headquarters were rather blasé. They didn't really know about Virgin and thought it just another local soft-drink brand.' But she garnered support from one or two Brits at the meeting and they helped her warn the bosses: 'This isn't just anyone – this is Richard Branson, who has a lot of clout and can build a major brand. We need to stop this as soon as possible,' she told them.

While Coca-Cola had few worries about a regional brand competing in a local marketplace with Coke and its other products, it didn't want to face another competitor such as Pepsi. My dining companion revealed how a team came to England to set up another team to ensure that distributors and shops were all given extra incentives to sell Coke – and keep us off the shelves. I heard later that the number of Coke people trying to stop us was bigger than the whole of our team in Virgin Cola! We truly were the underdogs.

After gaining a peak of 75 per cent of sales at Tesco and over 10 per cent of total UK market sales, sales started to decline. Coca Cola's SWAT teams were beginning to punish us. Coke started discounting cola more cheaply than bottled water – an offer we couldn't match: we simply didn't have the money. The only way to make money on a commodity where the price is so low is to ensure that you sell huge volumes – that's what the Coca-Cola company does. Coca-Cola threatened small retailers that they would take out their fridges if they continued to stock us. They also hinted that they would withdraw Coke altogether from the same retailers.

Our Coke escapade led to a number of articles asking whether Virgin had a proper strategy in place. A *Business Week* cover article questioned whether we had the ability to manage Virgin's 'chaotic' empire. Well, of course we had. We were a way-of-life brand, offering a consistent and enjoyable experience to our customers whether they were flying the Atlantic or making a mobile phone call. Virgin wasn't chaotic – it was utterly focused on the job of realising its core values in many diverse sectors.

Colas are a drink young people enjoy, so we figured a Virgin Cola would be a good idea. Coca-Cola is a huge corporation, and since Virgin is all about outfoxing the big guy, we leapt at the opportunity to take them on. Colas are pretty much indistinguishable as drinks, and much of the customer's enjoyment comes from brandishing their favourite brand; the Virgin brand was popular, so how could we lose?

We lost by ignoring the gaping hole in this otherwise rather solid-sounding proposition: as a cola manufacturer, we weren't the people's champion. They already were. *They* were getting their product into people's hands, every day, everywhere. *They* were offering their product at an unbeatable price because they had the biggest economies of scale on the planet. *They* were offering their customers a rather nice soft drink into the bargain. And their brand name was so ingrained in people's minds that when they asked for a Cola, they'd call it a 'Coke'.

Yes, Coca-Cola played hardball against us. But we had already lost. We still produce Virgin soft drinks, but in a much more targeted and niche way. And Virgin Cola is still the number-one cola drink – in Bangladesh!

I notice that Red Bull has launched its own cola. I know it will take them some time and a large tranche of money to win significant market share. But then, as a drinks company, this is their core business.

And perhaps the best thing to come out of our Virgin Cola escapade was a brilliant new company called Innocent Drinks, run by some entrepreneurial guys who were at Virgin Cola and saw a gap in the market for fresh fruit smoothies and have now built a business worth several hundred million dollars. While still with Virgin they set up a stall at the V festival to have revellers sample their products. They had two bins: a 'yes' bin and a 'no' bin. They asked people whether they should give up their full-time jobs to start the company. People tested the product and by the end of the day, the 'yes' bin was overflowing. Our loss, but even if it isn't a Virgin Company, I get a real surge of satisfaction to know that these guys cut their teeth in a Virgin business and made it work.

Back in 1971, when I was more gung-ho, I wrote in my notebook: '*We don't need lawyers.*' But over the years, stating our agreements in clear and unambiguous terms has proved, again and again, to have been vital for our success. Our contract with T-Mobile, in particular, turned out to be a vital document for us. Incurring unnecessary legal fees can ruin your start-up, but the answer, I now think, is not to ignore the lawyers, but to get the basics right from the very beginning. Any start-up business should sit down and take a long hard look at its legal agreements.

Our Virgin Mobile business was going exceptionally well in the UK. There was an incredible buzz – we were hitting the bullseye of the UK youth market with funky and irreverent adverts and great deals. Tom Alexander and the team were single-minded about the business and piling on thousands of new customers and there was a sense of fun. In the first three months of 2003 the turnover was exceeding £1 million a day.

Our television adverts were scooping awards for innovative marketing – and we were stealing market share from Orange, Vodaphone and even our network partner, T-Mobile. In the UK, we were able to use the American rap superstar Wyclef Jean for a cult advert. In it, he unwittingly signs a contract that leads him to being bound as a trailer park sex slave. In an attempt to escape he is subsequently imprisoned for 'breach of contract'. The underlying message of 'Be careful what you sign' demonstrated the benefits of switching to non-contract Virgin Mobile.

For all of us at Virgin Mobile, however, that advert had acquired a second, private meaning.

Our original deal had T-Mobile putting in the network, and Virgin arranging handset procurement, marketing and the Virgin Mobile brand. It all worked smoothly – until a new American executive, Harris Jones, arrived on the scene in Britain. He really set the cat among the pigeons.

He was smart. He looked at our original contract and saw we had a joint company worth £1 billion, of which Virgin owned 50 per cent: a fantastic success story in which both parties were doing well. Harris

Jones – and ultimately his bosses – were desperate to obtain our shares and were willing to try a number of different tactics to get hold of them.

What was their problem?

They saw the Virgin Mobile deal as just another cost, because for every customer on Virgin Mobile, T-Mobile paid us a monthly marketing fee. This payment was a termination charge which T-Mobile collected from other networks to connect their callers to Virgin Mobile's customers. Virgin Mobile was entitled to this termination fee, even though we didn't own the network infrastructure. It was in black and white in the contract.

T-Mobile were saying that the terms of the contract were legally questionable. While we thought the agreement was crystal clear, going to court over this was frightening: T-Mobile was a substantial business and had pockets deep enough to fund an expensive litigation. Every day spent dealing with lawyers is not only costly, it's hugely time-consuming for key executives. Our relationship soon became very sour indeed, and our cherished flotation looked increasingly remote.

The case ended in the High Court in London – and T-Mobile lost. The judge, it was reported, said that T-Mobile's conduct was 'deserving of moral condemnation'.

The head of T-Mobile in Germany handled the fallout well. He was good enough to invite me over to Germany so that he could apologise to me in person – a decent gesture, and one we appreciated. After many months, we managed to secure an out-of-court settlement with Harris Jones's former bosses in Germany and with a new UK team led by his successor Brian McBride. Due to the court ruling they had to sell us their shares for £1 (Brian framed the coin in a presentation case!), and they offered Virgin Mobile a new airtime contract that it still operates with today. Thanks in large part to him, we managed to steer our way towards a stock-market flotation.

The lesson of all this is that you need to get your basic business contracts properly sorted out. *It's always worth getting the contract right in the first place.* And be prepared, on occasions, to go to court to defend the company. I'm afraid that when you draw up a contract for a joint venture, you have to take into account what might happen if there is a falling-out – or, worse still, when someone is trying to screw you. It would be lovely if all business could be done with a handshake – and I have done plenty of successful business this way in the past – but there are unscrupulous people out there, and you have to guard yourself and your business. We have never lost a major court case in forty years of doing business. In the GTech case (where I was awarded substantial libel damages), the British Airways case and the T-Mobile case, we have stood by our decision always to fight our corner.

Protect your reputation. Don't be afraid of making mistakes.

These are the rules I live by. They ought not to contradict each other but many businesses wrongly assume that they do. Yet there is no denying the risk that mud sticks, and a damaged reputation in business can follow you around for years. You can deliver on every promise, keep your word, deal fairly, show forbearance – and the world can still throw you curveballs that mess up your reputation. And long after you have learned your lesson and moved on, others will still be harping on about this or that misfortune, this or that error. I've known plenty of talented and trustworthy business people who have carried the shadow of past errors around with them, and whose careers have suffered as a result.

There is no way to solve this problem, but there are ways to mitigate its effects. Certainly you should *never* keep your head down. That will do you no good at all – it'll simply confirm someone's lousy opinion of you.

I would say, first of all, that you should improve your communications. At Virgin, we take a great deal of care to keep the press up to date with what we're doing. Aside from maintaining a high profile, this helps decent journalists put any old, bad news in context. Our culture of openness also prevents bad news from building up a head of steam before it reaches the public. The public is actually pretty forgiving of most business errors except hypocrisy, and stalling almost always backfires.

We also practise what we preach. We look for people with exciting, dynamic CVs, not spotless ones. We're not pushovers, but we're happy to take chances with people, to move them around, to see how they tick and where they fit in. We don't pin the blame on people, or marginalise them when things go wrong. This culture pays dividends the longer we're in business, because eventually people realise that we're a company that knows how to deal with its problems, and is willing to take chances.

Over the years the Virgin brand has earned the reputation of being *bold* and *unafraid*. Isn't it extraordinary how few brands communicate fearlessness? Commercially, our reputation for fearlessness has been like gold dust. It turned our battle with Coca-Cola, which was commercially bad for us, into a story that, in brand terms, strengthened customer loyalty.

An error-strewn reputation is more damaging as rumour than it is in face-to-face dealings. Satirical magazines like *Private Eye* are always horrified to discover how many successful and famous friends stick by figures who are supposedly 'disgraced'. But that's not so surprising: individuals are better than groups at judging someone's character.

Your friends are your allies in the battle to improve your reputation after a knock-back. They will not only advocate for you; they will front for you. Their reputations will help yours recover. Distinguished people aren't stupid, and cultivating someone to take advantage of their reputation isn't going to wash. But they are, to a fault, generous and understanding. (They've been through the mill; they know what life's like.) So don't be afraid to ask the senior figures in your circle for advice and help.

I know what I'm talking about here because in 2004, when we were considering options for the flotation of Virgin Mobile on the London Stock Exchange, one of the perceived risk factors was *me*.

Investors usually have short memories. But the elder members of the City of London pinstripe-and-braces brigade recalled that I had taken the Virgin Group on to the stock market with huge fanfare and expectation in November 1986, and then, after the great market crash of October 1987, I offered to take it back into private hands again. I could feel the thick, red letters stamped on my forehead: 'Health Warning: This Man is Dangerous.'

The flotation of Virgin had attracted more applications from the public than any previous stock market debut, aside from the massive government privatisation of gas, electricity and telecoms. Nonetheless, my first experience of Virgin as a publicly listed company was one of the most miserable times of my business life. I became very disillusioned with the constant round of analysts' meetings and investor roadshows. I hated being accountable to institutional shareholders who didn't appear to understand our philosophy – and I know a lot of executives working in plcs have a certain sympathy for my viewpoint. But nobody was forced to 'take a bath' when we changed tack – and our investors got their original stake back plus a healthy dividend.

What happened was this. In 1985, our fledgling Virgin Atlantic airline found itself entrenched in a transatlantic price war, and our cash was being squeezed. My advisers at the time convinced me that we needed to expand the equity base of the group. Don Cruickshank took on the task of organising an initial public offering for Virgin's music, retail, and vision businesses, which were combined into the Virgin Group plc, a public corporation with 35 per cent of its equity listed on the London and NASDAQ stock markets.

Looking back, it was a funny sort of offering. Virgin Atlantic was considered far too risky an investment and was excluded from the share offering. So were our nightclubs, Virgin Holidays and Virgin

Cargo. Yet Virgin Atlantic became Britain's second largest long-haul airline, Virgin Holidays the number-one long-haul holiday company, the clubs have made a fortune and Virgin Cargo grew to handle nearly 100,000 metric tonnes of cargo by 2000!

Early in 1986, Don and Trevor Abbott, who was brought in by Don as finance director, raised £25 million in a private placing of convertible preference shares from Morgan Grenfell. There was no legal commitment to convert this to equity in the event of a flotation, but it all seemed remarkably easy. In the public sale, the financial institutions would convert their preference shares into 15 per cent of the listed business, and we would create new shares for other investors, raising a further £30 million. This still gave me 55 per cent of the Virgin Group, while outside investors held 34 per cent. The business, which twelve months earlier Coutts Bank had nearly forced into insolvency, was valued at £240 million. Some of the cash raised was moved into Voyager, the company set up to invest in Virgin Atlantic.

During early 1987, we used money from the flotation to plot the takeover of EMI Music from Thorn EMI, by building up our shares, and to open an American music subsidiary, Virgin Records America. Naturally, both projects soaked up our capital. Then the stock-market crash in October 1987 hit us – and I made a mistake. I continued to buy shares in EMI as they were plummeting. Don Cruickshank and our non-executive directors raged at me: 'Richard, you cannot do this. You are throwing away good money after bad.' It was just the sort of thing we should have been doing if we'd had deeper pockets, but we didn't.

As the world recovered from the October shock, I expected the share price to jump back after we announced our results, more than doubling profits from £14 million to £32 million for the year ending July 1987. But the price of our shares had fallen along with everybody else's, from our flotation price of 140p to just over 70p. Double your profits, halve your share value: this was barmy logic. In July 1988 we told the market that we were conducting a management buyout – and at the original price of 140p per share. I didn't want to let down the army of smaller investors – including many close friends – who had put their savings and faith in our business. We took out a £300 million loan to do this, which meant that our gearing was very high. My dream of taking over EMI Music came to an end there and then. The City of London had misunderstood our business – we would now go off and become one of the largest groups of private companies in the world with several quoted investments to boot.

In 2004, I hoped that the flotation of Virgin Mobile in the UK would enhance our already considerable rehabilitation in the eyes of the City.

From early on there had been speculation in the business press that we would float, with the *Sunday Times* calling Virgin Mobile the new jewel in the Virgin crown. But there were a few wobbles as we headed for our stock-market flotation in July – mostly caused by external market conditions, which made it difficult for firms to become listed on the London market.

Ironically, we were due to float in the same week as Premier Foods, the makers of Branston Pickle, which gave the newspapers a chance to dust down their 'BRANSON PICKLE' headlines.

How would investors view the return of a major Branson business in July 2004? This time round, the circumstances were entirely different. I had learned a great deal about business in the intervening years, and I knew that, while my bearded and smiling face was used in the newspapers, I choose not to be a board director of any of our public companies, and therefore would not be in direct control. Corporate governance was a whole new ball game in 2004, and from day one, Virgin Mobile was set up and acted like a plc-in-waiting.

A highly experienced team of corporate business figures was brought in to help Tom Alexander so there would be no replay of the 1980s. Charles Gurassa, chairman of TUI Northern Europe, and prior to that chief executive of Thomson Travel, joined as chairman, and Caroline Marland, a non-executive director of Burberry and Bank of

Ireland, Rupert Gavin, well known for his work as head of BBC Worldwide, and David Maloney, chief financial officer of Le Meridien Hotels, all joined the board as non-executive directors. These were heavyweight players who would steer the team as they joined the FTSE 250 index.

Tom Alexander and his team, aided by the non-executive board, had experience and pedigree. They required my backing only as a significant investor, and, of course, for the Virgin brand; so they let me be honorary president!

Our financial numbers were very good, and Virgin Mobile had been run scrupulously for the market. I knew that the 1987 experience might put off one or two investors. Well, so be it: there was no one forcing people to invest if they didn't like us.

On 30 June 2004, Virgin Mobile announced its intention of seeking a full listing of its shares and all Virgin Mobile employees who had worked for the company for more than a year received a gift of free shares. JP Morgan and Morgan Stanley acted as book-runners and sponsors and with Investec Securities they also acted as underwriters.

On 7 July 2004, we said that the indicative price per share would be between 235p to 285p, making the business worth over £1 billion at the top end of the valuation. Not a bad return, I thought; perhaps we were being too optimistic. As the market worsened, we had to temper our expectations, and on 21 July Virgin Mobile announced an offer price of 200p per share, valuing the business at £811 million, with proceeds of £125 million and share capital of £500 million.

I could hardly complain, particularly given the difficult markets which had seen several other IPOs abandoned during the year. The Virgin Group made around £400 million from Virgin Mobile being floated on the London Stock Exchange, and has invested this money in new Virgin ventures in the United States, China and Africa. Memories of 1987 and the 'Branson Factor' never became a serious issue – and Virgin Mobile has continued to grow.

*

When life isn't going well, it's very hard for a company to stay flexible enough to meet the challenge. Virgin Mobile USA has been trading punches in a fierce market since the beginning. It has pretty much done everything right – and it's still by no means out of the woods.

What delights me is the way the company has continued to innovate its way out of trouble. A defensive, conservative, cautious mindset – a natural enough reaction when things get tough – can kill you stone dead in a competitive marketplace. *When your very existence is threatened, you have to change.* This is one of the hardest lessons to learn in business, because it's so counter-intuitive. Plus, as you'll see from Virgin Mobile USA's experience, it's just plain hard to do.

We'd had a brilliant start in 2002 and were kicking ass. Virgin Mobile USA was giving young Americans the features they wanted, while offering a straightforward price plan with no contracts to sign and no fine print. But by 2005, the prepaid mobile phone market was a dogfight. After four years, Dan Schulman and his team were finding conditions tough. Bigger competitors – with deeper pockets – started to squeeze Virgin Mobile USA, targeting the prepaid customer.

Dan responded with great products. Our Flasher V7 flip phone had a flash camera, two-way picture messaging, 'superphonic' ringtones, downloadable games and custom graphics, and it was Virgin Mobile's first handset to plug into our new higher speed network. The price was great, too. And somehow it still wasn't enough. It was costing us more and more money to win market share.

The American team had taken out a large loan to make an impact in this vast territory, and it looked at one stage that defaulting might be a real possibility. To add to their woes, they had supply problems, and pending legal action with Virgin's major handset supplier, Nokia. I heard from Dan that employee morale was draining away, as our planned IPO was pushed further and further into the future. Bonuses were slashed and the very viability of the company was in question. Shareholders were concerned. One thing was for sure: our current strategy wasn't sustainable.

Dan spent a weekend alone and came up with his new manifesto, Virgin Mobile Rising. It was his clarion call to the company and to himself to regain the leading position and focus on a set of radical actions. Keep four million customers sweet. Resolve the debt and morale issues. Sort out legal matters with Nokia, Freedom and Telcordia. Relaunch the business. All within six months.

It was outrageous. It was gutsy. I loved it – and so did his team.

In 2006 Virgin Mobile USA overhauled itself. The brand underwent a complete revamp, as did the handsets, as did the distribution network. New services like Sugar Mama (a way to earn extra minutes), Stash (a prepay debit card) and ReGeneration (a charity network to assist homeless young people) built on emerging youth trends. By the end of July business was improving dramatically. Even against Cingular, who also had low-price handsets, Virgin was able to grow its market share. The customer base rose to 4.6 million, an increase of 20 per cent, and revenues went from negative to positive. Virgin customers sent or received 1.5 billion text messages, one from every customer every single day of the year. In addition, they downloaded 15 million ringtones and 2.5 million games. By December 2006, Virgin Mobile USA customers were using 950 million minutes of mobile phone time. That's a lot of chat.

We got ready for our trip to Wall Street. On 11 October 2007, Virgin Mobile USA announced its initial public offering, selling 27,500,000 shares of Virgin Mobile USA, at $15 a share.

No one ever said business was going to be easy, though – 2007 was Virgin Mobile USA's first year of profitability, with a net income of $4.2 million. But five months after the flotation, things were not looking so good. The US stock market was going into a tailspin caused by the sub-prime mortgage crisis and the collapse of Bear Stearns bank. Recession loomed. The share price was hit by a general downturn in the market and increased competition. Some analysts were beginning to question the MVNO model – and our stock price hit $2 a share. This was a disappointment to all of our investors. But I was convinced it would bounce back.

Dan, too, was upbeat and clear about Virgin Mobile's future prospects. 'We think we have one of the most attractive value propositions in the market, and that our business is well positioned for the future,' he told investors. I agree. Throughout its five-year operating history, Virgin Mobile USA has driven industry innovation and I believe that if it keeps its nerve, and continues to simplify and evolve its products and services, it will generate increasing demand.

For all its troubles – or perhaps because of them – I am incredibly proud of Virgin Mobile USA. The company has had the guts to innovate its way out of trouble. As the poet Robert Frost said: 'The best way out is always through.'

Dan knew that, and really bit the bullet. He knew that if a company needs reinvigorating, it needs a complete shake-up from top to tail. He knew not to confuse the intense physical retune of a company relaunch with the corporate comb-over of a mere rebranding exercise. He knew to address the basics – to clear the company's debts and settle its legal issues. And he knew to keep his staff onside with full, honest, direct corporate communications.

Virgin Mobile USA deserves to succeed. And if you follow its example in difficult times, so do you.

On the evening of Sunday 17 February 2008 I took the ribbed motor launch from Necker Island across to Biras Creek in the North Sound of Virgin Gorda. The daylight was fading and there was a brisk breeze, so I was wearing a cashmere jersey; not my normal attire in the Caribbean. But I felt a chill – a chill of despondency.

With me was Ryan West (known to everyone on Necker as Westy), Nicola Duguid, my then personal assistant, and Professor Dan Kammen. Dan and Westy had come to tell me how our sustainable tourism project on neighbouring Mosquito Island was progressing.

Dan's energy lab at Berkeley, University of California, was undertaking some computer modelling for us to create a low-carbon island holiday resort: all windmills and solar panels.

But my mind was elsewhere, and I was terribly disappointed. Five months of hard work by dozens of people across the Virgin Group had just come to nought, and I was mourning one of the most audacious deals we had ever concocted. The numbers were big, and the risk to the brand created over forty years was huge. There could have been serious repercussions for the brand if we failed to turn the business around. But I knew we had done our preparation. I knew success had been within our grasp. And I knew we could have done a good job. Now, of course, nobody will ever see the results.

We had lost our bid to rescue the embattled Northern Rock bank.

As we gathered on the jetty I said: 'Right, chaps, I've just heard that they're nationalising Northern Rock. So if it's all right with you, I think I'm going to get drunk.'

This story illustrates so many of the positive points I've tried to make in this chapter and throughout the book. Nevertheless, when the stars are set against you, there really may be nothing you can do. Blame and recriminations offer a spiteful sort of short-term comfort, but they're toxic, and can only only stunt your future enterprises.

The opportunity emerged in August 2007 as the international credit crunch began to bite. For many months I had been watching closely as the situation tightened, and I eventually decided to sell all my non-Virgin personal shareholdings in the stock market for cash. It turned out to be a wise move: I was luckier than many with equity in Northern Rock. Over the next few weeks, problems began to unfold as the mortgage banks were unable to get loans. But we didn't expect one of the biggest collapses in British banking history.

Jayne-Anne Gadhia, meanwhile, was up to her eyes in mud – though in a good way. On Sunday 16 September she was with her friends, Susan and Rosemary, being pampered at the Stobo Castle health spa near Peebles, outside Edinburgh. The Sunday papers were talking about the collapse of Northern Rock, and Jayne-Anne pondered that Virgin could do something with this . . .

She sat up, dropped the paper on the floor and cast around for a phone.

She called Gordon McCallum.

'Don't be daft,' was his initial response. 'It's a step too far.'

That evening she blasted off a follow-up email to Gordon and Stephen Murphy.

> *Hi there*
>
> *Call me insane, but I have been thinking hard about how we might take some advantage from the current situation at Northern Rock – and help out at the same time. I think there are a number of opportunities – ranging from the possible to the outrageous.*
>
> 1. *Accept that the big balance sheet providers will take the assets and look to take the systems etc. for a decent price.*
> 2. *Do a deal with a Citi or BOA [Bank of America] where they buy the company but we put in the brand so they get a Virgin-branded retail presence in the UK.*
> 3. *Talk to Northern Rock and the Bank of England direct. Richard could be used as frontman to make some sense of the crisis. Northern Rock could be rebranded Virgin and the Bank of England stand behind the current loan facility. We could withdraw from mortgages for the time being and focus on savings to rebalance the balance sheet – and with Richard fronting a saving campaign – Branson making sense of the current crisis – it's all now about increasing savings and reducing debts etc.*
> 4. *Whatever happens, I think we should do some research into who people would trust with financial services now. I bet the answer will be – Richard Branson.*

On the one hand I know that this all sounds pretty batty, but on the other hand – discontinuities in the system make it right for change – and I think we could do something, if Richard was able to speak to Darling or Brown to ask how we can help.

What do you think? I've restrained myself from copying this to Richard until I got your views.

J-A.

Gordon's reply was his usual mix of caution and common sense. 'I think 1. is interesting and the rest is batty! Let's talk tomorrow morning.' Stephen was equally cautious.

Jayne-Anne decided to phone me directly. She asked me if I'd seen the queues outside Northern Rock's branches on the news.

I certainly had.

'Well? Do you think we should give it a go?'

'Screw it,' I said, 'let's go for it.'

You can only get into pole position by giving something a try. Over many years, Virgin's business aim has been to find a strong position in a game-changing market. We've done this in the record business, media, telecoms, health clubs and the airline industry and will soon do it in space travel. We put ourselves out there, searching for new opportunities. And we know that they are more likely to come our way if we get ahead of ourselves and prepare the ground first.

Next day Jayne-Anne talked through her 'batty' ideas with Peter Norris, one of our long-term advisers, and a man who had run Barings. Peter said straight away that Virgin should start to look at the idea seriously. By now Gordon and Stephen had got their breath back and were over the shock – it was time to think how best to assemble a team to take on this enormous task. Our Northern Rock adventure had begun.

The following day I phoned Matt Ridley, the chairman of Northern Rock. I told him we would love to see how we could help save the bank. Matt is a charming man. He appeared delighted to take the call:

'This is great news, Richard. The Virgin brand is just what the bank needs,' he said. 'Of course, you do realise you're going to need literally billions of pounds?'

'Ohh, yes,' I said. And I thought to myself: *Billions? Did he really say billions?*

'I'm confident that can be arranged,' I said. Well, of course he said billions. He was a bank.

'I fully understand,' I said, and by then, with sweat beading my brow, I really did.

The bank's position had become public at 8.30 p.m. on Thursday 13 September 2007, when the BBC reported that Northern Rock had asked for and been given emergency financial support from the Bank of England. The funding facility was finalised in the early hours and announced to the London Stock Exchange at 7 a.m. Within hours of opening, long queues began to form outside Northern Rock branches across the UK. The website collapsed and its phone lines were jammed. This was shocking news: the first run on a bank in the United Kingdom since Victorian times.

There was a great deal to admire in Northern Rock, and I wanted to protect and save what was good about it. When the run on the bank began I watched the television pictures of the queues along with everybody else. Now, the queues were undeniably disturbing, they were the story. But being in the businesses I'm in, it won't come as any surprise that I also had my eye on the front of those queues, where Northern Rock spokespeople were trying to reassure some very worried customers. I admired the way the staff turned out at the branches and dealt with people as they demanded their money back. They stood right in the front line, calmly advising customers. I heard from inside that everyone had come in to help – it was all hands to the pumps.

The bank had weaknesses: yes, they had got themselves and their customers into a whole heap of trouble by borrowing short in the money markets for long-term mortgages. But hindsight is easy: the bank had been popular with intermediaries – the financial advisers who recommended the bank's mortgages – and they had very modern systems in place. It was an engine that was fine in its way – but too hungry for the road it was on. It had run out of petrol. Our job was to see how it could be made to work again on a more environmentally benign fuel than the short-term money markets.

First of all, we needed to put together a winning team. While much of the media interest was to focus on me personally in the coming months, it won't surprise you to learn that I've neither the time nor the skills to run a bank. As far as the rescue team – a formidable group of people led by Jayne-Anne Gadhia, the head of Virgin Money – saw things I was very much in the background. Each evening I would ring Jayne-Anne for a catch-up, and to see if there was anything I could do.

Stephen Murphy appointed James Lupton of Greenhill to help us in London, along with Peter Norris's firm Quayle Munro, and Andrew Balheimer of top law firm Allen & Overy – we had the makings of our team. We needed to know how to deal with a company the size and scale of Northern Rock. 'Do you really think we can get this?' Their answer was that if we could secure the funding, then it was made for us. But only if we could get funding.

So I was given the task of drumming up support for our equity consortium. One of our team dubbed it 'dialling for dollars' – and certainly I was able to use some top-flight contacts to pull people on board. I also made a number of more personal calls to ensure there would be goodwill towards a private rescue bid – I was given the green light at the highest level.

We built up a business plan to explain how we would turn Northern Rock into the Virgin Bank. (I had toyed with the idea of calling it Virgin Rocks, doffing the cap to our rock-music origins; Jayne-Anne gently but firmly dissuaded me.) My first port of call was AIG, the insurance group who sponsor Manchester United Football Club. They were very keen to support us. It was a flying start. We went on a roadshow, presenting our plans to the big global banks. Our long-standing relationship with the Royal Bank of Scotland paid dividends – they requested that we deal with them, and their partners, Citigroup and Deutsche Bank, exclusively. This was a brilliant boost for us. We now had in place a possible investment of £11 billion (yes, billion!)

On Friday 12 October 2007, we unveiled our consortium of heavyweight financial backers. Our team included Wilbur Ross, the veteran distressed debt investor; AIG, the world's largest insurance company; First Eastern Investment, led by Victor Chu; and Toscafund, the hedge fund led by Martin Hughes and chaired by Sir George Mathewson. (Sir George, the former chief executive of the Royal Bank of Scotland, was very kindly acting as our senior adviser while we looked for a chairman.)

The Virgin team went to Freshfields, the London law firm, for an initial meeting with the Northern Rock management team, when Adam Applegarth, the beleaguered chief executive, was still in situ. Jayne-Anne told me later that she had been hugely impressed with the Northern Rock team's willingness to divulge information, and with their diligence in trying to sort out the mess. Following this meeting, Northern Rock opened their data room to the Virgin team.

But now there were other competitors eyeing up the bank. Investment firms Olivant, Cerberus, JC Flowers and Five Mile were all up against our plan. It appeared that this was going to be a competitive bid and, given the credit crunch, the battle for funding was likely to be fierce.

It was clear to us all that we needed a credible senior figure to pull the project together. So Jayne-Anne allotted me the task of persuading Sir Brian Pitman – the leading banker of his generation and a man of huge knowledge – to become our chairman.

I had worked with Sir Brian for years on the board of Virgin Atlantic and through our connection with Singapore Airlines. I like and admire him. At seventy-six, his brain is as sharp and focused as ever. He is on the board of Carphone Warehouse, and ITV, and is a senior adviser to Morgan Stanley. Stephen and Jayne-Anne had spoken and met with him several times as we refined our proposal. He was extremely reluctant to get involved and told me it would be difficult to turn the bank around.

But I pestered him and he eventually relented. He would, at least, hear us out.

Jayne-Anne went down to his home in Weybridge to give a two-hour presentation. He saw enough to realise our bid was credible. He understood, too, that it required a man of his gravitas to shape it. He made some welcome suggestions to the plan, and came up to London a couple of days later to meet the team. But he still wasn't saying yes.

The pressure on us grew. Lee Rochford, Royal Bank of Scotland's Managing Director of Financial Institutions Securitisation (I wonder how he describes himself at parties?) phoned to say that in order to support us they needed to be assured that we would have a suitably qualified chairman. So Jayne-Anne called Sir Brian in Surrey asking him once again to consider. Finally, he agreed. It was a coup. Jayne-Anne phoned Lee to reveal the name. He was delighted: 'That's fantastic news.'

Sir Brian attended all our key meetings – including sessions at the Bank of England, the UK's Financial Services Authority and the Treasury – and he was by far the most distinguished and experienced of all the senior bankers who attended these sessions. Our credibility was established.

In the face of the credit crunch and the sub-prime problems in the United States, our recession planning needed to be faultless. First of all, it had to satisfy the regulators. Our bid chairman was a stickler on that. This was the question we had to ask ourselves, if we were to protect the downside: 'What would happen in the worst-case scenario, in which the housing market in the UK goes into a deep recession?'

The question Sir Brian was posing was a poignant one, as well as a practical one. Once, when Jayne-Anne asked him why he had agreed to join us, he said there were a number of reasons – but one was that he remembered how Northern Rock had looked after miners' families during the strikes of the 1980s. Apparently they stopped asking for mortgage payments while the strike was on, and risked lots of bad debt. But they lost nothing, and the miners and their families kept their homes. Sir Brian said that a business with such an honourable history deserved to be rescued.

Our plan was to inject £1.25 billion of new cash plus Virgin Money as a business. The cash would have come from Virgin, Wilbur Ross, Toscafund and First Eastern, and the plan was to allow the existing shareholders to participate in a rights issue that would enable them, on very preferential terms, to recoup their investment over the coming years.

Unfortunately, it had still to dawn on Northern Rock's shareholders what a bad state their bank was in. Their general feeling was that ours was a poor offer. It wasn't, as became all too clear. We really were being about as generous as we could possibly be – especially given the need to introduce so much new capital to satisfy the regulator's requirements. (Of course, I don't blame the shareholders: as I said earlier, hindsight is easy.)

Two leading hedge funds made it clear to the government that they would vote against the Virgin deal and force nationalisation if the government chose us over their own rescue plan. I feel that kind of rhetoric began to force the prime minister's hand; despite the need for a quick deal, the government couldn't be seen to support us and have the shareholders vote against us. The process was going to be a long-drawn-out one, but we were all set up to work it through.

We reported that without an injection of new capital of £1.25 billion, Northern Rock bank would not be able to withstand a recession of the magnitude of the early 1990s. We disclosed our reasoning and our figures to the FSA and they appeared very happy with our work and prudent assumptions. Indeed, this is my answer to those who suggested that I was only in all this to mug the British taxpayer of billions of pounds at little risk to my own business. Sir Brian explained this to me in stark figures several times. 'We have got to lose £1.6 billion in total as the consortium before the taxpayer loses anything.'

Nevertheless, we were confident. Our plan showed that we could repay all the debts by 2010. By early 2009, according to our figures, Virgin Bank would have lost £300 million; it would break even by 2010, and grow after 2011. This was an enormous risk for all of our equity providers, and for me personally. Virgin's normal rate of return in business is around 30 per cent. The returns here would be about half that – but applied to huge figures. I was entering alien territory. Stephen and Gordon talked me through the process and we weighed up the risk to the group. We all agreed we would press on.

We had to do many presentations to our equity consortium to keep them with us. Late in the day Jayne-Anne presented to Martin Hughes of Toscafund. Given the increasing cost of funding, she wondered if we would need to make people redundant. Martin was adamant that we should carry the cost of excess staff until the business was thriving again – he just didn't want the spectre of job losses to mar our bank. Like most really successful people I've met, Martin was more interested in doing the right and proper thing than the easy and expedient one.

Every night at 6 p.m. the Virgin team hooked up for a conference call led by Stephen and Gordon. It was our opportunity to catch up with each other and agree the next steps. Ours was a collegiate approach, using the wisdom of seasoned banking professionals, each of them a veteran of a significant merger deal. No one else had this treasure chest of knowledge, and I was extremely proud that the Virgin name could attract such top-notch people. In business, this kind of team support is in surprisingly short supply.

Wilbur Ross was a hard taskmaster. Jayne-Anne sat up till the small hours on a number of occasions as he stress-tested her on all the downside scenarios. My business view is always to protect the downside – and this was one of Virgin's biggest ever gambles. Wilbur was much more interested in how much he could lose, rather than how much he could gain. In major bids like this, involving billions of pounds, success comes from identifying the downside – and covering it – far more than planning for the upside. Wilbur wanted to make sure that we were prepared for every eventuality. He became convinced that we were. Sir Brian, the FSA and the Bank of England agreed, and declared us their preferred bidder.

The hedge-fund investors – who had been betting on the share price – were livid at the prospect of us taking over. As we approached Christmas, the credit squeeze was getting tighter and tighter. All over the City, major banks were announcing problems caused by a lack of liquidity. While our lines of funding with RBS and their partners were still open, the cost of that funding was getting more expensive. We began to look at our numbers and we all agreed it was becoming too expensive to borrow. It was starting to look unattractive for us – and we considered withdrawing. It was then that the Bank of England and the government stepped in and offered support by suggesting 'wrapped sovereign bonds'. These were bonds or gilts issued by the government and paid for at a commercial price. All of the bidders would have access to this funding, and so the merits of each proposal could at last be considered with a degree of objectivity.

This would certainly ease the pressure on us, because we knew our bid was already in very good shape.

True, we would as a consequence face stringent European Union restrictions on fair trading. If we were getting government-backed bonds, this would give us an advantage over commercial banks, and we would have to be restricted when competing with them, until we'd paid these loans back. This was only fair, and we had no problem with it. The government said that there would be no dividends until the UK taxpayer was paid back. This, too, was only reasonable: Virgin would have repaid the money back to the taxpayer before we took anything.

The Virgin team were interested and waiting for a term sheet to come out from Goldman Sachs just as I was heading out to China on a high-level business trip with senior British business figures and Gordon Brown, the prime minister.

We were delayed in leaving because of the emergency landing of British Airways' Boeing 777 at Heathrow. They had lost power in both engines as they descended, and through the immense skill of the pilot the plane had crash-landed on the grass before the runway saving everybody on board. I've had my run-ins with BA over many years but you have to hand it to them: they employ first-rate flight crews. The atmosphere on our flight was one of quiet elation, the surroundings reminding us of the life-saving efforts of the 777's captain and first officer.

When we arrived in Beijing, I phoned Jayne-Anne asking if the Goldman Sachs package had come in yet.

'Yes, it's just come through.'

'Good,' I said.

'What's been happening on the flight?'

'What do you mean?'

'It's all over the news that you and Gordon Brown have been having private talks about Northern Rock.'

'Ha ha.'

'No. Not "ha ha". What are you up to?'

There was a long pause.

'Jayne-Anne, please tell me you're joking about this.'

'It's on the news now,' she said.

There were forty journalists at the back of the plane, and one of the rival consortium's PR advisers. Gordon Brown had passed through the plane to talk to them, pausing to tell me what he then told them: that he'd be issuing the Goldman Sachs term sheet to all the bidders within the next twenty-four hours.

That was it. Nothing else. At any time. Never mind in front of forty journalists and a pack of hedge-fund managers who wanted me out of the picture!

Yet the entire China trip was to be coloured in the British media by a supposed 'sweetheart deal' between me and Gordon Brown. The herd instinct of the British media did lasting damage to our chances. There were even cartoons of Gordon Brown being in my pocket – and I being in his. Whether it was malicious or simple over-exuberance, I'll never know. We were told that the prime minister and the Treasury still favoured a private sector deal, but I think the whole Chinese episode must have influenced his team's eventual thinking.

The media played a major role, even beyond the China trip, in the whole evolution of the Northern Rock story. During the crisis, Bryan Sanderson, now Northern Rock chairman (after Matt Ridley's resignation), told Jayne-Anne that every paper had a journalist dedicated to the story and that they were being told to come up with a new story every day – that made for too fertile a field of gossip!

The Treasury didn't help matters when it started negotiating in the press, too. John Kingman, the civil service power broker in the Treasury charged with running the show, actually told our team that, in any decision made, the government would have to take account of the view of Robert Peston, the BBC's business editor. Now Robert is a very likeable guy and a good journalist, but we thought it was odd that he often had information about our proposal before we were told!

The most bizarre coverage for Jayne-Anne followed an early-evening call she had with Kathryn Griffiths at the *Daily Telegraph*. Like everyone else, Griffiths wanted to know how much Virgin would earn out of brand licence fees. She was told that it would be an arm's-length amount similar to that charged at other companies – including Virgin Media. That meant about 1 per cent of income – which, given the problems with Northern Rock, amounted to very little each year for years to come. Next morning the *Telegraph* Business-page headline screamed: 'BRANSON TO MAKE £200 MILLION FROM FEES FOR ROCK'. Our press team asked them how they had concocted this figure, and were told it was calculated over twenty-five years! It all contributed to the idea that I was trying to make a fast buck. When Jayne-Anne later went to Newcastle and talked through the numbers with the Northern Rock management team, David Jones, the finance director, asked why we had excluded the licence fee for using the Virgin brand. But we hadn't! He just couldn't believe the amount was so tiny as to be irrelevant. Even Sir Brian, in his interview with the *Financial Times* in early February, stressed the returns would be unexciting and that nobody 'will make a killing'.

He went on to say: 'We've satisfied ourselves that with the capital we are putting in we'd have enough pure equity in this thing that, if the worst came to the worst, the shareholders would lose money, not the taxpayer.' Yet the whole Branson–Brown 'sweetheart deal' notion began to grow arm and legs. It even reached Prime Minister's Questions in the House of Commons on Wednesday 23 January.

David Cameron, the leader of the Conservative Opposition, asked Gordon Brown about the taxpayers' exposure under the prime minister's bond scheme. It became part of a political boxing match between a new prime minister on the ropes and an Opposition leader determined to throw some mischievous punches.

'Let us be clear: the rescue package is as much for his reputation as it is for the business. If the bonds are not paid back, and if Northern Rock fails to meet its obligations, what is the total exposure? How much?'

'The loans and bonds are secured against the assets of Northern Rock, which, as everyone understands, has a high-quality loan book. It is our intention to get the best deal for taxpayers: they will get their money back, and make a profit,' said the prime minister.

Cameron then claimed the figure was £55 billion – a neat rhetorical trick, achieved by lumbering every household in the country with a hypothetical second mortgage!

If the press around that China trip was extremely damaging to our bid (and it was) so was the political point-scoring in Parliament. The Liberal Democrats were particularly aggressive, hiding behind parliamentary privilege to insult and belittle us.

Vince Cable, the MP for Twickenham and deputy leader of the Liberal Democrats, sounds an amusing guy and he's been an excellent performer in the House of Commons. His sound bites have enlivened proceedings in the British Parliament, but then, in the House of Commons, libel laws don't apply: he can say pretty much what he wants to.

And he did: 'Can the Chancellor tell us what Mr Branson is going to contribute? My understanding is that he is proposing to put in £250 million in kind, not cash, to acquire a bank worth £100 billion, or forty times that value.' A bank worth £100 billion!? If so, it certainly wouldn't have been in trouble.

Being able to come out with this sort of thing unchallenged clearly went to his head, because he went on to claim that I had been involved with this 'sweetheart deal' with the government. He talked about 'nationalising the risk, and privatising the profit'. Then he cast aspersions on me personally saying that I was not a fit person to run a bank – and that I had a criminal record gained when I was nineteen. This was untrue, of course, and the only reason he knew of my stupidity was because I'd chosen to be open about the story in *Losing My Virginity* some forty years after it had happened. I do hope he paid the full cover price for his copy.

I appealed to Nick Clegg, the new leader of the Liberal Democrats, asking that they depersonalise the campaign. Sir Brian Pitman and Jayne-Anne Gadhia offered to meet Vince Cable – but he refused to see them, insisting on meeting me.

On Monday 4 February, the announcement of Olivant's withdrawal piled more political pressure on chancellor Alistair Darling. His hope for a bidding war between Virgin and Luqman Arnold's private equity group simply fizzled out. The *Financial Times* headline summed it up

– 'OLIVANT ABANDONS ROCK AT 11TH HOUR' – and he was reported to be 'stunned'. Olivant's proposal had attracted the support of Northern Rock shareholders including SRM and RAB, the hedge-fund investors, who had amassed 18 per cent of the bank. They were opposed to the Virgin deal because they simply weren't going to get as much out of it.

At the very last minute, we were asked to increase our government guarantees and add an extra £100–200 million for equity warrants. This was stretching it for us, and in the same week I came across a lot of comments that we were 'getting the bank on the cheap' and 'benefiting from the upside, without taking downside'. This was news to me.

Indeed, towards the end of the whole process, Stephen Murphy spoke to Wilbur Ross who made it clear that as the government were seeking to tighten all the terms, the risks in the deal were getting more substantial while the returns were now becoming marginal. Wilbur warned that he could not accept any further reduction given his responsibilities to his investors. We had to respect this as Wilbur is a hugely experienced investor in international markets, and he and Tosca were our key investor partners. The government was (rightly) seeking a massive amount of new capital to protect the UK taxpayer, but wasn't recognising that this has to be rewarded for the risks involved. That position was never going to work.

In the end, I think the very thought of a business – despite taking the risks – eventually making a return on its investment threw Gordon Brown and his beleaguered Chancellor of the Exchequer into a panic.

The prime minister took the decision to nationalise the Northern Rock bank at 2 p.m. in Downing Street, after he and Alistair Darling concluded there was no other option. Their announcement was not diplomatically handled. Our only surviving rivals for the bid, Northern Rock's own internal management team, were still answering questions about their rescue plan when Gordon Brown declared his decision.

After our disappointment I received a cordial phone call from Gordon Brown, requesting that I didn't make too much noise and nuisance about the decision. He told me that nationalisation was the right option. In the back of my mind I couldn't help but wonder whether the UK's press hysteria about me being on a trip to China with the prime minister had put the kibosh on our chances. Still, I did as I had been asked: I didn't make a fuss. I issued a statement saying we had submitted as strong a proposal as we could, and that I was 'very disappointed'. And I was certainly disappointed enough to feel I deserved those drinks at the Biras Creek bar that night.

On reflection, the whole Northern Rock saga represents to me a case of the government looking for the most politically expedient solution and not planning for the long term. Virgin, as a private company, had been willing to take Northern Rock off the government's hands and make it work again. We could have developed a brilliant bank, the Virgin Bank, out of it, and I am confident we would have generated new jobs by doing so. As it is, the Labour government will be forced to shrink the company quickly, cut the jobs and get the money back to limit any political fallout. There isn't much innovation or product development in this route and certainly not more competition in the banking market – and the poor old taxpayer gets all the downside risk.

But governments and civil servants can't run businesses – that's been proven a depressing number of times all over the world, and for years in the UK we had daily experience of their ineptitude every time we boarded (or weren't able to board) what they laughingly called a 'train'. Business is not in their make-up. To be fair, it's not their job, any more than running a bank single-handedly would ever be mine.

And that, of course, is the point: *I was never going to run the bank*. I know my limitations. I know what I'm good at, and what I'm not good at. I would never pretend that I could run a bank – and that's why we built a credible banking team. Jayne-Anne Gadhia of Virgin Money, Gordon McCallum and Stephen Murphy of Virgin Management, Sir Brian Pitman, Sir George Mathewson, Wilbur Ross, an immensely successful US investor in difficult turnarounds, and advisers such as James Lupton and Peter Norris. We had assembled a formidable team of serious bankers and investors and in the end we were the only real show in town. Our lawyers had a better understanding of the company's legal position than the company's or government's own advisers, while James, Peter and their teams ran rings around their opposition. My vision was to make it possible that the bank could be saved, by finding really good people to run it.

Nationalising Northern Rock? I think it was the wrong decision which will haunt not only this government but whoever is elected to hold the reins of power in Britain for years to come.

I spent the day after nursing my poor head. The press cuttings were filtering through and we received a number of emails and calls from well-wishers. The Chancellor sent me a note thanking me for Virgin's interest and our offer but reiterating that nationalisation was the best option for the bank.

I couldn't and can't agree with that, and it saddens me to think of all the good work that's been undervalued, and all the opportunities that have been lost.

Inasmuch as it was in me to feel anything that day – aside from the throbbing in my head – I felt, and I still feel, a great deal of sympathy for the people working within Northern Rock. The staff were tremendously decent people caught in the middle of a public nightmare. They worked every hour, every day of the week, for many months, and they remained upbeat. I'm positive they would have enjoyed being part of the wider Virgin family.

And Jayne-Anne's own team played a blinder too. Virgin Money's finance director, Dave Dyer, and its strategy director, Matt Baxby, worked with total commitment. They more than embodied the Virgin spirit and put a great many personal and family matters on hold while we aimed for the prize.

Jayne-Anne phoned me on the Tuesday after the announcement. I was worried about her. She had been a stalwart, driving the process for us, plus she and her husband Ashok had a five-year-old daughter to look after. Jayne-Anne had spent a hell of a lot of time away from home, her weekends were taken up with some hefty reading of reports and number crunching, and most nights she worked long past midnight. I thought she might be very let down.

'I hope you're not standing on top of a building and about to jump,' I said.

'Oh, don't worry, Richard,' she said chirpily, 'I've spent the weekend looking over the figures of Bradford & Bingley and Alliance & Leicester.'

My head began to throb again. A lot. 'For heaven's sake, *why*?'

'They both look ripe for a takeover. Listen . . .'

That was the kind of spirit that cheered me up. At Virgin, we move on.

What if you can't move on? What if there is nowhere to move to?

Assuming you're not burning other people's money in their faces, you could always perform the hardest trick in the book of business tricks: get very small, very specialised and very expensive.

I would absolutely count this as innovation, and of the highest calibre: you're taking a large operation and finding ways to scale it down, retarget it and remarket it, all the while adding bucketloads of value to justify the hike in price. And it's very hard to do – not least because you're in so much pain as you're doing it. (Indeed, your old business is dying around you.)

What is the first thing we do at Virgin when we're faced with a problem? We get together promptly to look for the answer to a single question: 'Is there a way out?' And we then go right to the endgame and ask: 'What is the ideal way out of this problem for everyone?'

You need to become 100 per cent focused on trying to find that way out. If it's a major problem, give it 100 per cent of your time and energy until it is sorted. Work night and day to resolve it, and try to delegate everything else that is going on. If, having done this, you fail to resolve the problem, then at least you know you've done everything in your power you can. Move on. If it means taking a hit, then take it on the chin. Don't even think about it again. *If you're hurt, lick your wounds and get up again. If you've given it your absolute best, it's time to move forward.*

As I write this the economy is deteriorating; it may be that some of you will be faced with this task in the near future. Good luck. And may the next chapter, which is all about innovation, give you some serviceable ideas.

Innovation

A Driver for Business

In 1986 I gave an interview to a British music paper. The headline was 'BRANSON'S BOMBSHELL'. I said that we were planning to put every album and single on to a small portable computer box and that the listener would be able to buy it and play any record they wanted, listening through mini-headphones. I said it would revolutionise the music industry – and people believed me. I got frantic phone calls from some major record company bosses pleading with me not to launch such a device. They told me it would blow away the record industry. Then I pointed out the date. It was 1 April – April Fool's Day. When the editor of the paper found out, he wasn't amused.

Fifteen years later, Apple sold its first iPod.

Already, in this book, we've talked a lot about innovation. *The best, most solid way out of a crisis in a changing market is through experiment and adaptation.* Businesses surf the waves of changing circumstances, and I can't offhand think of any industries whose best players are not constantly engaged in reinvention of one sort or another.

Making changes and improvements is a natural part of business, and for sole traders and very small companies, the distinction between innovation and day-to-day delivery is barely noticeable and unimportant. It's all just business, and creative, responsive, flexible business comes easier to you the smaller your operation.

Larger operations command more capital, and so, in theory at least, their range of possible actions is greater. But complexity soon gums up the works of an organisation as it expands. (One marvellously backhanded Chinese curse runs: 'May you employ more than a hundred people.')

This is the point at which entrepreneurial functions become separated from management functions. This makes a lot of sense – as you'll see when we look at different forms of business leadership in the next chapter. However, the separation of day-to-day business from the motive energy that birthed the company does cause problems. Suddenly, innovating is seen as something extra, something special, something separated from the activities the company normally engages in. This is when niggles become endemic, intractable problems; morale declines; and the business begins to lose its way in the marketplace.

Virgin's management style is unique, designed to both empower employees and avoid a culture of fear. A couple of other companies encourage new ideas even in their day-to-day operations. These are very different companies from Virgin, and I admire both of them immensely.

Since 1976, with design and ease-of-use its business mantra, Apple has simply kept inventing and improving. The sale of over 100 million iPods and three billion downloads from iTunes is proof of their success. While other businesses have been caught in the free fall of the record industry revolution, Apple has been able to fire up a new generation of listeners, not just with music but with podcasts, radio shows, TV shows, movies . . .

Steve Jobs and his colleague Steve Wozniak both had a passion for gadgets and began as electronic entrepreneurs in 1970. Six years later they were listed in the *Fortune* 500 rich list. In 2008, Apple had a market capitalisation of $105 billion, ahead of Dell and just behind Intel. The original Apple Mac, which was released in 1984, was described by Steve as 'the fastest and most powerful computer ever placed in the hands of a large number of people'. It was a transformational product. Steve later stepped back from the sharp end of the business – which promptly started to go into reverse. He returned as its saviour.

He is seeking perfection all of the time, and from that original mouse-driven Apple Mac, through to the iPod and the revolutionary iPhone, he has pushed the frontiers of technology in a creative way. And Apple's products have transformed people's lives. On Apple's campus at Cupertino in California, innovation is driven by a combination of perseverance at tackling large, intractable problems and, as a *Harvard Business Review* article in February 2006 described it, Steve Jobs playing his part as the 'great intimidator'.

By all accounts, Steve is a difficult man to work with because of his impossibly exacting standards, but his co-workers are filled with a sense of 'messianic zeal' to gain Steve's approval for their work. He is meticulous about the details and zealous about protecting all the new features that give his business that vital edge. That's leadership.

Apple is an iconic global brand that inspires emotional attachment. Yet the logo is only very subtly embossed on their products. Steve Jobs and his team know exactly how to design, manufacture and then deliver high-quality products to the market.

Steve immerses himself in the marketing campaigns and product launches himself he has chosen to be both the manager and the entrepreneur, and in his case he has been successful playing both roles. He's a rare animal. Perfecting the fine art of delegation is normally essential when you're running a large company. Steve is more zealous than he needs to be, but it seems to work for him. It gives the public and investors confidence that the admiral is at the helm – with his hand firmly on the tiller. Steve has that rare business quality: the acute intelligence to see what the public wants. You can tell this by the way Pixar Animated Pictures, which he co-founded, has had a stream of blockbusters which have earned a stack of Academy Awards, including such successes as *Toy Story*, *A Bug's Life* and *Finding Nemo*. Pixar's family films have grossed more than $4 billion at the box office. Steve was there when it merged with the Walt Disney Company in 2006 and he remains on Disney's board of directors. His unrelenting genius is at the heart of everything Apple does and, in my view, this places Steve in a business class of his own.

While I acknowledge that Apple's products have transformed lives – and you only have to walk along a street to see the ubiquitous white earpieces of the iPod – I reckon it is another 'Invented-in-America' brand that has made the most significant difference to the shape of our connected world. I have been asked: 'What is the greatest business invention of the last fifty years?' That's a tough question because you need to factor in the mobile phone, DNA testing, the personal computer and the Internet, but I think the winner has to be Google's powerful search engine.

Google has allowed ordinary people to find things out much more quickly. It has led to more immediate choice – and increased consumer power – and a freer flow of information, knowledge and ideas. It is far more than just a search engine – it has become an engine of change. Google's mission is 'to organise the world's information and make it universally acceptable and useful'. That's a noble ambition. It has allowed political, cultural and interest groups to flourish. It has brought the democratisation of information on to a global scale – something that was unthinkable just ten years ago. It has also brought a great deal of fun into our lives.

I'm honoured to be good friends with both Larry Page and Sergey Brin, the founders of Google. I was flattered to be asked to officiate at Larry and Lucy's wedding on Necker. Larry and Sergey won't mind me describing them as geeks – indeed, with them it's a badge of honour – but they both have strong personalities. Their characters complement each other when they are working on a project. They get on very well and never, ever disagree with one another in front of staff, clients or investors. In the world of business, this requires remarkable self-discipline. If they have a disagreement, they will wait until everyone has gone out of the room and only then will they discuss the matter. They are bound together better than the best marriages, and their personal chemistry is an intrinsic part of their business success.

Today Google attracts the brightest technical talent. I love the idea that employees are encouraged to generate *and develop* new ideas, and that technical staff spend 20 per cent of their work time doing something they choose to do. By giving their people ownership over their work in this way, the company and its customers have benefited enormously. Among many other innovations, this scheme has brought us Gmail, Adsense, Google Earth, Google Maps and Google News, which aggregates headlines from around the world. The company excels at IT and business architecture. It continually conducts experiments to test its system, and then improvises and improves, and it has a backbone of people who are acutely analytical.

Sergey and Larry understood early on that they are not managers. Their trade now is in finding ideas and turning them into businesses or other enterprises. While they conceived Google and built it, they also found a brilliant CEO in Eric Schmidt, who runs the company on a day-to-day level. Eric was the CEO of Novell, and he also sits on the board of Apple. He is steeped in the technology world but he knows how to deal with financial matters and the investment community. This is a classic example of how the roles of entrepreneur and manager can be separated – a theme explored further in the next chapter. At Google, both sides of the business are given room to breathe. Eric's day-to-day management of the company allows Sergey and Larry to commit themselves to the search for new ideas – and to enjoy some of their wealth!

One of our Virgin team was visiting Google's HQ in Mountain View and told me they have an enormous whiteboard detailing the strategy of Google. It is Google's Master Plan and there are thousands of ideas on the board, all contributed by the employees. One of the key tasks along with 'Hiring network engineers' and 'Hiring hardware engineers' was 'Hire Richard Branson'. I don't need to be hired: I'm always happy to help Sergey and Larry.

On April Fool's Day 2008 we announced the launch of Virgle, a partnership between Virgin and Google looking at creating a community on Mars in the next fifteen years. We were advertising for volunteers to travel on a one-way ticket to Mars. It was concocted over dinner at Necker when we talked seriously about the creation of a human colony on Mars and what it might look like. We then pondered who we would invite. Our announcement made headlines around the world and had dozens of blog sites buzzing with activity. Were we joking? Of course we were joking. Mind you, fifteen years before Apple started selling iPods, I was joking about portable digital music players. With that in mind, we've registered the Virgle brand – just in case . . .

Innovation can occur when the most elementary questions are asked and employees are given the resources and power to achieve the answers. That's how Virgin America did it. While the legal team fought to convince the Department of Transportation that Virgin America was indeed a US-owned carrier, the Virgin America design and finance teams focused on taking care of business, and that was the business of creating a totally different and better flying experience. *What does a great travel experience look and feel like? How would it be different from anything else US travellers have experienced? What would it take to knock their socks off?*

Building an entirely new way to fly required a team of specialists who respected each other's expertise but didn't hesitate to fight for what they believed was important, who worked in close proximity round the clock, made decisions swiftly, and passionately believed in their vision for the customer. Ironically they themselves *were* the customers!

While understanding that the airline was to be under US control, Virgin USA CEO Frances Farrow was convinced that the issues the flying public truly cared about – the actual product and experience – should be without equal in US skies. Her first focus was to go after the best talent for customer service and design, and where better to look than people leaving Virgin Atlantic?

As I've said before, Virgin employees, after they've started a shiny new Virgin company or run a mature one with aplomb, are worth holding on to because they love the brand they helped build and their experience and knowledge of the brand are priceless. New companies are a great way to keep them challenged – and to keep them within the family.

Adam Wells, a whizz-kid from Virgin Atlantic's design team which had created the award-winning upper-class suites, and Todd Palowski, Virgin Atlantic's customer service specialist, were brought in as part of the original customer and product insight team. They were quickly followed by talent of the likes of Charles Ogilvie, a cutting-edge interactive entertainment guy.

This small but dedicated group began to dream big. The team didn't inherit drab legacy planes and they weren't stuck in the status quo. They were empowered with the Virgin brand to do things differently; there was no other way to create a completely different experience. *What if we got rid of check-in lines? What if we turned the airplane into a living room? How can we give control back to passengers? What should we put in our toilets? How can airplane seating express freedom? And how can we express that freedom from the moment passengers reach the ticketing area?*

Flying is generally a passive experience. From the moment you enter the airport, you are told what to do. Claim your boarding pass here. Put your luggage there. Stand in line, take your belt off, remove all liquids ... The onboard experience is no better. If you're lucky, the cabin crew flips on a heavily edited movie that no one really wants to watch. And that's followed by a trolley of unhealthy snacks that blocks you from the loo.

What you don't have is freedom. The Virgin America team believed they could find a way to give it back to you, and they did. (Sorry, they're geniuses but even they couldn't make check-in go away.) They designed a liberating experience, one in which you could genuinely do what you wanted with your flying time. You want to work on your laptop? Open it up and go, there's plenty of room. Running out of power? Plug it in, charge up your computer and play a game while you're at it. Want to chat with your cousin who is a few rows back? Try seat-to-seat chatting on the inflight entertainment screen using the QWERTY keyboard at your armrest. Feeling peckish? Order a sandwich from your seat, and a flight attendant will deliver it to you *when you want it*. Want to listen to music? Create a music playlist? Watch a movie ... in Mandarin Chinese? Go for it. It's all there right in front of you.

You will not get bored on our flights.

So innovation has to be appropriate for your business. It must fulfil a need, and it must give you an edge over your competitors. Our food-ordering system was an extension of our service philosophy, the idea that the cabin crew wanted to give passengers control. No airline in the world but Virgin America offers on-demand food ordering. We decided that free airline food was a failed model. Free is not necessarily good; customers have low expectations and the airline is pressured to slap down the absolute bottom-quality snack. But our team asked some questions and offered a simple solution: if you pay a little bit, you will get what you want. Customers had passively accepted the norm of free peanuts and then nothing at all ...

The Virgin USA brand team did some research on Virgin's US customers and learned that they tend to be open, ambitious, very social and up for trying new things. It says something about you if you choose to fly with Virgin. You can think of flying as being trapped on a plane with strangers but we think our passengers have more in common with each other than they would with passengers on a legacy carrier. The team liked the idea of giving people a real opportunity for community creation, whether it's on the entertainment system or chatting with the person next to you or texting someone a few rows away.

We knew broadband was coming but couldn't time it, and we needed a stopgap to invite people to chat and interact in the cabin. So Charles put chat rooms and seat-to-seat chatting in the inflight entertainment system, with keyboards at every seat. It's a totally new way of stretching out and interacting while being in a confined space. And through those little seat-back entertainment screens, we created a social community. It didn't hurt that our small new airline's tight-knit cabin crew was friendly, remembered repeat passengers and helped to make each flight feel like a party.

While the commercial team was about to order millions of dollars' worth of planes, the brand team was at the next desk demanding a brighter shade of white from the seat supplier. The supplier had never had this sort of request before; in fact, seat-back colour choices ranged from ten shades of beige to the same of purples and greys ... but no white, and definitely no whiter-than-iPod white.

Lighting on planes tends to be harsh and grim, so Adam designed a mood lighting system with special controls that was custom-developed for us, a first for aeroplanes. Because no whiter-than-iPod white option was available, we gave the seat-backs a unique coating, giving the lighting a sleek surface to reflect off and washing the cabin with soothing light; it was a deliberate visual experience to give the impression of space and freedom.

These simple details are the stuff of Virgin. If that's what business professors call innovation, fine. Innovation is often what you didn't know you wanted until you got it. Now the other airlines look outdated and neglected, so they will have to catch up to our innovation. And so the cycle of competition goes.

Like any Virgin company, the Virgin America team were surrounded by, learned from, and influenced amazing specialists. Colleagues are your best resource at Virgin companies: open and thoughtful people to bounce crazy ideas off – which don't seem so crazy when the person next to you shares your vision and can help you realise it. The Virgin brand demands people like that, people who are going to ask tough questions and demand excellence and something different.

Could the team have worked as effectively in a different setting, a different company? They were indeed extraordinary but the circumstances were equally unusual. The team weren't motivated by getting ahead – there was no corporate ladder and they weren't inspired or intimidated by a bureaucratic hierarchy. They were empowered and they owned the product, and they would have to live with it once it launched. Because the brand is known for being a leader and going against the grain, there's a bit of pressure to innovate – not just for the sake of innovation but truly to deliver something better.

Virgin America also benefited from being the underdog. The airline was a start-up minnow fighting the legacy sharks that wanted to keep its planes grounded. This do-or-die mission was motivating.

Innovation doesn't necessarily mean being first or biggest, but being the best. We weren't the first carrier to introduce low-cost fares to Americans. We aren't interested in flying into every airport in all fifty US states. We want to offer travellers an excellent flying experience to a small but growing number of urban point-to-point centres. We have a model that gives us the flexibility to navigate these turbulent times.

We want people to enjoy flying again and that's why Virgin America continues to focus and innovate on the customer experience.

Customers are talking about Virgin America. They're writing in their blogs about a vacation and how it started with a flight on Virgin America and how much fun they had on their flight or how clever the safety video was. They're uploading on their Flickr pages snapshots of themselves on our planes or the inflight entertainment screen.

This tells me we're doing a pretty good job of it so far.

The power of research and development is great – too great just to be let out to graze on the existing market. Governments and powerful philanthropists have understood this for centuries, and have tried, often quite successfully, to harness innovation to their own long-term purposes. I am becoming more and more involved in questions of how we can best direct capital investment to address the problems which we know are round the corner, but which are not yet driving the day-to-day responses of the market.

Schemes to encourage advances in a particular field are not new, of course. The first recorded prize created by the British government was launched in 1714, offering financial incentives to the inventor who developed a device capable of measuring longitude within half a degree of accuracy. This was vital work at the time, because European seafaring nations, including Britain, were finding themselves caught up in increasingly violent skirmishes with each other – all because they couldn't agree on the location of borders and treaty lines in territories far away from their home shores.

Fifty-nine years later the prize was won by John Harrison, a self-educated Yorkshire clockmaker. The prize – £20,000, a vast sum for its time – made his family's fortune.

I've always liked the idea of prizes. Even if a prize isn't awarded because the competitors fail in their attempts to win it, the very fact that there is a target to aim for can drive an idea forward to early maturity. As focus points for venture capital, technical innovation and entrepreneurial ambition, prizes are hugely valuable. And as we've been discovering at Virgin Galactic, our space-tourism operation, prizes like the Ansari X Prize capture the public imagination, providing the commercial applications of the future with a firm foundation.

Indeed, success in the world of aviation has been built on winning trophies. In December 1912 Jacques Schneider – a French industrialist and a fanatical balloonist – offered a trophy for a seaplane race. This was the Schneider Trophy. To secure it – and to pick up 75,000 francs in prize money – a pilot needed to win three races in five years. In 1919 Raymond Orteig, a New York City hotel owner, offered the $25,000 Orteig Prize for the first non-stop transatlantic flight between New York and Paris. It was eventually won by Charles Lindbergh in 1927 – while the Schneider Trophy was still up for grabs. In 1925 the UK's air ministry formed a racing team at Felixstowe, Suffolk, and commissioned the designer Reginald Mitchell to develop a monoplane to compete for the Trophy. The result was the Supermarine S5, which spawned successive improvements. The S6B broke the world speed record by flying at 407mph, a record that remained unbroken for fourteen years – while another direct successor, the legendary Spitfire fighter plane, probably saved Britain from invasion by Nazi Germany.

Prizes are not the only way to encourage research and experiment. Tax breaks serve innovative businesses well. Various schemes have been rolled out by successive governments, with varying degrees of success. In the private sector, the new generation of entrepreneurs emerging from Silicon Valley and elsewhere in the world are keen to encourage new ideas to help them achieve their philanthropic goals. Some of their schemes are incredibly ambitious. You need to be aware of these developments, and I hope that, as well as offering a few lessons about innovation, this chapter will serve, in passing, as an introduction to some exciting and fast-developing areas of business.

*

Like so many leaders and heads of state, from Blair to Mandela, President Mikhail Gorbachev was a persuasive salesman. 'Richard, you are known in Russia as a very brave adventurer, surely you would like to be a cosmonaut?'

In the aftermath of the Soviet Union's implosion, Gorbachev was sweeping away all the symbols of the inefficient and discredited communist regime. In the Kremlin, the free market was the buzz, with Margaret Thatcher its flag-waving hero. And it was Thatcher who told her new-found Russian friend that I was worth meeting.

So here we were now, at the Livadia Palace, once the imperial home of Tsar Nicholas and his wife Alexandra, in Yalta on the Black Sea. This was the Italianate residence where Churchill, Roosevelt and Stalin met to redraw the map of Europe at the close of the Second World War. The Russians were very keen to persuade me to help open up this beautiful area for tourists – and earn them much-needed hard currency.

A few days later, I was flown by helicopter to Star City at Baikonur in Kazakhstan for a VIP tour. As a Westerner, it was a privilege to be allowed into this secret world. Here were the creators of the Sputnik satellite, the Vostok, Voskhod and Soyuz manned missions, the Salyut space station – and of the ballistic missiles that had once threatened us. This was where Yuri Gagarin blasted off into space in April 1961 to make history. And now a new breed of Russians occupied this place, negotiating with all the entrepreneurial zeal of a Palo Alto deal-maker.

These guys offered me a once-in-a-lifetime opportunity: to sit in a capsule on top of a Russian rocket and be blasted into space. They were giving me the chance to become the first ever space tourist.

Of course, there was a price tag.

Over $30 million.

At the time Virgin had a high-level ballooning project called Earth Wings and a Soviet cosmonaut was coming to join our team. I was very keen to do business with the Russians – all good grounding for the future when I planned to start a low-cost Russian airline – but the price tag for this junket – $30 million! – was astronomical. It felt immoral to me, the idea of spending that much money on myself.

It's certainly far too much for one individual to fork out for a trip into space. Yet that remains the going rate if you want to spend your annual vacation at the International Space Station. It seems a fortune to pay when there are other priorities in life. It made me question the ridiculous economics of putting people in space – and it sparked my search for the big-business breakthrough that would make space travel a more realistic proposition for many, many more people and be able to get crucial science and technology into orbit at an affordable price to really make a difference to life here on Earth.

I passed up my opportunity, but others were more than willing to pay the price. Dennis Tito (who actually has a scientific background working as an engineer in the Jet Propulsion Laboratory in Pasadena) became the first civilian to go into space in 2001. Tito was followed by Mark Shuttleworth in 2002, Greg Olsen in 2003, Anousheh Ansari in 2006 and Charles Simonyi in 2007. All said the experience surpassed their wildest expectations. As I write this, English-born Richard Garriott, the son of an astronaut, is expecting to fly into orbit in late 2008. He will be only the sixth paying customer. Half a dozen people in space, at a total cost of nearly $200 million – that isn't very good, is it?

Thirty million dollars isn't space tourism. It's private exploration by rich individuals subsidising a Russian mission. The chances of a tourist going into space are currently one billion to one. I want to shorten those odds drastically. I want to see if taking people into space could become a working business proposition and also create a new technological platform for science, satellites and other human activity in space. There is no doubt though that tourists need to be the first stepping stone on our journey.

Our initial task has been to establish the likely demand for what we have in mind. In a new field, this can be hard. What questions should we ask, and how should we interpret the answers we get back?

Market consultancies are a mixed bag, on the whole. You should definitely see what they have to offer, but please, never neglect your own reading and thinking. Consultancies, like any group of experts, are best given something to chew on, and the more insight and detail you can provide about your needs and questions, the more useful the advice you will get back.

I can't deny that, in our hunt for sound advice, our passage has been smoothed by the fact that space has such huge commercial potential. Apart from Virgin Galactic, there are others anxious to become involved in commercial space: there is Jeff Bezos, who made billions selling books and other goods in cyberspace with Amazon.com; the Las Vegas hotel magnate Robert Bigelow, who is now developing a large inflatable space-hotel; John Carmack, the computer-games creator behind hits such as Doom and Quake; Elon Musk, the founder of PayPal, who has set up SpaceX, a commercial orbital transportation service.

Such is the demand for high-quality research in this sector, consultancies have grown up dedicated to encouraging and shaping its emerging markets. In 2002, a survey performed by Zogby International for Futron, one of the leading space consultancies, began to look seriously at the market for space tourism. Their reports suggest that from 2011 there will be 2,000 tourist astronauts a year, and that by 2021 as the cost comes down, there will be around 15,000 a year, by which time the potential revenue from this business is $676 million per annum.

Zogby arrived at these figures by interviewing thousands of very wealthy individuals. My vision is to make the experience of sub-orbital flight open to many more people. Virgin Galactic only needs two flights per day at three different sites to break through the Futron survey barrier and, with all things going well, this is a highly conservative estimate. My own prediction is that by 2019 the price of a trip into suborbital space will drop to a level that will enable hundreds of thousands of people to experience and enjoy a flight into space. For someone in Europe or America it will be as simple as a decision of whether to go on holiday to Australia or up into space. A figure of under $100,000 is eventually achievable. But even if Futron's survey is correct, Virgin Galactic will still be a successful business.

Virgin is ideally placed to move into the space industry. We have the expertise and experience of moving millions of people around the globe, safely and securely. What the Virgin brand will do – unlike any other in the commercial space market – is establish in the public mind that space tourism is for them: a service industry that's going to be a lot of fun, while being as safe as people can make it. The brand also helps to give the team global credibility as they build out the business to include environmental science work in space, satellite payload launching and astronaut training.

In March 1999, Will Whitehorn registered Virgin Galactic as a company – and our hunt for technology to get us into space relatively cheaply began in earnest.

For years, however, I had been keeping tabs on anything and everything to do with the vexed business of getting off the ground and into space. I wanted us to be first in this sector, in the same way that I wanted us to be first in the biofuels market. And just as we've toyed with some very unlikely biofuels over the years, we've witnessed the launch of some pretty crazy prototype spacecraft!

This is the unseen part of business, the part that nobody ever discusses because, to be fair, there's not a lot to discuss. *The secret to success in any new sector is watchfulness, usually over a period of many years.* It's hard to spin waiting and watching into a vibrant business lesson, but if there's one thing you take away from this chapter, let it be this: that Virgin's sudden emergence as a leader in cutting-edge industries was decades in the making. You need a huge amount of sheer curiosity to make it in a new sector.

Our search for a way into space led us into a brave new world of exotic materials and untried designs, bristling with spin-offs and business opportunities; a thriving community of small companies and driven individuals, motivated by prizes, supported by engaged and well-informed philanthropy.

It was a strange experience. Having considered myself a small entrepreneur all my life – all evidence, airlines and the rest of it, to the contrary! – it was dizzying for me to find myself looking at business through the other end of the telescope. Yes, I was looking to set up my own business – a small commercial space company – but at the same time, I could see that the capital I had to hand could make a real difference in this sector, encouraging other small businesses to develop.

I was now not merely innovating in an existing market; I and people like me were actually helping to create the market. This posed the old question in a whole new light for me – how could we best make a difference?

The tipping point for commercial space travel came during the millennium with the announcement of the Ansari X Prize by space entrepreneur Peter Diamandis. The X Prize set a simple challenge to contestants: carry three people 100km above the Earth's surface, twice within two weeks. Peter had come to England to pitch the idea to me several times since 1997, and we thought a Virgin X Prize was a good idea. However, rather than sponsor a prize, we wanted to take the technology forward ourselves and build a business.

We made the right decision. We were playing to our strengths by developing our own company. That said, I don't think we'd be sitting here preparing for the launch of our first spaceship if it had not been for Peter's idea, his determination, and the huge generosity of Anousheh and Amir Ansari, who were the ones who ultimately donated the $10 million prize.

The Ansari X Prize had twenty-nine entrants, but only three serious contenders. Of these, just one had managed to acquire serious funding – *SpaceShipOne*.

Burt Rutan's company, Scaled Composites – based in Mojave, California – unveiled the existence of its space programme on 18 April 2003. Burt's *SpaceShipOne* was to be carried into the upper atmosphere by a mother ship – a lightweight plane called *White Knight* – and launched in flight.

On 17 December 2003, we finally got confirmation of what had become an open secret in aviation circles – Paul Allen, a reclusive billionaire with a passion for science fiction, was Burt's financial backer for the *SpaceShipOne* project. That day, *SS1* broke through the sound barrier during its first manned test flight. On 21 June 2004, Mike Melvill flew *SS1* above 100km altitude, and this was a significant breakthrough, dispelling the myth once and for all that manned space flight was the sole domain of huge government programmes.

I calculated that Paul had spent about $26 million to achieve winning the $10 million X Prize. So I wrote to him in January 2004 proposing a fifty-fifty joint venture.

Dear Paul,

May I congratulate you on the latest flight. From the footage I saw it looked magnificent. I should be delighted to work with you on taking the project forward and helping turn it into a serious space-tourism project. I'm hopeful that with the strength of the Virgin brand and our team's marketing skill and your technological skills we can not only get your investment back but earn enough to take the project forward into even greater heights. Our suggestions are these: 1) that initially we together spend the necessary funds to create a three-man craft (along similar lines to the test craft) but with large windows. We spend these funds to make it safe but don't apply (at this stage at least) for FAA certification. This craft should be ready to take passengers in 18 months. We put aside $100 million each over three years to achieve this. 2) We start marketing in a major way to coincide with the last flight before the X Prize flight. We offer 1,000 trips at $200,000 per trip. This would result in $200,000,000 and should be sufficient to get our total investments back plus have a fund *left over to take the project to the next stage (possibly a six-seat craft at more affordable fares).*

I suggested the name Virgin Galactic Airways and thought we could start taking deposits in the summer. I said: 'We have a team which I believe can manage this well.'

While running an actual airline in space didn't appeal to Paul, he loved the idea of developing a six-seater commercial space plane. Will Whitehorn and Alex Tai, a former Virgin Atlantic captain, flew to Seattle to meet Paul's advisers. Jon Peachey, Virgin's investment director and a Galactic board member, went with them. Peachey was the moneyman, with strict instructions to keep Will's and Alex's enthusiasm under control!

The first deal didn't work for Paul's company, but we resumed discussions a little while later and this time things progressed well. Both sides were conscious that the Ansari X Prize was looming, and we needed to complete the deal quickly if the new company was to get the benefit of the publicity. Eventually Virgin negotiated with Paul Allen to buy the rights to use his technology – just three weeks before the X Prize! It was a terrific deal for us because the Virgin Galactic branding would now be on *SpaceShipOne* during the ceremony in the Mojave in October. This would give us worldwide exposure – and it would deliver a message that we were now a serious player.

The last week of September 2004 is one I will always cherish. We launched our 125mph Pendolino tilting service in the UK. We gained plaudits from the President of Nigeria for the launch of Virgin Nigeria. And I was on the platform at the Royal Aeronautical Society in London with Burt to announce the launch of Virgin Galactic. We signed a historic $21.5 million deal for the use of the technology with Paul Allen's company, and announced that we had developed a $100 million investment plan to develop a prototype commercial six-seater spaceship at Burt's factory in Mojave.

Burt Rutan is an engineering genius, years ahead of his time. Do you remember *Voyager*, a plane that looked like a flying catamaran and flew around the world on a single tank of fuel in 1986? That was Burt's design. It was the largest all-composite aeroplane ever built, and the father of much of Scaled Composites' later work and of *SpaceShipTwo*. That plane was *woven* from glass, graphite and aramid, and bonded with epoxies and resins. Once heated in an autoclave, the compound became immensely strong and far lighter than pressed aluminium.

SpaceShipOne was constructed from equally exotic materials. In fact, there was very little about its design, fabric, execution and flight behaviour that *wasn't* exotic. Take the engine: a revolutionary rocket-motor design that will be used in *SpaceShipTwo*, and one without which commercial space tourism simply wouldn't be possible for us.

It was Burt's unique take on an old idea, of course: a dual-propellant system with a liquid oxidiser and a solid fuel. The solid fuel lines the case of the rocket. The liquid oxidizer is injected at the head of the motor and then ignited. The surface of the solid fuel reacts, combusts and turns to gas. And because the propellants are separated they cannot mix in the event of a leak. Consequently, they cannot explode. Most serious systems failures on rockets over the years have been fatal. Not so here: Burt's spaceships are very failure-tolerant.

And they're cheap. Once all the engineering and design has been done, cranking them out on a production line is a relatively simple business. The solid fuel is rubber. Once the igniter motor starts the rubber burning, nitrous oxide is added under pressure, producing a flame. The gas expands through the nozzle and provides instant thrust.

The rocket motor will give us just enough push to tip the craft into suborbit. After this the motor shuts down, and the spaceship coasts into space for a few minutes. It reaches the top of its arc and then starts to fall back down again. Just like tossing your keys in the air, once they reach the top, they start to come down.

And another lovely thing about this engine. It's green. Well green compared to any other form of rocketry from the ground. Fly into space with Virgin Galactic and we'll be releasing less CO_2 than the equivalent of a person flying from London to New York and back on an upper-class ticket. NASA's Space Shuttle has the same environmental output as the population of New York over the average weekend!

Mike Melvill, a long-time friend and associate of Burt, was the pilot as *SpaceShipOne*, tethered to its mother ship *White Knight*, took off from Mojave Airport's Civilian Aerospace Test Center on 29 September 2004. It was a shaky ride, which required brilliant skills from the pilot. *SS1* reached its apogee of 337,600 feet, or 103km. This was space.

On 4 October 2004, *SS1*, with test pilot Brian Binnie at the controls, was launched from its mother ship and soared into suborbit, reaching 367,442 feet above the Earth. For Binnie, it was a flight and a day to remember for the rest of his life. He had become an astronaut.

For Burt Rutan, it was the culmination of his life's work. *SS1* had won the Ansari X Prize.

At Virgin, we believed the success of this tiny spacecraft revealed commercial possibilities, and so we decided to license the technology of *SS1* and its mother ship, *White Knight*.

On 27 July 2005, at Oshkosh, Wisconsin, Burt and I announced the signing of an agreement to form a new business. It was agreed that the new company would own all the designs of *SS2* and the *White Knight Two* launch systems that were being developed at Scaled Composites. The new business, the Spaceship Company, would be jointly owned by Virgin and Scaled. Burt's company would undertake all the research, development, testing and certification of the two craft, with Burt heading up the technical development team.

I believe Virgin's work with Paul Allen and with Scaled Composites is a great example of capital and inventiveness working together. From day one, we have, every one of us, been singing from the same song sheet. Our symbiosis is nigh on perfect. Burt's genius is being challenged and stretched and will be well rewarded, even as our investment of capital produces a fantastic return. I think – setting aside the huge financial risks involved in doing anything new – the relative ease of doing business in this sector is due partly to the environment; the enthusiasm is tremendous. I also think it has to do with the fact that Virgin considers everyone involved, regardless of their capitalisation, as an entrepreneur. We're all, in our own way, moving into unknown territory, and so we're all sharing the same experience.

The commercial success of *White Knight Two* and *SS2* will open doors for our business. A single shuttle mission can carry 23,000kg into orbit at a cost of around $450 million. We are working towards the day when *White Knight Two* will be able to take 12,500kg of payload to 50,000ft, and then blast it into low Earth orbit. This will give it the highest drop capability in the world, and opens up a whole array of commercial possibilities for localised weather satellites, carbon-emission measurement and cheaper zero-gravity training for tomorrow's astronauts. In the future, *SpaceShipTwo* and its successors may be able to take payloads further out into space. While Virgin Galactic must concentrate on its original plan, these are all options for our business to grow its revenues and technology base.

While I want to take nothing at all away from the importance of prizes, I'm glad that in this instance, we chose to develop a company, rather than sponsor a cup. I think this emerging market benefits from Virgin's spirit of branded market capitalism. Virgin brings the public on board, it brings serious capital into play, and it keeps the field inclined towards small entrepreneurial ideas. We stand to make money by doing good, and in business, things don't get much better. And believe me, cheap access to space matters enormously if humankind is to have any hope of solving its problems here on Earth.

Even the most rarefied and exotic-sounding business environment works to familiar principles. Once our systems are proven, and our first space travellers are talking enthusiastically about their experiences, I believe the floodgates will open. A major reduction in costs will come when the insurance industry sees how safe space travel is becoming. More venture capitalists will sense that there is a buck or two to be made; their funds will, in turn, support further expansion. We might even see some commercial space companies listed on the New York Stock Exchange or in London.

Frankly, space – outer space – is there for the taking. The risks of failure are high and you will need to churn ideas at high speed to attract funding. On the other hand, there are plenty of ideas to explore. Materials science and biotechnology are both throwing up possibilities faster than businesses can find applications for them, so an appetite for learning is vital if you are to take advantage of new opportunities in these areas. That, in turn, requires you to take a real interest in people, and what they're up to, and how you might be able to help. You are not going to strike gold in this sector on your own.

Reality shows about business are becoming much more popular. *Dragons' Den*, in particular, makes excellent viewing, not least because it focuses on the more exciting side of business – coming up with, assessing and testing new ideas. The business panel is comprised of successful millionaires, and while the programme makes some token gestures towards how scary these people are, I think it's pretty clear to everyone that they're a courteous, lively bunch who bring a sense of adventure to their work. Some contestants are well prepared and have worked out their pitches; others are thrown to the Dragons, gobbled up and spat out. But it's a wonderfully positive show: it's amazing the number of interesting ideas and schemes that people come up with.

At a meeting in Downing Street a while ago, I was asked by some emerging Russian business leaders if I could help with some informal education about the practical aspects of capitalism. I scribbled on a bit of paper: '*Russian Dragons' Den: Must Launch*'. As I walked along Downing Street after the meeting, a *Times* newspaper photographer about sixty to seventy feet away snapped the bit of paper and then blew it up. This ended up headlined 'BRANSON TO CONSIDER LAUNCHING DRAGONS' DEN IN RUSSIA'. I still think it's a good idea – but I'm sure the BBC, who commission the show, are on to it.

Everywhere I go, I'm deluged with business ideas. A few years ago I would sit with a pile of business ideas in front of me and work my way through them. For example, there was a charming offer from a Spanish gentleman, written in perfect English. He told me that he would like to work with me to create Virgin White – a washing powder. He reckoned this would be a wonderful product and, of course, he might have been right.

Some of the proposals we get are brilliantly thought-out, down to the last detail, and offer us a good share of the market. Others are simply handwritten scribbles, often marked 'Private and Confidential', saying basically, 'Dear Mr Branson. I have had this idea for a great product which you might like to launch – it is Virgin Tomato Soup in a tin can. I think it would be a very popular product. I look forward to hearing from you.' What can you say about that? That Mr Heinz and Mr Campbell already have perfectly good products? I never like to be rude. I've looked back and discovered that we've had about a hundred proposals to set up – yes – Virgin White. So you might think your idea is original, but there are other people out there who might have been there before you.

I never want to blunt anyone's passion or enthusiasm but over the last thirty-five years we have run the rule over almost every single idea you can think of. We are bombarded with ideas: some half baked – like Virgin Beans – some plain crusty – like Virgin Breadsticks – and, among them, some real ringing successes – such as Virgin Mobile.

I've come to think of our search for ideas as 'Showgirls to Stem Cells'. Indeed, we have always looked at sex and health as being pretty fundamental parts of the Virgin brand.

The ageing of the 'baby boomer' generation in a number of wealthier nations means that people can no longer expect their own national welfare systems to prop them up in terms of pensions and healthcare. In the UK, the National Health Service can only come under increasing strain. In the future, there's going to be a need for supplementary and supportive health services, which might deliver the extras and the non-life-threatening services that would give people a better quality of life. This isn't a political view, or even a business pitch. It's stark reality. The NHS can no longer be expected to do everything. There are too many of us, and it is simply unreasonable to expect a single organisation – however visionary – to adopt every single new procedure, however expensive, however rarefied, and roll it out to everyone. It's just not doable.

This, anyway, is the big picture. Virgin's supportive role is quite modest but, we hope, targeted in a way that will support and sustain current public services. We want to offer non-urgent complementary services that combine physiotherapy, dentistry, optometry, diagnostic testing and scans. Given the surge in the number of fit and active people in their forties, fifties and sixties with a lot of disposable income who want to travel and see the world, it seems crazy not to offer them the opportunity to invest in their own well-being. It is an evolutionary step for us, too – to consider the healthcare of the first Virgin generation!

In addition, and with the awareness that there are many regulatory issues and ethical ones to look into, we are exploring the highly contentious field of stem cell research. Stem cells could open up breakthroughs in treatment in years to come. As I jotted in my notebook: '*Stem cells are the essence of life. They have potential to develop into any other cells. Given the right conditions they can create not just a heart – a heart for you.*'

We've researched the harvesting of stem cells from the blood stem cells of human umbilical cords. We've set up a Virgin cell bank storing stem cells for forthcoming generations, and we've invested in a genetic testing service which might be able to predict certain conditions and diseases. I've spoken to several scientists at the cutting edge of this field, including the head of a company called ViaCell, a clinical-stage biotechnology company whose raft of experimental cellular medicines might one day beat cancer, neurological diseases, diabetes and muscular dystrophy. My view is that difficult ethical questions are there to be answered – again and again, if necessary, as the years go by and morals and fashions change – and that anything that can save lives in the future is certainly worth studying.

Virgin – like all the best entrepreneurial businesses – is really looking for something fresh. If you think we're going to make millions together launching a washing powder, tomato soup or even three-legged women's tights (yes, we've had that: you tuck the spare leg into your underwear and use it if you ladder one of the other legs) then perhaps you need a different entrepreneur.

The other thing you'll need – in spades – is luck. The business-school gurus tend to underplay this commodity, presumably because the power of chance undermines every other business rule they teach you. But trust me on this: *luck is essential*. There aren't many chief executives who admit to simply being in the right place at the right time. Yet the business world is littered with the broken careers of those who were in the right place at the *wrong* time and screwed up. Certainly Virgin Mobile – the fastest growing company in history to reach a billion-dollar turnover – was propelled by a huge slice of good fortune.

But then, chance favours the prepared mind. Gary Player, the South African golfing master, used to say that the more he practised, the luckier he became. Yes, the rub of the green (or should that be the red?) played a significant part in Virgin Mobile's success. But never forget we doggedly stuck with our interest in mobile phones, and were constantly searching for the gap in the market. When a gaping canyon revealed itself, we were ready.

Right now, the world could do with some luck. Climate change will be a serious business challenge for our lifetimes and well beyond.

Companies are already starting to make major changes, but things aren't progressing nearly fast enough. We need advanced control technologies and clean energy alternatives to start delivering much sooner than we ever anticipated – and we haven't even developed a fraction of what we need: ultra-efficient water heaters, improved refrigeration and freezers, advanced building materials, heating, ventilation, insulation, cooling, rainwater harvesting . . .

Some terrific products have already emerged. Smart windows that adapt and maintain comfortable temperatures. Super-efficient LED lighting. Energy-saving improvements in building design. Sensor technology to help us use scarce resources more wisely. Even a new breed of super-smart robots. (Bill Gates tells me this technology is as exciting as the nascent personal-computer industry was in the mid-1970s.) According to a *Scientific American* report in 2008, by 2055 a $1,000 personal computer will have as much processing power as all human brain power combined. By then we could probably do with the help.

Then there are next-generation hybrid cars (the latest being encouraged by Peter Diamandis, the founder of the X Prize and now the Automotive X Prize) that emit less pollution. There are colonies of wind farms, on- and offshore, sea barrages and solar panels. There are technologies emerging to capture carbon from power stations. Parabolic mirrors, deployed in Africa's deserts, provide green electricity. There are huge investment programmes looking at biofuels such as cellulosic-based butanol that don't eat away at our vital food supplies. And many of these excellent schemes have been evaluated by Virgin's Investment Advisory Committee.

In business, as in life, you can't afford to be afraid of doing the wrong thing. This book is littered with accounts of my and my colleagues' successes and mistakes. Virgin Fuel's first biofuel investment was in manufacturing plants that make ethanol from corn. Given what's happening to world food investment at the moment, we can all agree that that was going to be a non-starter! But as we saw, from that not-so-good idea, good ideas have grown. Remember: success in business never comes from inaction. Have I been lucky in business? You bet. But most people, most of the time, have the same amount of luck. It's what you do with it that counts.

Innovation is what you get when you capitalise on luck, when you get up from behind your desk and go and see where ideas and people lead you.

'It's idyllic here – would you mind passing me the sunblock?' I asked my wife, as we both lay sprawled out on our sunloungers. Joan and I were having a romantic anniversary break in the Maldives, and the Indian Ocean was a shimmering mirror of turquoise. It was wonderfully warm, with a gentle sea breeze, and the only sound was the lapping of the waves on the pure white lagoon sand.

'There you go. You'll smell gorgeous with this one on,' she laughed as she handed me the bottle.

It was a factor 30 organic coconut-based lotion and my arms, legs and tummy glistened after I applied it. Joan was right, I had acquired the aroma of a molten king-size Bounty bar.

My novel wasn't very exciting – so I replaced my sunglasses to read the ingredients on the bottle instead. I'm always on the lookout for ideas and almost anything can kick-start your thinking. I began contemplating the irony of our globe. Here was one of the most beautiful places in the world – and over 80 per cent of it is less that one metre above mean sea level. Global warming and rising sea levels meant catastrophe for this piece of heaven on Earth. Was there a solution? Perhaps part of the answer lay in the bottle I was holding . . .

Rising population combined with climate change are the main challenges facing our world – and aviation contributes about 2 per cent to industrial global warming (agriculture is the main culprit). On 21 September 2006, I stood next to the former US president Bill

Clinton, and pledged to commit all the profits the Virgin Group made from our transport business over the next ten years to combating global warming. At the Clinton Global Initiative in New York, I said: 'Our generation has inherited an incredibly beautiful world from our parents and they from their parents. We must not be the generation responsible for irreversibly damaging the environment.'

On CNBC's *Power Lunch* programme, I repeated my pledge. 'Obviously we are in the transportation business and we do our fair share of spewing out CO_2 ... We are pledging that any money that comes back to the group in the form of dividends, share sales or flotation, that 100 per cent will be invested in tackling global warming. We expect over the next ten years to put aside around three billion dollars.'

My notebooks for the weeks following my announcement are spiderwebbed with figures and arrows and exclamation marks as I tried to understand the economics of the fuel debate.

Less than a week later, on 27 September, Virgin Atlantic unveiled an initiative to reduce carbon emissions from aviation by up to 25 per cent. Our airlines use around 700 million gallons of fuel a year. I wanted to cut back on this consumption and floated a few ideas. At the time, I knew these were ambitious targets. What if our planes were towed to the runway before the engines were started? We proposed starting grids for planes at airports, and a method of landing planes called the 'continuous descent' approach, which meant a saving in fuels. We also pointed the finger at Europe's air traffic control system, which is punishing the environment by keeping planes on holding patterns in the sky. (There are thirty-five separate traffic-control organisations in Europe; there's a single one for the whole of the US!) Virgin Atlantic was working to pull together the airlines to make commercial flying more environmentally friendly, and by 2008, many of the world's airlines – now faced with growing criticism over their contribution to global warming – had begun to adopt these procedures to save vital aviation fuel.

Of course, we could all stop flying tomorrow. But that's not only an unrealistic idea, it's politically and economically disastrous for millions of the world's poor. If you stop people going to Africa, say, you will only increase the hardship of the people there. Many African nations have been building up worthwhile and profitable tourism ventures. You only need to look at Kenya in 2007, and how tourism dried up after the disputed presidential election results and the massive loss of jobs that followed, to recognise the industry's importance, and the destabilising effect the loss of tourism can have on a nation.

The global economy now depends on aviation and tourism, two of the world's most important industries. They have grown exponentially over the last forty years and have kick-started the economies of many developing nations. I can't see how we're going to stop this and return to the Stone Age. People love to travel. It broadens the mind and increases international cooperation and understanding. Ironically, eco-tourism is often the best way to protect sensitive environments such as rainforests.

Slowly the aviation industry is waking up to a harsh reality: the status quo is no longer sustainable. The airframe-makers – and indeed the engine-makers – must keep searching for quieter and cleaner engines. The other issue for all airlines remains the sustained high price of oil – indeed all of our Virgin airlines have felt the pinch as fuel costs have risen. Virgin's fuel bill went up by several hundred million dollars between 2004 and 2006. Cutting back our consumption of fossil fuels isn't a lasting solution, however. At best, it merely postpones the coming crisis.

What is the solution?

The key to saving our environment is to create a new breed of cleaner energy sources and fuels that do not damage the atmosphere, do not lead to deforestation, and do not eat up vital food stocks that the world's growing population will need to eat. The recent backlash against biofuels has lumped all kinds of energy and fuel initiatives together, without considering the individual arguments. But not all drugs are bad – compare aspirin with heroin – and the same argument applies to renewables generally. While I know they probably won't provide the overall answer, I believe we have so far not even begun to find out what biofuels might be able to deliver.

Burn any organic matter – and that includes coal and oil – and you release carbon dioxide – CO_2 – into the atmosphere. Coal and oil are what happens to vegetation when it's compressed in the earth over millions of years. If we used living vegetation – sugar cane, willow trees, peanuts, corn, coconuts – instead of these 'fossil fuels', then we wouldn't be loading the carbon of previous ages on top of the carbon already in our environment. There's a phrase I like which sums up this view: 'Don't dig up the dead.'

Synthetic fuels have been around since the 1910s, when fuel alcohols first went into mass commercial production. Before Prohibition in the US, cars were run on the stuff – but since ethanol is a type of alcohol, the practice was eventually outlawed for fear that people would drink it.

Vinod Khosla, the man who founded Sun Microsystems and one of the most influential investors in California – indeed, the United States – believes that ethanol is likely to be the future fuel of cars, and a far more practical option than hard-to-handle hydrogen. However, ethanol – which would otherwise be a suitable alternative for traditional aviation fuel – freezes in temperatures above 15,000 feet.

For nearly a century, the unsuitability of ethanol seems to have put the dampers on research into alternative aviation fuels. When I first started to look into this area, I was astonished at the lack of progress or interest in this field. Had no one seriously thought of putting biofuel into a plane?

Apparently not: when I first mentioned in 2006 that we were looking for a jet engine fuel that was clean, we were laughed at and mocked by environmentalists and engine manufacturers alike. People said it was absolutely impossible. It's worth remembering that as recently as the 1950s, some airline people – including the American aviator Charles Lindbergh, then working for PanAm – didn't think the jet engine had a future in commercial aviation. Step changes, driven by business imperatives, do happen – but they need a catalyst.

Our first port of call was Rolls-Royce, the world's leading jet-engine makers, based in Derby. We tried to get them interested in biofuel development, but they were pursuing a different path, improving the efficiency of their engines. More than that, they told us that the fuel we wanted to develop was 'impossible'. So we went to GE Aviation, one of their rivals, and makers of jet engines for Boeing and Airbus airplanes. They did want to help us. And with them on board, we got Boeing Commercial Airplanes interested too. At last, the key players were engaging in the hunt for clean fuels.

Many of my notes from around this time are highly technical, as I tried to wrap my head around molecular structures, enzyme activity, the chemical formation of algae . . . The really dizzying part, though, was trying to get to grips with the sheer scale of the fuel economy. Our transport needs for the next two decades are still likely to be met by liquid fuels to drive the internal combustion engines in our cars, boats and generators. For any alternative liquid fuels to be a viable option, we need massive amounts of feedstock – the raw material to make the energy – and it has to be cheaper than – or at least comparable to – traditional fuels.

Our studies found that cellulosic biomass meets both these requirements, as does waste from agriculture, municipal sewage and animals. This is where new businesses must emerge, and investors such as the Virgin Green Fund and Vinod Khosla are spending billions of dollars on this bet. It is not simply the feedstock but its collection, transportation and processing which needs to be tackled so that the end product is competitive with gasoline. This brings lots of opportunity – and many blind alleys. I'm going to take you down a few unlikely avenues now to give you an idea of the scale and complexity of the biofuel sector, its sheer pace and the effort that's being invested.

Inefficient corn ethanol started the ball rolling in the United States, aided by massive government subsidy, while the Brazilian experience has long since proven the viability of sugar cane. Brazil has over thirty-five years' experience of using it as a fuel, and in 2008, its cars consumed more ethanol than fossil fuels. The primary feedstocks for the production of renewable fuel are sugar from sugarcane, and starch from corn, the source of most US-based ethanol. Corn ethanol has become a major concern because of its impact on food production. In Asia, tapioca, potatoes and other starches can also be used. But I cannot now see the benefit in growing food and using it for energy when people around the world are starving and basic food prices are rising elsewhere.

So I became interested in the discussion regarding the tonnage per acre of plants with no food value. Prairie grass, willows, corn stalks and wheat straw all can be used to manufacture cellulosic ethanol. I spoke to John Ranieri, vice president of biofuels at the chemical giant Dupont. I was interested in how the big players were tackling this. John's a very sound guy, and he gave me some excellent advice and information. He told me about Dupont's strategy to bring biobutanol and cellulosic ethanol technologies to market. This led to discussion with Ian Ferguson at Tate & Lyle, the sugar giant. We began to think that the Dominican Republic might be a suitable place for a sugar refinery and then considered a prairie-grass plant in Louisiana. Our research also led the Virgin Green Fund to make an investment in Gevo, a world-class biofuels company that converts biomass into butanol. It was important to invest in the development of many clean energy solutions, not just one.

We talked to Iogen, which was already turning some of the Canadian prairie's vast cellulosic waste into ethanol and had a 40-million-gallon plant making E10 biofuel for cars. We spoke to Cargill, one of the world's largest food and agricultural companies. We went to Brazil to look for joint venture partners.

We even played with coconuts.

Now, coconuts will never solve a global energy crisis. But they have a few things going for them. For a start, they thrive on sandy beach areas in the tropics, where other plants don't grow well. The market for copra – coconut flesh – has been falling worldwide, and so has the price, leading to declining incomes in regions heavily dependent on copra production, so it would be great to find another use for this important crop. The low return for the harsh work involved with the cutting and drying of copra has pushed many rural farmers into other cash crops, leaving unharvested coconuts lying on the beaches. It may be that the harvesting of coconuts on a large scale can bring much needed income to these areas.

Coconut oil in engines is not new. It was used in the Philippines during the Second World War when diesel was in short supply. Today, on the islands of Vanuatu in the Pacific Ocean, an Australian entrepreneur, Tony Deamer, has succeeded in using coconut oil in fuel for motor vehicles. Potentially, this enterprise could help to revitalise the market for copra and have wide-ranging environmental benefits as well. Tony, together with a local coconut-oil producer, has been negotiating with the government for a reduction of duty on coconut oil-based mixtures. In Vanuatu, the local electricity company UNELCO has been using diesel blended with coconut oil to run a large (and now pleasantly perfumed) four-megawatt generator.

I did some basic sums and quickly confirmed what we all suspected, that the sheer labour of breaking into the things and scooping out the flesh made coconuts an unlikely player on the world biofuel scene. Coconut oil was, however, an excellent local solution.

In general, I think that the debate about biofuels gets too easily hung-up on this or that single 'solution', its merits and demerits. We don't have to find a single biofuel that will do everything for everyone. What we can and should develop is a suite of solutions that work well in different places, for different purposes, and at different scales. It should, for example, be possible to cut dramatically the human carbon footprint by introducing bio-ethanol for cars and buses. Flying will require a major breakthrough, however.

That's why it was important to us that we prove, in principle, that we could fly a commercial airliner on biofuels. To demonstrate this principle, it didn't strictly matter what biofuel we used, or whether or not it could be scaled up. It just had to keep a Boeing in the sky. On Sunday 24 February 2008, we flew *Cosmic Girl*, a Virgin Atlantic Boeing 747–700, on a test flight from London to Amsterdam. A 747 has four engines, and in one of the engines, for the first time, we used, not fossil fuel, but a mixture of coconut oil and oil from a related fruit, the Brazilian babassu nut. No modifications were made to either the aircraft or its engines to enable the flight to take place.

The demonstration flight, piloted by Captain Geoff Andreasen, Virgin Atlantic's chief Boeing pilot, took off from Heathrow at 11.30 a.m. and arrived in Amsterdam at 13.30 local time. It was a quiet, intense affair: during the flight, technical advisers on board monitored readings and recording data for analysis. The flight was a success: we had shown that it was possible to fly a plane at 35,000 feet on cleaner fuels. Now the challenge was to develop a biofuel that would scale up, and that wouldn't eat into the food supply.

That work continues. Imperium Renewables, who manufactured our experimental fuel, have since opened one of the world's largest biodiesel refineries at Grays Harbor, Washington State, in the United States. It's capable of producing up to 100 million gallons of biofuel per year. The company has formed a subsidiary in Hawaii to develop another biodiesel production facility, which will likewise provide 100 million gallons of biodiesel fuel a year, using locally produced feedstock, including coconuts.

Meanwhile John Plaza, president and CEO of Imperium, is overseeing the development of a 'second generation' bio-jet fuel, harvesting algae which can be grown in fresh or sea water. I think that, for us, this approach promises a great deal.

Some people have asked why don't I give straight to charity the profits I have pledged to clean technologies and renewable energy. But that won't do the trick. There is a time for giving in a charitable way, but where there are business opportunities to be had, one is much better off harnessing the might of the commercial sector to one's cause. Given our rapidly rising population and the consequent environmental pressure, our solutions have to be technological as well as social. I'm not saying: let the market dictate everything, and all will be well. Quite the opposite – I'm saying: let's use our position in the market for the greater good and prove there is money in greener technologies. That's what Virgin Green Fund is trying to do.

Business has a duty to continue to push the boundaries. In the next ten years, we'll all head into unknown territory. There will be a vast increase in our demand for energy – yet I believe we may well have passed the point of 'peak oil', and that it is now starting to run short relative to demand. Carbon fuel prices look set to remain high, and alternative fuels are urgently needed. It is not beyond the wit of man or woman to come up with an answer. And if we go into this for the right reasons, in a concerted way to tackle climate change, we will, on the way, definitely create some very exciting and successful new businesses and technologies for the future.

Most of them will be small businesses. If the complex and often overheated debates about climate change have taught us anything over the years, they've taught us that local solutions and small initiatives punch well above their weight, while broad-brush initiatives get horribly bogged down in their own complexity, and very often have unintended and sometimes damaging consequences. I say this as a global businessman, working at a global scale on global problems.

Big initiatives – like Virgin Fuel's project to develop a clean aviation fuel – depend on small initiatives – like the coconut-oil-powered cars on Vanuatu – for their development. No one is going to solve global warming by edict, and at Virgin, we never forget that, in business, small is beautiful.

Entrepreneurs and Leadership

Holding on and Letting Go

In 2004 I did a programme called *The Rebel Billionaire* for Fox Television, where I was nice to people and then had to whittle them down to a winner. It only got seven million viewers but it really helped our brand in America.

In one episode, I told a participant we were going to be the first to go over the Victoria Falls in a barrel.

Annie Taylor was the first person to conquer the Niagara Falls in Canada, riding the 170-foot drop in an airtight wooden barrel in October 1901. Since then many other daredevils have copied her achievement. But the Victoria Falls in Africa – at 360 feet – is more than twice as high, and much more dangerous, with jagged rocks at the bottom. I asked one of the contestants, Sam Heshmati, if he was ready for the challenge of going over the falls with me, in a barrel I said had been specially created by NASA.

Were we going to do this thing?

Bravely, Sam nodded. We got into the barrel. A large crane lowered us into the fast-flowing river, a few metres away from the drop. A two-minute countdown began. It seemed an eternity, Five. Four. Three. Two . . .

A split second before we were due to plummet, I shouted: 'Stop! Hold on just one moment, I want to show you something.'

So we got out. And I showed young Sam the bottom of the falls. I pointed at the rocks below.

'Sam,' I admonished him, 'you were ten seconds from certain death. You shouldn't blindly accept a leader's advice. You've got to question leaders on occasions.'

Fast forward three years. I'm in Las Vegas announcing the new route to San Francisco with Virgin America. Someone has had this idea for a publicity stunt: they're going to drop me on a wire, dressed in black tie, from the Fantasy Tower at the top of Palms Casino, into the midst of the cocktail party taking place on the ground below.

Now, I've abseiled many times before, so this stunt is actually something I should feel relatively comfortable with, even though I've never before been dropped off the side of a building at 100mph. But it's an October day, and it's windy. I'm looking at all the harnesses and wiring used in the *Spider-Man* movies . . . and there's something about all this that's making me feel uncomfortable. And as I stand there on top of the tower, minutes before the leap, I know what it is: *I'm far too close to the building.* So I say to the technical team: 'I'm sorry, I need to go to my room.'

Everyone thinks I'm chickening out. But I just need to *think*. Four hundred feet. A windy day. And I'm being dropped almost within touching distance of the building . . .

There's a knock on my hotel-room door. It's our Virgin America publicity people.

'Would you mind just coming up to the roof to do the press anyway, Richard?'

I know I'm being suckered, but I can't get the words out to refuse. My legs carry me upstairs and there is the stunt team boss, assuring me that the wind has died down a little. It doesn't feel like the wind has died down at all. Indeed, it feels a damned sight windier to me. But these people are professionals, right? And everybody is counting on me to do this thing, right? And I don't want to disappoint people, right? And suddenly I'm hurling myself off the top of the building. I hurtle down, and on the way down I hit the casino. Twice.

I reach the bottom, utterly dazed and very sore. Have I broken my back? I just hang there like a rag doll while free airline tickets – part of our stunt – rain down unnoticed on the appalled guests now crowded around me.

Sam, you can consider yourself fully paid back for that joke we had at your expense. My backside hurts. My trousers are ripped to shreds. The press get some pictures of me looking rather grey and dishevelled. I should have listened to my own advice.

True leadership must include the ability to distinguish between real and apparent danger.

This is as true in business as it is in ice climbing, ballooning, mountaineering or powerboat racing. You need to understand the challenges to your enterprise and face up to them. Equally, you have to resist the temptation to overreact at the first sign of trouble.

Since I've been littering this book with tales of our own successes, mistakes and lessons, I hope you'll forgive me if – for once – I illustrate this last point by giving you an account of someone else's mistake.

On 14 February 2007, the combined company of NTL, Telewest and Virgin Mobile relaunched as Virgin Media, creating the largest Virgin company in the world. For the first time consumers could get everything they needed from one company – we were the UK's only quad play of TV, broadband, phone and mobile, offering the most advanced TV-on-demand service available, V+, our high-spec personal video recorder and really fast broadband Internet access.

Overnight, Virgin Media had become the UK's most popular broadband provider, the largest mobile virtual network operator and the second largest provider of pay TV and home phone. We were taking on the Murdoch empire.

Rupert Murdoch has wielded more power over a longer period of time than any other businessman on the planet. The Australian, born in Melbourne, built a newspaper empire in his homeland, expanded into Britain in 1968, and snapped up Dow Jones in the USA in 2007. His satellite television empire straddles the globe, and his newspapers are hugely influential. Rupert Murdoch is someone to be feared and admired in equal measure.

Rupert is now in his late seventies, and while he still has immense energy, it is his two sons, Lachlan and James, who are poised to take his place at the helm. In November 2006 James, the chief executive of British Sky Broadcasting, heard that Virgin Media were planning to acquire a majority stake in ITV, Britain's first and largest commercial TV station.

Deeply worried that the combination of Virgin Media and ITV might give Sky a very serious run for its money he tried to stop us. How? He bought 17.9 per cent of ITV's shares – at a cost to Sky's shareholders of £940 million.

At the time, he was generally praised by the press for pulling off this deal – but it turned out to be perhaps the biggest mistake of his otherwise stellar career.

The media world – and the politicians – knew that his move was anti-competitive, and he had only done it to stop us getting ITV. To that extent, he may have succeeded. James Murdoch's intervention had, for the time being, frustrated our plans to take over ITV.

The intervention led to a war of words between us, legal action and a decision by Sky to withdraw content, such as *Lost* and *24*, from our Virgin Media service, at significant cost to itself in terms of lost advertising income.

Soon after BSkyB bought the stake, Virgin Media complained to the Office of Fair Trading, arguing that competition in the UK TV market had been impacted. The Secretary of State referred the acquisition of a 17.9 per cent stake to the Competition Commission.

James Murdoch bought ITV's shares at £1.35 each, overpaying in the market to secure them from two large institutional investors, who promptly then went back into the market and repurchased positions at about £1.10!

On 29 January 2008, the Competition Commission ruled that Sky must cut its stake in ITV from 17.9 per cent to below 7.5 per cent. BSkyB, having paid 135p a share, could now be forced to sell below 50p. And ITV's share price continued to fall. In July 2008, the ITV shares were worth only 40p each.

So what's the cost to BSkyB of that share purchase? At a share price of 40p it would be in excess of $1.3 billion. James's mistake was to overreact to what Virgin was doing. He could see that Virgin Media was going to be a threat to the Murdoch media empire and that we would do well. Virgin Media's aim was to give Sky a run for their money. But I don't think it would have damaged Sky in any dramatic way – certainly not nearly as much as he's lost trying to stop us.

Once you've been able to assess the level of danger in any given situation, you must be able to honestly gauge your own strengths and weaknesses as leader. You need to be able to recognise what you can do as an individual – and how you inspire and motivate other individuals to cooperate willingly to get the job done.

How to achieve this? Well, for starters, this is something that should – no, *must* – be written into every business plan: *This company will have lots and lots of parties and social get-togethers.* Parties are a way of galvanising teams and allowing people to let their hair down. They have to be inclusive and encouraging, and then they are an excellent way of bringing everyone together and forging a great business culture.

I used to invite everyone in the Virgin business to a party at my home in Oxfordshire – but unfortunately it became too big. At the last one we held – over three days – we had nearly 60,000 people. We put on fairground rides, sideshows, hamburgers and hot dogs, and rock bands – all paid for by the Virgin Group. I stood at the entrance and made sure I shook everyone's hand. My hand was swollen and rather painful after two days of this, but it was worthwhile. Today we have smaller gatherings, and I aim to get to as many of them as possible.

The Virgin Blue party, meanwhile, has become a glittering, red-carpet event – raising thousands for charity in Australia. The event is organised, set up and served by Virgin Blue people. It's headed by Jane Tewson, who established Comic Relief in the UK and lots of other charity projects, and who has been working in Australia with Aboriginal people. I donate a week's holiday in Necker Island in the British Virgin Islands as a major auction prize, and one trick I use is to get the runner-up, who has bid perhaps A$80,000, and the winner, who's paid A$90,000, both to pay A$85,000 and both go to Necker together. It's forged some great friendships. We also raise A$100,000 by letting someone name one of our aircraft, and all that costs is the paint job. It's easy money for charity and fantastic for staff morale.

I think governments should make parties completely tax-deductible, with the proviso that every time there's a knees-up, shindig, disco or rave, the proceeds go to charity. That's the deal. It should be much more than just a fun night for everybody. A night when everybody gets merry is good, but it's even better if you can combine it with something that makes a difference to others. Music events, fashion shows, sports contests, anything that gets people together and is enjoyable can be rolled out across every business – just don't let anyone use the charity's money to pay for the drinks!

A poor leader can make life hell for so many people. Leadership is not about a person sitting at the top of the tree, making all the decisions and expecting everyone to do as they're told. That's hardly leadership: it's more like dictatorship.

I have huge admiration for the British version of the TV show *The Apprentice*, in which people compete for a single job with Alan Sugar. The camerawork is slick, the editing is clever, the music is great. The power of television is immense, and if it's capable of inspiring people to treat business with excitement and enthusiasm, that can only be a positive thing. Frankly, anything that can be done to inspire young people to give it a go has to be worthwhile.

But I have one issue, and that's with the way Alan has to say, with a frown, at the end of each episode: 'You're fired!' It's in his contract because it makes good television. And it's cobblers. The whole competition is structured around the fear of being fired. While this does make it interesting for the viewer, it is not, in my opinion, how businesses should be run.

Where *The Apprentice* is successful is in its wider portrayal of the modern business world. There are few jobs for life any more. As individuals we need to be positive and sell ourselves. Most of those taking part in the show will have a better grasp of this than is apparent on camera. They know that failure is not something to fear. They know there are other options, other places to work.

So here it is important to stress that *there is a fundamental difference between an entrepreneur and a manager.* They are often contrasting people and it's crucial to realise this. Although I'm sure there are entrepreneurs who could make good managers, my advice would be: don't try to do both.

Entrepreneurs have the dynamism to get something started. They view the world differently from other people. They create opportunity that others don't necessarily see and have the guts to give it a go. Yet an entrepreneur is not necessarily good at the nuts and bolts of running a business. I admit that this is not my true forte – and recognising this weakness is essential for the entrepreneur. The annals of business are littered with stories of the driving force trying to run the business on a day-to-day level – and failing dreadfully.

Good managers are worth their weight in gold. People with the acute psychological know-how to smoothly organise and handle the pressures of an ongoing business venture are the glue that binds the business world. My notebooks are full of contacts and names of people who have been recommended or whom we seek out to come and be Virgin business managers. Cherish them, and give them a proper stake in the business, because they deserve a big share of any success. Once the entrepreneur has the company up and running, they often need to pass the baton on to the manager. The creator's job is to find someone with expertise who understands the vision and is prepared to follow the path.

The entrepreneur's job is effectively to put themselves out of a job each time the new company is up and running. Then they can step aside and free themselves up to be entrepreneurial in a different business. It is generally asking for trouble for an entrepreneur to stick around for too long, trying to cover both roles.

In a small business, you can be both the entrepreneur and the manager while you are getting it going. But you need to know and understand everything about that business. And I really mean everything. *An emerging entrepreneur should sign every cheque.* Examine every invoice, and you'll soon appreciate where your money is going. Even in a big business like the Virgin Group, I sit down now and again and sign every single cheque that goes out, and I ask my managing directors to do the same. For a month. Sign everything for a month every six months and suddenly you're asking: 'What on earth is this for?' You'll be able to cut out unnecessary expenditure quite dramatically when you do that.

As a small-business person, you must immerse yourself 100 per cent in everything and learn about the ins and outs of every single department. As you get bigger, you will be able to delegate, and when people come to you with their problems, they'll be surprised how knowledgeable you are and how much practical advice you can offer. The reason you're knowledgeable is because in the early days of the business, you learned all about it. This is how business leadership is achieved. There are no short cuts. Remember my earlier description of Brett Godfrey at Virgin Blue who insists that all of their senior managers spend time doing the different manual jobs like luggage loading. (I needed a physical after my stint!)

And as the business gets bigger, you will have to decide if you're a manager or an entrepreneur. If you're a manager you can stay with that business and help it grow. If you're an entrepreneur, you need to find a manager. Then you should move on, enjoy yourself and then set up your next enterprise.

Nothing in business is quite like the early, frenetic days of an ambitious start-up project. There's always an amazing buzz about this kind of thing. It's high-octane and high-risk and it builds a tremendous spirit and camaraderie which takes everyone through some very trying times. I've seldom seen people work harder than in the initial stages of a new venture. Once a business matures and is established, it can become more challenging to retain that excitement. What we do at Virgin is not let businesses get too mature. If you can keep the businesses relatively small, people will know each other within the organisation and feel like part of a team.

It's then down to the leadership of that organisation to keep making sure that people are challenged and motivated. Jack Welch, a great business leader, who transformed GE into one of the world's leading corporate powerhouses, was constantly evolving tools and methods in search of continuing growth. He encouraged managers to start each day as if it was the first day in the job. He said that managers were often afraid of change – and they must embrace it. I agree with Jack on that.

We never let people sit on their laurels, and we keep on trying to improve things. The minute Virgin Atlantic was voted 'The airline with the best business-class seats in the world' in the UK Airline awards, our designer was already beginning to work on the next seats in order to beat our own expectations rather than our competitors'. You must either stay ahead of other people, or stay ahead of yourself, all the time. If you really put your mind to it you are normally going to find a better way. You have to keep on questioning the way people do things.

Looking back over the personal notebooks I have kept for more than thirty-five years, I don't think there has ever been a letter from my office which criticises the staff or an individual. Now and again I've disagreed with something and suggested changes in behaviour. But the Virgin Group has always tried to look for the best in people. That way, you get the best back.

A plant needs to be watered to flourish and people need encouragement so that they can flourish. If this sounds precious, so what? It's true. When someone says something nice about any of our Virgin ventures, I feel great. I'm flattered. When someone has a go, it knocks me back. We've developed a thicker skin over the years, but I hope we haven't lost the sensitivity to do things properly. If witless criticism can deflate me, after thirty-odd years of business success, then what a fool I'd be to go around ticking off other people. People say business is a cut-throat affair. Certainly it's a tough game – we talk about 'the competition' for a reason. And, yes, sometimes people play dirty. But nothing in my years with Virgin has eroded my habit of saying thank you to people or praising them. I was brought up in England by parents who praised and encouraged me a lot. Why would I behave differently to others?

Right across our business we have a philosophy of encouragement. Our people are very rarely criticised. If someone makes a howling mistake, usually they don't need to be told. They know.

One of my weaknesses is that I find it very hard to tell someone that their services are no longer required in the business. It's an unpleasant obligation, and one you absolutely must not shirk. If you're a small company, it is vital to do it personally. You really have to see the person face to face rather than get someone else to do it. I think, generally, a personal explanation of the situation is appreciated, and it helps the individual you're letting go to move on.

Of course, if you actually *enjoyed* firing people, there'd be something wrong with you. Jack Welch made a point of continually weeding out the people at the bottom. Alan Sugar and Donald Trump aren't afraid to fire people either, though I doubt they go about it quite the way *The Apprentice* would have us believe. There's a machismo about the way some managers talk about hiring and firing that I find downright repugnant. A senior person at Apple rather proudly says in his speeches about firing people that 'I'd rather have a hole than an asshole.' My philosophy is very different. I think that you should only fire somebody as an act of last resort.

If someone has broken a serious rule and damaged the brand, part company. Otherwise, stop and think. Indeed, these days you have to. There are a lot of legal and employment issues to take into consideration before you even go down that route. This can be frustrating, but to be honest I don't think it's the nightmare that some managers make it out to be. People respond to their surroundings. If someone is messing things up royally, offer them a role that might be more suitable, or a job in another area of the business. You'd be amazed how quickly people change for the better, given the right circumstances, and how willing they are to learn from costly mistakes when offered a second chance. If you've over-promoted someone and it hasn't worked out – which happens – then offer them their old job back rather than firing them. It's your fault for over-promoting them. Not theirs.

A lot of companies these days call themselves 'families'. Usually, this is just an embarrassing bit of public relations flannel. I think companies can be like families, that it's a good approach to business, and that Virgin's created better corporate families than most. We've done it by accepting the fact that we have to think beyond the bottom line. Families forgive each other. Families work around problems. Families require effort, and patience. You have to be prepared to take the rough with the smooth. You have to put up with your troublesome siblings. They're your family: you can't just throw them out on the street.

The higher up you go in a company, the more perilous your job position is if you don't perform. In football, dropping out of the Premiership – or failing to get into the Champions League – can be disastrous. The board of directors, or the club chairman, must hit upon a formula for success, and the buck has to stop with the coach. Sacking the coach is easy. The hard part is making sure you're getting someone better than the person you're dropping. In football, that doesn't always seem to be the case.

I often read about chief executives, managing directors and large company bosses who are told to resign from their high-profile companies by investors because they have made a hash due to poor business decisions. In the United States, for example, we've had Angelo Mozilo, the CEO of Countrywide Financial, Citigroup's boss Chuck Prince and Merrill Lynch's Stan O'Neal all departing with $100-million-plus compensation packages despite their businesses being caught in the sub-prime mortgage meltdown.

Too many top executives are given massive payouts and allowed to walk away, leaving others to sort things out. I think the opposite should happen. In most cases, leaders should stay on until any problems are sorted out – or a solution found – and then they can go and with a fraction of the money they would earn if successful.

Decent leadership is about explaining clearly and unemotionally why a decision has been taken. This applies just as much to a large company when there are lots of jobs at stake. For a business to survive under extreme pressure it must take decisive action. And when there are a lot of redundancies, that can hurt the pride and self-esteem of a lot of hard-working individuals.

After the terrorist attacks on New York City, Washington and United Flight 93 on September 11, 2001, our 'Council of War' met each day to look at the unfolding situation. I see from my notebooks that my first phone calls – of many hundreds made within those vital hours – were to our bankers, to let them know of the cash position; and to the UK government, seeking their support and encouraging a common approach. We also had to talk candidly to other airlines to get a proper picture of events, so we needed temporary anti-trust immunity – we didn't want to be accused of working in consort. I called the New York mayor, to pass on my condolences.

Transatlantic air travel stopped and I pleaded with Stephen Byers, the Transport Secretary, not to let the position of Britain's airlines be weakened when the US government was supporting its own national carriers. We didn't get the same cushion of support as the American airlines – and we couldn't and didn't hide in Chapter 11 administration. If Virgin Atlantic hadn't responded decisively to the Twin Towers attack, then we would certainly have gone out of business. We began renegotiating our bank lending and our aeroplane contracts and we did everything necessary to cut our costs. We had to reduce our US capacity by a third, and so we began looking at other international routes instead, such as launching into Nigeria, China and India. Then we had to relay the bad news: reluctantly, we were letting 1,200 Virgin Atlantic people go. It was the first mass redundancy in Virgin's history. We offered our people part-time work, job sharing and unpaid leave. We also tried to find them work in other parts of the business. Our managers made tough decisions that hurt many people, but we promised to get them back on board as soon as conditions improved – and, thankfully, most returned.

Dealing with Virgin Atlantic's flight engineers was particularly difficult for us. A breed of aviators with a passion for flying, they had considerable skill, and were tremendously loyal and committed to our company. And here we were, putting them out of a job.

If your rival airlines introduce planes that require only two people in the cockpit – that's the captain and first officer – rather than three, as was still the case with Virgin Atlantic when we had the flight engineer on board, then you're faced with a serious business issue.

The reliability of a new generation of planes and the increasing sophistication of fly-by-wire systems meant that airlines could reduce the number of flight crew in each cockpit and, in the process, save a great deal of cash. Unfortunately, the flight engineers were the victims of progress and obsolescence in the airline industry. There was no longer any need for them, and we had to tell many of our engineers that they had to go. It happens sometimes. It's horrible. And there is no way around it. If we hadn't done this, we wouldn't have been competitive.

Over the years in the Virgin Group our diversification has been a bonus. We've been able to move people around our various companies, offering different jobs until things improved again. But this wasn't easy with our flight engineers. They had extremely specialised skills and we didn't think that converting them to commercial pilots would work for us. Our captains and first officers were normally highly experienced pilots who had spent up to ten years on short-haul flying.

Since we were saving cash by laying these people off, they deserved the lion's share of the savings in their redundancy pay. It was far more than the legal minimum and I think most of them appreciated the gesture. It was a decent package. The engineers thought it fair and – just as important – so too did their colleagues who were staying on with the company.

Many elements of leadership can be prepared in advance, planned and rehearsed. You don't have to be Winston Churchill to be a good leader.

That said, I think there is such a thing as natural leadership. It takes a certain generosity of spirit to trust people, and to judge their merits and limitations fairly. It takes not a little bravery to bear bad news to people. Optimism, openness to possibilities and sheer self-confidence – some people have more of these qualities than others.

So, in addition to the practical steps you can take, I think there is a huge amount to be gained in following the examples of great natural leaders. You can certainly read about them; but you should also be asking who among your circle is a leader you can learn from. I am hugely privileged to have met some great natural leaders in my time. Some are internationally famous; many are not. To describe all the help, influence and mentorship I've been sustained by over the years would make another book, so for now, let me just tell you about one important figure in my life: Nelson Mandela.

When people think of 'Richard Branson', they tend to think first of all about Virgin's involvement in the music industry. It's a piece of our heritage we're extremely proud of. When I cast my mind back to what shaped me most as a businessman, however, I find myself remembering an even earlier phase of my career; and I recall my brief, fortunate and illuminating adventures in journalism.

What, after all, could be better for a young man searching for answers in life, than to go around interviewing people? I was never going to be a great journalist, but one skill I did have was being able to keep my mouth shut. I let the people I was interviewing do the talking. I was also quite unembarrassed when it came to asking what, in hindsight, seem naive and obvious questions. Both are skills I've carried into business, and they have served me incredibly well. The ability to listen, and the willingness to stick your neck out and ask the obvious question, are criminally underrated business essentials.

I was brought up in the mid-1960s and this was generally a caring and compassionate time, when a lot of young people became socially aware and began to understand how the world treated minorities, what their rights should be, and how a fairer deal might change things. From the other side of the Atlantic, I followed with fascination the struggles of black Americans against racism, discrimination and economic inequality.

In March 1968, I was proud to be marching to the US embassy in Grosvenor Square in London in protest at US involvement in the Vietnam War. I strode side by side with left-wing firebrand Tariq Ali and actress Vanessa Redgrave, and I remember the fear when the police on horseback charged us with truncheons and tear gas. I was also invigorated by the thought that young people were doing something direct and positive. And through the prism of *Student* magazine, I – a privileged English public schoolboy – heard for the first time about the horror of Africa. I learned a little about oppression, and disease, and famine. *Student* campaigned against the horrific Biafran War in Nigeria, and we used harrowing photographs by Don McCullin, the celebrated photojournalist whose *Sunday Times* images would go on to define the conflict in Vietnam and Cambodia. We helped bring to the public's attention the plight of millions of children dying of starvation who were caught up in the civil war.

The autumn issue of *Student* in 1968 was awash with anger: the black American ghettos were exploding with violence; rioting students were throwing cobblestones at the police on the streets of Paris; Russian tanks had crushed the Prague Spring in Czechoslovakia; Vietnam was withering under a rain of bombs. There was so much to cover. I remember we had Gyles Brandreth writing on America, and a report from Vietnam by a fresh-faced seventeen-year-old Julian Manyon – now a veteran ITN foreign correspondent – in which he interviewed a North Vietnamese doctor about the death of Vietcong soldiers through dysentery. But it was the interview I conducted with the American black militant writer James Baldwin which shocked me to the core. If you are harbouring any doubt in your mind about the value of naive questions, read this. Look what he made of my stumbling questionnaire. I would never have elicited such fire had I been less direct.

What kind of education did James Baldwin have?

'At school I was trained in Bible techniques. I received my education in the street.'

Were there good schools in America?

'How can there be? They are built by the white state, run by white powers and designed to keep the nigger in his place.'

Can the white man give you freedom or must the black man take it for himself?

'The white man can't even give it to himself. Your record has not been very encouraging. I DON'T EXPECT YOU TO GIVE ME ANYTHING. I am going to take what I need – not necessarily from you, this is your myth – but I intend to live my life. I am not interested in what white people do. White people are not that important. What one is fighting against is not white people, but the power standing between a person and his life. It is as simple as that. It is not a race war, it is a war between poverty and privilege, freedom and imprisonment.'

I was transfixed by what Baldwin was saying to me – his vitriolic yet restrained anger at what he saw as the inequality of life.

In *The Fire Next Time*, written in 1963, he had predicted that in ten years' time we would see the end of white supremacy. I asked him if he still believed this.

Baldwin replied: 'I didn't say it in quite that way. I said that this was a prophecy – and the prophet may well be right. I am telling you that Western societies are visibly in trouble and are visibly crumbling.'

'Under pressure from the black man?'

'Under the weight of their own lies.'

This was strong, urgent stuff for a white, teenage editor. It was an anger that I could not understand, because I had nothing to measure it against. I wanted to help change the world, but what did I know about the world?

Fred Dube, a black African, born in Johannesburg, a social worker married with two children, joined the African National Congress in 1955. From 1964 to 1967 he served four prison sentences for sabotage, in Ladysmith in Natal, Leeuwkop in Transvaal, on Robben Island and in Groenpunt in the Orange Free State. He left for England in July 1968, and became a bank clerk in London. He told *Student* that the poverty, homelessness and malnutrition in his homeland all stemmed from one problem: South Africa's vicious and unjust apartheid society. Some time later I heard about the black activist Steve Biko, and then I encountered the name of Nelson Mandela. His parents called him Nelson because it sounded 'white', and they thought he would get on better in a whites-only society. He was viewed as a dangerous extremist by some in Britain but I began to know the truth about this incredible man.

When I first got to know Madiba – as he is affectionately known in Africa – I was always in awe and slightly nervous meeting him. Then when he smiled, his warmth and impish humour simply radiated into your heart: 'Richard, it is a great honour to meet you.' I soon learned that he says that to everyone on first meeting them! Here is a man who has suffered so much because of his colour and what he believes in. He was a victim of apartheid injustice, handed a life sentence at forty-six. His prison number was 466/64, which stood for the 466th prisoner admitted to the dreadful Robben Island jail in 1964. His cell was six feet square, the walls two feet thick. When he lay down his head touched one end and his feet the other. His first months in jail were spent with fellow political prisoners crushing rocks into gravel using a four-pound hammer. It was achingly strenuous and constantly painful. I have seen his cell – it must have been hell on Earth.

He says in his autobiography, *Long Walk to Freedom*, that 'Robben Island was without question the hardest, most iron-fisted outpost of the South African penal system. It was a hardship station not only for the prisoners but for the prison staff. The warders, white and overwhelmingly Afrikaans-speaking, demanded a master–servant relationship. They ordered us to call them baas, which we refused to do. The racial divide on Robben Island was absolute: there were no black warders, and no white prisoners.'

Yet I have never witnessed one scintilla of anger or indignation from the man.

His spirit is best captured, I think, in the address he gave, not long after being elected president, at the unveiling of a statue of Steve Biko. 'While Steve Biko espoused, inspired and promoted black pride, he never made blackness a fetish . . . accepting one's blackness is a critical starting point: an important foundation for engaging in struggle. Today, it must be a foundation for reconstruction and development, for a common human effort to end war, poverty, ignorance and disease.'

Here are the characteristics of great leadership, contained in a handful of sentences. The concern for people is here; so too the easy intelligence Mandela brings to the judging of individual merits. There's authority in these words, but they're not hectoring or bombastic: they create for us a clear, simple vision of what has to be achieved.

The unveiling of Biko's statue, sculpted in bronze by Naomi Jacobson, took place on 12 September 1997. Peter Gabriel and I were on hand – the only white faces in a crowd of around 100,000. I urged Peter to sing the song that had done so much to keep Biko's name alive. That rendition of 'Biko', backed by Nelson Mandela and a crowd of 100,000, is something I will treasure to my grave. From the moment Mandela came up to shake my hand and thank me for my support, I wanted to do something meaningful for South Africa, to help it recover from its terrible wounds. I wasn't a songwriter – and I didn't have to wait long for the call.

There is one characteristic of Mandela's leadership that isn't apparent from his speech, but it is typical of most of the great leaders I've met: they are all inveterate salesmen! Mandela is an entrepreneur through and through. He absolutely will not stop. Whenever we were together, Madiba seldom missed an opportunity to pull a few strings for his country. He was in London one time, having lunch with Joan, Holly, Sam and me and a few close friends, and afterwards I wrote in my notebook. *'No lunch or dinner ever goes by without him asking a favour for someone in need: He came to my house with his new wife, Graca Machel, and his daughter, "That was a delightful lunch, Richard, Now last week I saw Bill Gates and he gave £50 million in dollars." Gulp!'*

I am proud to say that Nelson Mandela has become a close friend. As we pass his ninetieth birthday, he has remained an inspiration to me as a human being and I have many cherished memories of time spent in his company. I think it's worth explaining how the former South African president's astonishing acumen for business, coupled with his sense of duty, helped his country. For Madiba knew that the 'long walk to freedom' for his black brothers and sisters meant embracing a positive economic future. While he recognised it would take many years – even a generation – to reverse the inequalities of racial discrimination, he had few qualms about seeking my involvement – and that of other business leaders – if he believed it would bring jobs and wealth to South Africa.

One occasion was in September 2001, just days after the World Trade Center atrocities in New York. Tourism and business travel had dried up overnight, the whole airline industry was in meltdown, and I was sitting in the bath thinking how the Virgin Group could deal with the immense disruption to Virgin Atlantic when he phoned. Madiba's voice was like an anaesthetic balm: calm and reassuring.

'Richard, you said that you wanted to help South Africa,' he said.

'Yes, Madiba. You know I'm willing to help,' I replied.

'Well, we have a problem . . .'

One of South Africa's biggest health clubs, the Health and Racquet chain, had collapsed. It meant the loss of 5,000 jobs. 'Do you think you could do something with it? Do you think you can save the people?'

I didn't really know if this was a viable business, but I went with my gut instinct, and my desire to support a man I revered. Also, I trusted Madiba: in another life he would have made an astute corporate financier!

I rang Frank Reed, the Virgin Active chief executive, and Matthew Bucknall, his finance director, who ran just three large clubs in the UK. Would they be prepared to take on an ailing South African business nearly eight times their size? There was a palpable gulp from Matthew – but he then said they'd jump at the chance. Brilliant! Within hours we were able to put a rescue package together – rebranding the whole business Virgin Active. I called Madiba back to say we were definitely on board.

But money was tight for us and we needed to raise funding, so we approached the UK private equity company Bridgepoint Capital who agreed to take a 55 per cent stake in a deal worth £110 million, leaving Virgin with 36 per cent, and Frank, Matthew and the team around 8 per cent. When Gordon McCallum heard about the speed of the transaction he said: 'At this pace, we should rename the company Virgin Hyperactive.'

Our strategy involved keeping on as many people as we could, and retaining Health and Racquet's 900,000 customers, although we had to change the arrangements for many health-club users. They had been given free lifetime membership, in return for signing up with a big upfront fee – fine until the new memberships dried up! We judged, correctly as it turned out, that nearly all of the members would agree to start paying a monthly subscription provided we gave them a first-class health-club experience and fixed the dilapidated gyms that had been starved of investment.

The rescue gave us a fantastic footprint in South Africa from which we have continued to expand. By October 2005, Virgin Active was in a better financial position – having doubled in size and expanded into Italy and Spain – and we were able to buy back Bridgepoint Capital's 55 per cent share for £134.5 million.

*

When Nelson Mandela was president of South Africa he knew his diplomatic position. South Africa's re-emergence as a nation was reliant on China's increasing strength and its investment as an economic superpower. He didn't want to offend China. And he never ever did.

Once free from the burden of presidency, of course, Madiba was his own man again.

In November 2004, I was in Johannesburg at the CIDA City Campus, the first free campus for black students from townships and rural areas who cannot afford education. I was with Kelly Holmes, the double gold-medal Olympic runner, the singer Estelle, and the team from Virgin Unite for the launch of an initiative called Women on the Move, which focuses on empowering young women across South Africa. After the ceremony I stayed on to listen to the Dalai Lama, the exiled Tibetan leader, who had been invited to speak at CIDA. It was his third time in South Africa and he spoke with verve, compassion and gentle humour. He smiled as he welcomed people from all religions, the non-religious, and black, white and brown alike. I was enthralled listening to this deeply spiritual man appealing for peace and justice.

He said: 'If you wish to experience peace – provide peace for another. If you wish to know that you are safe, cause others to know that they are safe. If you wish to understand seemingly incomprehensible things, help another better understand. If you wish to heal your sadness or anger, seek to heal the sadness or anger of another. Those others are watching for you now. They are looking to you for guidance, for help, for courage, for strength, for understanding and for assurance at this hour. Most of all, they are looking for your love.'

There was nothing the Dalai Lama said that day that could possibly have incited the Chinese authorities. He simply asserted that the gap between rich and poor was morally wrong.

I had been with Madiba at his home the previous afternoon, and I asked him why he had never met the Dalai Lama. He frowned and told me it had been too political. The South Africans didn't want to upset China over their activities in Tibet. But I thought it would be good to get these two wonderful elders together – and that political expediency should not bar them from meeting.

'You're no longer president, Madiba,' I said. 'He can visit you as a private individual. He's staying only a few blocks away from here.'

Mandela smiled and looked across at Zelda le Grange, his assistant and adviser. I could tell that he was persuaded. Later the next day, Zelda invited me to join them for the get-together I had suggested – but I found myself declining this extraordinary invitation. I felt it should be a special occasion between two inspirational people, and that no one else should be present. That night, after the meeting, we got the following message from Wendee, who works for the Dalai Lama: 'On behalf of the entire delegation, thank you for setting up what may be the first and last meeting of these two giant spirits ... The meeting lasted an hour in deep discussion.'

There are many things in my life that have given me satisfaction. But the union of two iconic figures in Johannesburg will be a moment I will cherish for as long as I live. And that meeting began to strengthen the idea Peter Gabriel and I had had: to bring together a group of wise global elders ...

Necker Island, January 2004

Dear Madiba,

An idea – yes, I'm sorry – another idea. Out of the most wonderful day – the 46664 concert [in November 2003 – a declaration of war on Aids in South Africa] – Peter Gabriel and I were inspired to write to you.

As well you know, in an African village there are elders who the rest of the village look up to. We believe that the Global Village needs to equally tap into our elders. You told us then that it had been easier for you to gain the trust of the generals negotiating in

Rwanda, as they said talking to you was like talking to a father.
We would like to set up a small body of the most respected
'Elders' in the world and as you are accepted as the most
respected person of all today, we would ask that you become the
father figure to this organisation and the first Elder.

Einstein once said: 'How I wish that somewhere existed an island for those who are wise and of goodwill.' I said it would be wonderful if the Elders could meet somewhere like my own Necker Island two or three times a year to discuss how they could help tackle the pressing issues of the world.

We would suggest that the Elders are initially chosen by yourself,
and then in the future chosen by the world community, giving
them added legitimacy on the world stage. None of them would
be current politicians. The Council of Elders would comprise
12 men and women. Four of these could stand down every three
years. The new four could be voted in from a shortlist selected by
the Elders through channels like the Internet, television, post and
email. They would represent a broad spectrum of the world's
people.

Peter and I said that the first worldwide vote would encourage people to think globally, to feel part of events and engage with a world beyond their borders, culture and religion. As the United Nations represents the governments of the world, the Elders would represent the hopes, aspirations, fears and dreams of the people.

The Elders would have at their disposal a 'Growing Tree' – an
army of people worldwide who have retired, or who have the time,
who are willing to give their time and expertise to help tackle the
problems of the world. Whether setting up an Open University for
Africa or India, tackling conflicts, diseases or poverty. They would

also help mentoring programmes. They would be a huge
educational resource.

The aim from the start was for the Elders to be a group of global advisers and not to instruct people to do things. They were to be individuals, and not simply representatives of a country or state. They were to be beyond party politics and free to speak what they saw as the truth.

I appreciate that you would have difficulty finding much time
yourself but it would give enormous credibility to the future of
the Elders if you were to give it your blessing and be its founding
father.
   I would pledge myself to find the time and resources to help
organise it behind the scenes and to make sure it becomes a force
for good in the world and hopefully continues for many years to
come.
Kind regards,
Richard

Nelson Mandela loved the idea. It appealed to his entrepreneurial instincts. He agreed to become its founding Elder, along with his wife Graca, and they issued invitations to the eleven people in the world he felt had the greatest moral authority.

I'll never forget walking out of Madiba's home with Jean Oelwang after he and Graca had made the final selection of Elders. I had a wonderful feeling that this was the start of one of the most hopeful and inspiring ventures in my life. I also felt so blessed to be able to spend time with two true global leaders. Graca and Madiba share the extraordinary ability to lead with humility, honesty and an unfailing focus on those whose voices are not yet being heard. Madiba frequently reminds us that if something is not going to make a difference at village level, then we shouldn't be doing it.

With Virgin Unite's support, we then went on a journey of creation, reaching out to people all over the world to shape initiative and build support. We had two glorious weeks during which Archbishop Tutu and ex-President Carter helped Peter and me to host a range of different groups on Necker – from scientists, to philosophers, to entrepreneurs, to front-line leaders. As with the development of any business idea, there were moments when we thought: what are we doing?, and then that magnificent moment when it all clicked into place and we knew that this was going to be something that really could make a huge difference in the world. We also wove in some fun – impossible not to do with the cheeky archbishop there to keep us all on our toes. One of my fondest memories from this time is of Peter and me teaching him to swim in the beautiful waters surrounding Necker.

I will never forget the speech Madiba gave to everyone when we first brought the initial group of Elders together at Ulusaba:

> *Let us call them Global Elders, not because of their age, but because of their individual and collective wisdom. This group derives its strength not from political, economic or military power, but from the independence and integrity of those who are here. They do not have careers to build, elections to win, constituencies to please. They can talk to anyone they please, and are free to follow paths they deem right, even if hugely unpopular. I know that as a group, you will support courage where there is fear, foster agreement where there is conflict and inspire hope where there is despair.*

After this gathering the Elders decided they wanted to announce their existence to the world on Madiba's upcoming birthday on 18 July 2007. The team at Virgin Unite went into overdrive preparing for the launch and working with me to raise the funds we needed for the first few years – all in a little over five weeks! During this time, we had the opportunity to connect with an amazingly humble and sincere group of entrepreneurs and organisations who helped found the Elders. Their spirit in coming together behind this dream and the absence of any individual agendas truly captured the essence of the Elders. They have not only become partners in this initiative, but I'm also sure they will become lifelong friends.

As I write this, the other Elders are Madiba's wife, Graca Machel, a renowned advocate for women's and children's rights; the Anglican archbishop Desmond Tutu, who was a tireless campaigner against apartheid in South Africa; Kofi Annan, Secretary General of the United Nations from 1997 until 2006; Ela Bhatt, founder of India's Self-Employed Women's Association; Lakhdar Brahimi, the Algerian-born former ambassador who began life in his country's liberation struggle and then became a mediator in many Middle Eastern conflicts; Gro Harlem Brundtland, the former prime minister of Norway, who has made a significant impact on global society through her commission on the environment and sustainable development; the sociologist Fernando Cardoso, the former president of Brazil, who has fought hard for human rights in South America; Jimmy Carter, who brokered the historic Camp David peace accords when he was president of the US; Mary Robinson, former president of Ireland and a distinguished United Nations High Commissioner for Human Rights from 1997 until 2002; Muhammad Yunus, the Bangladeshi economist and Nobel Peace Prize winner, and founder of the wonderful Grameen Bank; and Aung San Suu Kyi, a fearless and outspoken critic of the military junta which dominates her Burmese homeland.

The Elders are, in essence, a group of immensely influential world figures acting like entrepreneurs who use their moral courage, wisdom and independent leadership to help tackle huge intractible problems. The beauty of the Elders is that they are at a time in their careers where they have no other agenda but that of humanity.

Once, whole empires were operated out of small rooms by a handful of oligarchs. Those days are effectively over, thank goodness, and certainly it's not anyone's plan to give the Elders political power! But what we do hope and intend is that the Elders can bring their influence to bear on the world stage, quickly and responsively, providing the peoples of this planet with a voice and a conscience.

So over these few pages, as I explain to you how the Elders work, I hope to convince you that *entrepreneurism is not something you ever grow out of; nor is it something uniquely fitted just to sole traders, or small companies, or even to modular enterprises like the Virgin Group. Entrepreneurism is – if this doesn't sound too pompous – a universal business virtue.* I mean that it can be applied to problems, challenges and opportunities *regardless of scale*.

The Elders have been assembled in much the same way that a Virgin company is created. We have facilitated their organisation, and have provided them with the means to work together. We've made sure there is a motivated administrative team. And we are ensuring that the Elders' name and brand is protected. It is important that the group develops a recognised single identity, to sustain it through frequent changes of membership and a constantly evolving roster of activities.

Peter Gabriel and I felt it was essential that we stepped back from this – that the Elders had complete independence and that their articles of association enshrined that complete independence. The Elders are beholden to nobody – and that includes the founders and any of the people funding them.

The twelve Elders are people with tremendous personal integrity. They are generally all over sixty years of age, and beyond ego. Their mission statement says that the Elders' role is to work to resolve global issues and alleviate human suffering. It has taken a huge amount of work to get the mission statement and the structure properly sorted.

As mentioned, we've brought together a wonderful group of entrepreneurial founders whose generous contributions ensure that the first three years' operating costs of the Elders are paid for, so that they can go on missions to places like Darfur and Kenya. The Elders are not paid for their work. They are able to tap into some of the leading conflict and dispute-resolution professionals from around the globe. The international stature of the Elders means that if they call on someone for specialised help in a project, then they will get an immediate response. Professional mediators will be able to do the groundwork before the Elders go into any area.

I hope that in 100 years' time – if it is run correctly – the Elders' group will still be in existence, and that people who have excelled in their lives, be they politicians, diplomats, humanitarians or business figures, can be part of it. When these good and worthy people get into the last fifteen years of their active lives, then the Elders can ask them to join in tackling global problems.

Does this extraordinary-sounding organisation motivate you to create and facilitate something similar in your own industry? I do hope so. After all, the idea for the Elders came in the first place from my nigh on forty years of business experience and Peter's experience starting up global organisations such as Witness. Every industry has its revered figures, people that companies and entrepreneurs go to for advice and sound judgement. Many of the great and good in business are living longer these days, they're living healthier lives, and more often than not their appetite for business is unquenched. Imagine how much mentorship, sound advice and even practical assistance is out there, waiting to be tapped. Imagine if your industry were supported by a network of revered business figures like Sir Brian Pitman.

I concede this isn't so much business advice as a call to arms – but if these pages have inspired you to consider the good of your industry as a whole, and how your organisation can contribute to the effective and responsible conduct of that industry, so much the better. The great and good in your business sector are a resource you should take seriously. Finding a way to harness that resource to best support and encourage your industry will add value to your brand – and what you learn will have a direct and positive effect on your business.

*

To be a serious entrepreneur, you have to be prepared to step off the precipice. Yes, it's dangerous. There can be times, having jumped, when you find yourself in free fall without a parachute. There is a real prospect that some business ventures will go smashing into the ground. It has certainly been very close at times throughout my own business life. Then you reach out and grab a ledge with your fingertips – and you claw your way back to safety.

Life has become too cosy for many, who have their lives mapped out by parents and teachers. It's all a bit, well, *comfortable*: off you go to university to study a course. Land a good job, get a mortgage, find a nice girlfriend, boyfriend, partner. It's a solid life – a good life in many ways – but when was the last time you took a risk?

Many people reading this book will be affluent. If you don't feel affluent right now, take a minute and think: the very fact that you could afford this book, or afford the time to take it out of the library – the very fact that you are able to read at all – marks you out as one of world history's richest and most privileged people. There's not that many of us, and we haven't been affluent for very long, and so we're not very good at it yet. Affluence makes us lazy. It makes us complacent. It smothers us in cotton wool. If your job's well paid, who can blame you if you're not willing to take a risk and, say, set up your own company?

The vast majority are very happy with this arrangement, and good for them. But if you want swashbuckling action in your life, become an entrepreneur and give it a go. Learn the art of trying to set up your own business. Which is the same as saying, learn the art of making mistakes and learning lessons.

Because if you want to be an entrepreneur and you *don't* make a few errors along the way, you certainly aren't going to learn anything or achieve very much.

People have a fear of failure, and while this is perfectly reasonable, it's also very odd. Because it seems to me that it's through making mistakes that we learn how to do things. Watch a musician practise sometime. Watch a baby figure out how to walk. Listen to a toddler speak. Skills like walking and talking and playing music emerge gradually, steadily, from a blizzard of (often pretty funny) mistakes. I think this is true of *everything* – that learning is about making mistakes and learning from them. And that is the fundamental reason that flying has become so safe in the twenty-first century; so safe in fact that sitting on a 747 to New York is safer than watching TV at home.

Now, I grant you that you may hit a limit, beyond which you *can't* learn from your mistakes. Don't expect a chart-topping album from me any time soon, or a recital at Carnegie Hall, or a sequence of sonnets, or any of the billion and one other things I'm never going to be great at. But that's not *failure*. That's finding out what you're good at. The world is much, much bigger than you, and no amount of worldly success is going to change that fact.

Failure is not giving things a go in the first place. People who fail are those who don't have a go and don't make an effort. Failures can't be bothered. There are few people who've tried something and fallen who didn't get enormous satisfaction from trying, and I've learned more from people who have tried and faltered than from the few charmed people for whom success came easy.

In my home country, the British education system has a lot to do with our fear of failure. I think it concentrates exclusively on academic achievement and downplays the other contributions people can make to society. I've huge admiration for scientists and engineers; whereas they are given due respect in Germany, the United States and Japan, in British society they tend to get a raw deal.

As someone who never went to university, perhaps I've a radical view of education. I am committed to excellence and expertise in business but I believe we need to show young people the value of wealth creation too. I think some university degrees could be finished more quickly – I've never understood why some courses have only two or three lectures per week, and why students are left to their own devices much of the time without much direction from tutors, lecturers and professors, who now spend most of their energy, it seems to me, chasing funding grants. But one thing is apparent to me: we still need a good deal more entrepreneurial thinking in our universities and colleges.

One of my greatest entrepreneurial heroes was Sir Freddie Laker. Freddie, who died in February 2006, aged eighty-three, lived his life to the limits. He was a tremendous person: a man of magic and mirth. He lit up a room and he was the ultimate salesman. An ex-colleague and close friend, David Tait, said he could sell a glass of water to a drowning man. Freddie was a huge inspiration and supporter of Virgin Atlantic and he was the godfather of cheap international air travel.

The first Skytrain flights took off from Gatwick to New York in September 1977. Although Freddie's airline was no-frills, the ticket prices were unbelievable. It was only £59 single to get to America – a third of the price of any of the other carriers. He made £1 million profit in the first year – and I was one of his regular customers as we expanded our Virgin Records business in America.

Skytrain were carrying one in seven transatlantic passengers – and Freddie was knighted in 1978. Then in 1982, the company went into receivership with debts of £264 million. He had borrowed heavily to buy fifteen new planes just as the pound plunged in value against the dollar, but worse than that, the major airlines had conspired against him, offering cheaper fares to undercut him. The airlines also threatened the airframe manufacturers, telling them not to sell to Freddie. His airline collapsed – with passengers still in the air.

In 1983, the liquidators Touche Ross started an anti-trust action in the United States, claiming $1 billion from ten major airlines – including British Airways, PanAm, TWA, and Lufthansa – who had got together to plot Freddie's downfall. The defendants settled out of court, negotiating a reported £35 million payment to Freddie's creditors – while he reluctantly accepted £6 million in compensation and retired to the Bahamas.

Three days before the collapse, in typical style, he said: 'I'm flying high – I couldn't be more confident about the future.' And David Tait recalls sitting next to Freddie as they flew out of Gatwick airport on an Air Florida flight ten days after the collapse. Below, jammed in wing tip to wing tip in the Laker hangar, sat Freddie's life's work, a forlorn cluster of grounded DC-10s still emblazoned with the Skytrain logo. But Freddie turned to his distraught partner and said: 'Don't worry, mate, it'll all work out just fine.'

His company was bust. Yet four-times married Freddie still knew that there was much more to life. He enjoyed reminiscing with me over a Pusser's rum and orange on his yacht in the Bahamas, and he relished a pint and a laugh with his friends.

It was on another Air Florida flight that he met an off-duty Eastern Airlines stewardess called Jacqueline Harvey. It was love at first sight – or first flight – and Jacquie made Freddie's last twenty years a lot more fun, erasing any memories of his airline's failure.

It was his business sayings that were so memorable for me.

'Only a fool never changes his mind.'

'Don't bring me your problems – bring me the solutions.'

And his most famous one: 'Sue the bastards.' Litigation lawyers the world over still celebrate that one! But it was about the best advice I got when I had to take on British Airways after their dirty tricks campaign against Virgin Atlantic in the late 1980s.

Freddie was never afraid of failure. He succeeded in life – and always gave it a go. That's why we named one of our planes the *Spirit of Sir Freddie*.

7 Social Responsibility

Just Business

Over the years, we've watched billions of dollars go into development aid and emergency relief. Yet, unbelievably, we still have well over 16,000 people dying every day from preventable and treatable diseases like Aids and TB, half the planet still lives on less than $2 per day, one billion people have no access to drinking water, and the list goes on and on. The fact that these problems persist is not due to lack of hard work and commitment from the social and environmental sectors; nevertheless, without normal market forces and businesses ensuring that the best ideas can be fully realised and communicated, what we end up with is a market of good intentions.

Through my travels over the last couple of decades, I've started to realise that the only way we are going to drive the scale of the change we need in the world is if we pull together some very unlikely partnerships with businesses, charities, governments, NGOs and entrepreneurial people on to the front lines. More often than not, the people most affected know the answers – we just need to listen to them. None of us can do it alone; we all have to put aside our differences and revolutionise the way we work together to ensure that we leave this world in good shape for at least the 'next seven generations', as is the philosophy of the indigenous people we are working with in Canada.

In this last chapter, I want to tell you about Virgin's adventures in the territory where business and making the world a bit of a better place meet. This has always been important to me and really began when I was eighteen and opened up the Student Advisory Centre on Portobello Road, helping young people with sexual health. Forty years later, it has changed shape a bit, but it's still there, and still in the same place offering counselling services.

When Aids first started to become a major issue in the mid-eighties we launched Mates condoms, combining our business and creative skills to get young people to wear a condom while still enjoying sex (well they certainly weren't going to be stopped!). We decided that this was so important that we would make it a social business and all profits would be ploughed back into extending the safe-sex message. The team did a great job. We even got the BBC to run an advertising campaign for the first time in their history, which significantly raised awareness of the importance of safe sex across the UK – all in a cheeky Virgin way. Here in the Caribbean, the slogan goes: 'No glove – no love'.

Several years ago, I realised that if Virgin really wanted to make a difference with some of the tougher issues facing humanity, we had to start pulling together everything we were doing. I knew that the only way this would work was if we put social responsibility at the core of what Virgin is. So we spent months talking with staff, customers and front-line organisations all over the world, and out of this we built a company philosophy of 'doing what is best for people and the planet' and created Virgin Unite. Virgin Unite has now become the entrepreneurial foundation of the group, working with our businesses and partners to develop new approaches to tackle the tough issues. It's really about ideas and people – finding the best of both and then helping them to scale up. Our fundamental belief is that doing good is great for business. It's not about the 'golden charitable cheque' but, rather, it's about making sure that we leverage everything we have across our businesses – especially the wonderful entrepreneurial spirit of our people – to drive change.

There is *such a thing as enlightened self-interest, and we should encourage it. It* is *possible to turn a profit while making the world a better place.* And, inasmuch as there can ever be answers to the problems of the world, capitalism – generously and humanely defined and humbly working with others who understand the issues and solutions – can create some of those answers. More about Virgin's ventures in this area later, but first I want to tell you about some of the people who have inspired me.

We've had many impressive and influential people come and stay with us on Necker Island. But the visit of Bill and Melinda Gates at Easter in 2001 provided me with plenty of inspiration for what I should be doing in a philanthropic way.

It takes a bit of time to get to know Bill Gates. He's cerebral and intense about all he does. This intensity made for an excellent game of tennis which ended in an honourable draw.

During his visit he spoke to me a great deal about the Bill and Melinda Gates Foundation, which in 2008 had assets of $37.6 billion, making it the world's largest charity and a force for immense good in troubled parts of the world. In 2006, the foundation handed out $1.54 billion in grants in three areas: global health, global education and programmes in America, including the creation of forty-three new high schools in New York City.

I wrote in my notebook: '*He's very involved with it. Not just giving away billions but reading up about African diseases and seriously trying to help with Aids/malaria/tuberculosis and educating people to use condoms.*'

At that time, the Bill and Melinda Gates Foundation had just overtaken, in the value of its trust fund, the Wellcome Trust – one of the UK's long-established charities, which has funded research into human and animal health since 1936 and was spending £650 million a year. Since then, the Foundation has grown dramatically and is now, by far, the largest charitable foundation in the world, alleviating poverty, disease and ignorance around the globe. Bill and Melinda have done such a brilliant job as 'venture philanthropists' that Warren Buffett, who pipped Gates in 2008 as the world's richest man, handed over much of his substantial wealth for them to look after.

My wife Joan didn't know what to make of Bill at first, though she warmed to him and enjoyed spending time with his wife, Melinda. Melinda was then in her late thirties, a charming and intelligent woman. She had amassed a huge amount of knowledge about malaria-carrying mosquitoes, tuberculosis, Aids and rotavirus, a severe form of diarrhoea that kills more than 500,000 infants a year. Effectively she was giving Bill a running personal tutorial on some of the key issues in global health. While Bill was interested in the actual microbiological science of vaccine research and finding a scientific solution, Melinda wanted to alleviate as much suffering as possible now.

I went sailing with Bill – discovering to my surprise that he used to race sailing boats – and he told me about the Microsoft Xbox, which he was about to launch on to the market to take on the Sony PlayStation. 'It's the biggest thing I've ever done,' he said. But he was thoughtful, and I sensed that his mission in life was changing. He had achieved so much with Microsoft, building it to become one of the most powerful businesses on the planet. In little more than twenty years he had changed the face of the modern world. Now he was turning his formidable brain to solving some of the apparently intractable problems facing our Earth. He told me he went to see Nelson Mandela. 'I said: "Most people think you're a saint. Tell me the truth. Did you hate the people who put you in prison?"'

'Yes, I did,' was the answer to Bill's question. 'For twelve years I lived off those people and I hated them. Then I realised they couldn't take my mind or my heart away.'

Bill was astounded and said meeting Mandela was a seminal point in his life: 'He taught me about living.'

That must have been quite a moment: the richest human in the world talks to the most revered human and acquires a new purpose and a challenge in his life. I think it may eventually go into the history books as a turning point – the start of something big.

In January 2008, Bill Gates was a guest at the World Economic Forum in Davos, in Switzerland. He said: 'We have to find a way to make the aspects of capitalism that serve wealthier people serve poorer people as well.' He has called this idea 'creative capitalism', saying that by harnessing the basic factor that drives capitalism – self-interest – creative capitalism can enhance the interests of the giver *and* the recipient.

I agree. I think capitalism is a proven system: it works. But it has got a lot of faults. Breathtaking wealth goes to relatively few people. This would not matter so much, were it not for the fact that the very poorest in society are destitute, lacking even the basic amenities for survival. This being the case, an enormous responsibility falls on a successful business leader. Leaders need to reinvest their wealth by creating new jobs or by tackling the social problems of the world (ideally, both – which is what makes Muhammad Yunus's microcredit movement so exciting).

History has thrown up no viable alternative to the free exchange of capital, goods and services, and the enterprise of law-abiding people. But capitalism as an ideology needs work and reform. Capitalism has to be more than the survival of the fittest.

My own fairly unexceptional view is that capitalism should pay far more attention to people and to the resources of this planet. I call it 'Gaia capitalism' for short, and as a tribute to the work of Professor James Lovelock, who has spent a lifetime tracing the life-sustaining connections between the living and non-living parts of the Earth. Human behaviour and human capital have to work with our planet.

More generally, entrepreneurs and wealth creators around the world must be a positive force for good. There is nothing unbusiness-like about sharing the benefits of your industry with happy, fulfilled people and a planet that is going to be there in all its glory for our children and grandchildren.

In 1997, while proposing a lottery scheme in Johannesburg, I called upon the world's business community to run their companies more ethically – and, to get the ball rolling, to adopt a zero-tolerance approach to bribery. Perhaps the most unethical and dangerous abuse of a company's financial muscle around the world is the use of bribes to secure contracts. If company directors bribe politicians they start a rot at the very top. Police, customs officers, tax officials and the judiciary will then start saying to themselves: if our bosses are accepting bribes, why shouldn't we?

In my speech, I kept my definition of ethics simple. Business ethics interest me, and ethical questions are less complex than some academics on business courses make out. I said we should all pledge to do nothing that we'd regret reading about in the press. In the developed world, we're extremely fortunate in having a free press. Being misquoted or misinterpreted can be frustrating, and a bad journalist can do a lot of damage, but set against the big picture, these are really just inconveniences. A free press is a society's conscience. You may, for instance, be trying to discourage a competitor. A scheme is sitting on your desk that would undoubtedly work. But it rides close to the wind. These things can get complicated, so you can't rely entirely on gut instinct. If the public and the media got to read this document, what would they do? Would they shrug, or laugh at your cheek – or would you and your company be vilified?

As we work to improve and reform capitalism, I think this connection between free commerce and free expression will become ever more evident. And whilst having a free press is a wonderful check, ideally it will be needed less and less as a conscience as we all start putting the well-being of people and the environment at the core of our business.

In June 1999, Nelson Mandela invited me to his leaving party and to the inauguration of his successor, Thabo Mbeki. At the banquet, my neighbour, a doctor, told me about her hospital – which receives more patients than any other in the world – and I agreed to visit.

The next morning I went to Soweto. After the previous evening's pomp and glamour, I was brought back down to earth with an incredible bump. The hospital was worse than she had described. The accident and emergency section was like a Vietnam War movie. The queue for medicines stretched for half a mile. I have a deep respect for South Africa and I wanted to help so much. This was a country with fabulous potential and people who were so warm and friendly. Yet a staggering 20 per cent of female South Africans coming into antenatal clinics now had HIV, she told me, and medicines were just not going to the people who needed them. We had already done some work with HIV/Aids in the UK and I was now determined to do everything in my power to stop this unnecessary human suffering in South Africa.

For some years, Virgin had been investing in companies to help drive the South African economy. Virgin Unite had also started to look at creating opportunities for young South Africans. One of my favourite examples of this is the Branson School of Entrepreneurship at the CIDA City Campus. This took off when CIDA's charismatic leader, Taddy Blecher, literally chased Jean and me down the street to sell me on the idea of forming a partnership to assist financially disadvantaged young people to start up their own businesses. As I write this, I have just spent my birthday with some students at the school. Their energy and positive spirit always inspires and humbles me. One after the other, they got up and talked about their small businesses, which began as part of the Branson School and now gave economic freedom not only to these young people, but also to their families and communities. This was the best birthday gift I could have asked for! I wrote down the following quote from one of them in my notebook:

> *One thing that I like about the Branson School is that it's a place where you feel like when you're there you get inspired – there's that inspiration that is drawn from the Branson School. You're always excited. The moment you get there, you forget your problems, and you just focus on growing your business. To all the beautiful Virgin people, I would like to wish you guys all the best, and I need to tell you something. Please keep on supporting the Branson School. We love you. Thank you.*

Even with this incredible next generation of South Africans starting to build a positive future, I could see that Aids was sapping the country's ability to function properly. A vibrant and dynamic economy needs healthy people to maintain the fabric of society for those who are ill, infirm and disabled, but there is a tipping point beyond which the levels of disease and death are so debilitating that any kind of enterprise is impossible. This was the situation that I could foresee arising in South Africa. And I wasn't doing nearly enough about it yet.

For me it was the story of Donald Makhubele, one of the waiters at our Virgin game reserve, Ulusaba, that gave the tragedy of Aids a human face. Donald was a poet and musician, a wonderful character who wrote eloquently about the local land and its people – and about his illness. His own testament was deeply humbling. He said: 'I'm a songwriter who writes about HIV and Aids . . . Let us work together as one, to be proud of ourselves and have the same purpose in order to defeat the enemy. This is not a disease but it is a war that is in Africa, aiming to destroy our continent.'

Donald died of Aids-induced tuberculosis. When he passed away I pledged that no other Virgin employee would die unnecessarily. I thought it was wrong that any of the hundreds of foreign companies operating in Africa should allow their people to die of Aids, and the same should apply to local companies.

At Ulusaba, we first had to show that we had no inhibitions about HIV. Nelson Mandela had told me about a time when he had visited some Aids orphans who lived in a hut. Instead of throwing the food over a fence, he ventured in and spent some time with the girls. As he walked back to the car, his driver was so scared of catching something from him that he jumped out of the car and ran away. He said that Princess Diana had done more than anyone by cuddling a young child with HIV – this simple act had been a huge positive step forward in Africa.

So Joan and I invited a wonderful doctor and extraordinary social entrepreneur, Hugo Templeman, to come and see us. We then gathered all our staff at the game reserve and took an HIV/Aids test in front of them. We tried to encourage as many people as possible to come forward and also take the test – and most of them did. Afterwards, we invited some young people with HIV to speak to all of us about how antiretroviral drugs had saved their lives.

In 2005, Virgin Unite worked with a partner to fund two films, created by Africans and translated into multiple languages, to show how the HIV/Aids drugs worked and how the human immune system worked. In one of our African businesses we found that 24 per cent of our staff had HIV, which meant nearly a quarter would die within six or seven years without drug treatment. I was shocked – yet we were typical of so many other businesses working across Africa.

I said our organisation would supply anybody working for us with free antiretroviral drugs. And then we rolled out the 0% Challenge across the whole of our Virgin business: that no staff should ever die from Aids, that no one else would become HIV positive, that no HIV-positive pregnant mothers would pass on HIV to their baby and that we would have zero tolerance towards any type of discrimination against people who were HIV positive. The 0% Challenge is not only helping to stop needless suffering, but also makes absolute sense for our business to ensure we keep our people happy and healthy.

I went on a tour of local projects fighting the spread of HIV and Aids. We asked to spend time visiting as many clinics as possible to see first hand the medical crisis – I was already well acquainted with the facts and figures of the situation, but I was keen to gain a better impression of the scale of the epidemic.

The images of that tour are still too harrowing for words. In clinic after clinic, the vision of hell was clear for all to see. The sight of row upon row of near skeletons, both men and women, often with their babies and children by the bed, was utterly appalling. And the waiting rooms were full of people waiting to get into beds where people had died just hours before. These were not hospitals. They were places where people went to die. And yet we knew that this problem could be tackled. We even knew *how*.

I wrote in my notebook: '*A pregnant mother with HIV or Aids giving birth to her child is likely to give that child HIV. For as little as fifty US cents the mother can be given medicine six weeks prior to birth, and the baby can have an injection six weeks after birth, and nearly 100 per cent of such children lead a normal life, free of HIV.*' Yet very few pregnant women in South Africa had access to these life-saving drugs.

All this troubled me deeply. As I returned regularly to South Africa to build up our companies, it seemed as if the HIV/Aids epidemic was getting worse. Since the first case in 1982, millions had died and the prevalence in South Africa was higher than anywhere else in the world. By 2006, the incidence rate in South Africa was up to around 29 per cent for females coming into antenatal clinics.

Those who know they have HIV must be given hope. They can't be consigned to a living death and told that their life will be extinguished in a horrible way in five years – seven if they're lucky. Antiretroviral drugs are a lifesaver. Before our zero tolerance campaign had started, one of our employees at Ulusaba had been reduced almost to a skeleton – he was barely a day away from death – when we managed to obtain the right drugs for him. A month later, he was back to normal weight. Three months later, he was back at work. If antiretroviral drugs are used properly, a person can live a full life. The drugs also cut dramatically the chance of that person spreading the disease. We decided to use our business skills to partner with some great organisations and come up with ways to help stop this health emergency. One of my thoughts was to help build clinics that can sustain themselves over time and start to administer drugs and ensure that condoms are distributed. Virgin Unite teamed up with Hugo Templeman, plus Brian Brink from Anglo American plc, the South African government and the US President's Emergency Programme for Aids Relief to set up the Bhubezi Community Health Care Centre in Mpumalanga – a brilliant example of the kind of public and private partnership that really works, where local health officials and the business community are working hand in glove to fight Aids more effectively.

Hugo's idea was to create a one-stop-shop for primary health care, to include a pharmacy, X-ray and obstetrics facilities, an HIV/Aids patient care clinic, and a laboratory. Hugo had not only built such a centre; he had helped create an entire economic infrastructure with basic utilities such as water, electricity, roads and even a bakery, a car wash and a nappy-manufacturing factory! Bhubezi was a great opportunity for Hugo to develop and extend his ideas.

In 2006, I returned to open the Bhubezi centre. In the interim, thousands more people had suffered and died from Aids and thousands more had become infected with HIV. Of course, I wasn't alone in my concern. There were dozens and dozens of worthy and learned organisations and donor countries working to eradicate Aids. In fact, the number of organisations actually helping out was crippling some of the effectiveness on the front lines. We spoke to one doctor who said that 40 per cent of his time and his staff's time was spent on managing over a hundred different funders. With this in mind, I worked with Virgin Unite to look at how we could set up a

'War Room' for sub-Saharan Africa to help better coordinate and mobilise resources in the fight against diseases.

During my trip in 2006, after some incredibly emotional visits to hospices and still angry at myself for letting Donald die, I decided that I could no longer be silent about the issue. Much to the dismay of the Virgin Unite team, who were worried that this would slow down or shut down our ability to progress with some of the projects, I went on national TV stating that I felt the leader of South Africa and his health minister were guilty of genocide and should be tried for crimes against humanity.

The next morning – 27 October 2006 – the *Financial Mail* reported: 'British billionaire Richard Branson has slammed President Thabo Mbeki and health minister Manto Tshabalala-Msimang for presiding over "a government [that] is effectively killing its own people".'

I stared at the report. Here I was, a supposedly non-political industry figure, commenting on key political figures in a country where I was doing business. From a purely commercial perspective, it certainly wasn't wise. But I felt, and still feel, *it's more important to do what you believe to be right in life*, and if this contradicts your business interests, so be it. Business can't be allowed to float above ordinary morality.

But this wasn't about me. This was about a country and a people and, yes, a leadership that I loved. I wanted the ANC to be remembered for the good work it had done for the country, not for turning a blind eye and effectively killing a large percentage of the population by refusing to accept that HIV and Aids are linked.

I immediately received a letter from President Mbeki and, much to his credit, he did not condemn me for speaking out, but instead engaged in a dialogue about what he felt needed to be done. He also offered an honest perspective on his views of the issues that South Africa was facing, from HIV to the lack of job opportunities. After several open and frank communications, we both had the guts to put our differences aside and agree to partner up on building the war room to tackle disese in sub-Saharan Africa. This was the first step on a journey that we hope will make a great difference. As I write this, I have just joined Priya Bery and Jean Oelwang from Virgin Unite for a week of meetings with the ANC government, some amazing South African entrepreneurs and many other health partners to prepare for the launch of the war room.

The war room will become a memorial to Donald Makhubele and all the countless others who have died of disease in Africa. It is also another example whereby entrepreneurial skills coupled with health expertise and knowledge from the front lines will together build a powerful force for change.

One day in April 2006, I received a copy of the starfish parable – from Starfish, a charity that focuses on the Aids orphan crisis in South Africa.

A girl walks along a beach, throwing starfish back into the sea, when she meets an old man. The man asks the girl why she is throwing starfish into the ocean. She says: 'The sun is up and the tide is going out, if I don't throw them back they will all die.' The old man says, 'But there's a whole beach and it runs on for miles. You can't possibly make a difference.' The girl picks up a starfish and throws it back in the sea. 'It made a difference to that one.'

What can you do to make a difference? And why should you do it?

If the account of some of our work in Africa has leapt rather dizzyingly from small-scale innovations to big-policy manoeuvres and back again, it did so for the very good reason that the scale of one's social investments *doesn't matter*.

What matters is that you operate as a force for good at every scale available to you. An Aids policy rolled out across the staff of your business is as important as an Aids policy rolled out across the entire Virgin Group, or across an entire nation. The important thing is to have the idea, and realise it, however modestly.

This includes looking at your future investment strategy to try to find business opportunities that will also help tackle tough issues.

Over the last five years Virgin Unite has grown into a platform to help all of us across the Virgin Group drive change. It brings everyone together with a common focus to try to do our best for people and the planet. Virgin Unite is making sure that it's not just me trying to do my bit, but instead the whole Virgin community works to do whatever we can – small or large – to make a difference.

These differences come in all shapes, depending on the business. With Virgin Atlantic, in their quest to become the most sustainable airline possible, they are looking at various aspects of the operation to see how they can reduce their impact on the environment. One thing I'm particularly excited about is the biofuels test they successfully completed a few months ago. Finding an alternative environmentally friendly fuel source will be one of the biggest contributions we could ever make as an airline.

Dan Schulman and his team at Virgin Mobile USA have worked with Virgin Unite, their staff, customers and young people in the US to come up with ways they can use their core assets to make a difference for the 1.5 million homeless teenagers in the US. It's still shocking that in such wealthy countries we are allowing teenagers to live on the streets. Virgin Mobile have used their text messaging communication channels, website, lobbying voices and anything else they can find to help build awareness of the issue and to raise money. They teamed up with singer/songwriter Jewel and Virgin Unite to lobby the US government who have now made November 'Teen Homeless Month'. This has been a great initiative not only for our partners, such as Stand Up for Kids, and the young people they serve, but also for the business. It has truly built a community among our customers, staff and homeless teenagers, who have come together to drive change and learn from one another.

Sometimes the businesses focus on their own programmes and other times they come together as a group to make greater impact. For example, one initiative we recently launched is finding and supporting the best grassroots ideas that have environmental benefits and also help to create local jobs, from employing Aboriginal people in Australia to practise their ancient land-burning techniques which minimise carbon output and protect biodiversity, to working in Kenya on an ecolodge that will help the Green Belt Movement sustain their reforesting projects. We hope that these smaller projects will scale up over the coming years, using the fight against climate change and the need to protect our natural resources as an opportunity also to fight poverty in the world.

Good small solutions are like gold dust as it's often possible to scale them up, or replicate them manyfold, so that they acquire global influence. Muhammad Yunus's Grameen Bank is a classic example.

So don't let relative scale put you off your goals. *Think realistically and creatively about what you can achieve.* You can do this whether you're a corporate manager or a sole trader – and what you learn by way of entrepreneurship will directly benefit you in your business.

If there is one line that could sum up all the varied and curious lessons I've learned in business, it's this: *scale doesn't matter – people do.* This thinking is reflected in some of my current work: creating small entrepreneurial 'war rooms' to tackle big issues. So let me show you, finally, how I'm working with Virgin Unite and other partners to set up a war room to help deal with the biggest, most elusive, most pressing and most abstract problem of all: climate change.

Reading comic books, when I was growing up, one of my recurring nightmares was the invasion of aliens from Mars. It was terrifying stuff: everywhere I looked, bug-eyed monsters were zapping humans with their ray guns. The sci-fi films of the 1950s such as *The Day the Earth Stood Still* and *The War of the Worlds* regularly showed our planet under attack. It was a horrifying prospect. The solution was invariably that all the world's nations had to bury their differences and get together to ward off a common enemy.

The equivalent of that alien invasion is already here. It's impossible to see, it's odourless, and it's everywhere. Our war is against carbon. Not an alien menace, after all, but – irony of ironies – one of the building blocks of life.

On the Celsius scale, zero is the freezing point and 100 degrees the boiling point of water. For the last 10,000 years, the average surface temperature of the Earth has been around 14°C. The hottest recorded temperature has been 58°C at El Azizia in the Sahara Desert in 1922. The year 2007 was the warmest on record.

But if the average surface temperature rises by 5°C – and scientists now say it will unless we wean ourselves off this business of burning fuels that release CO_2 into the atmosphere – then our planet becomes a hostile and arid place. We are now at 14.5°C – moving to 19°C will be disastrous. So we must act now.

Earlier this year, I was clearing out some possessions of the previous owner on Mosquito Island, which is being developed as a low-carbon ecotourist destination in the Caribbean, and stumbled on some old picture books written by Jacques-Yves Cousteau. Cousteau, who invented the aqualung, warned about the destruction of the sea. In the 1970s, he filmed a polluted section of the Mediterranean devoid of life, and these shocking images led to immediate environmental action.

In his first book, *Window in the Sea*, published in 1973, Cousteau posed the question: What happens if our oceans die?

If the oceans of the Earth should die – that is, if life in the oceans were suddenly, somehow to come to an end – it would be the final as well as the greatest catastrophe in the troublous story of men and the other animals and plants with whom man shares this planet.

With no life in the seas the carbon dioxide content in the atmosphere would set forth on an inexorable climb. When this CO_2 level passed a certain point the 'greenhouse effect' would *come into operation: heat radiating outwards from Earth to space would be trapped beneath the stratosphere, shooting up sea-level temperatures. At both North and South Poles the icecaps would melt and oceans would rise perhaps 100 feet in a small number of years.*

The calamity we are facing is not unknown, not unforeseen, not even surprising. Cousteau wrote his prophetic warning thirty-five years ago.

Every business around the world must now radically change its thinking. In every aspect of its operation, it must do much more to reduce the amount of carbon dioxide it releases into the air. And this won't be easy, since the endeavours of humans in agriculture and business, responding to the demands of consumers and customers, have been partly responsible for creating the problem in the first place.

As mentioned, all of our businesses are looking at how they can re-invent the way they operate to try to minimise the impact they have on the environment. This issue has personally captured my imagination and set me off on a journey to discover new approaches.

First, I had to muster the facts. Then I could look at the marketplace, and come up with a scheme. But I also needed an expert sounding board – which I found in both Professor James Lovelock, a man who is the environmental equivalent of Nelson Mandela, and Tim Flannery, an ecologist whose book *The Weather Makers* is the best guide to our current situation that I have read.

Scientists have been able to drill a deep hole into the Antarctic ice caps to collect core samples which they have examined. The ice samples contain air bubbles. From the amount of carbon dioxide in the air trapped inside these icy time capsules, they can tell how temperatures have risen over the years. The invention of the steam engine and the arrival of the Industrial Revolution in the 1780s in Britain began this cycle of the age-old process. But even more influential were the medical and social advances that gifted us clean water, sanitation, a better diet and inoculations against common diseases. Suddenly, there were more of us. The population of the world exploded, and continues to explode, and virtually everyone on the planet is consuming many times more energy than their parents ever did and we are now in 'deficit financing' of the planet – the ecological equivalent of sub-prime lending.

Before 1800 there were about 280 parts per million (ppm) of CO_2 in the atmosphere. Since then industry has burnt, smelted and forged, and humans have farmed, cooked and heated themselves with huge quantities of carbon. Still, for generations, there was equilibrium as vegetation used atmospheric carbon dioxide to grow. But now we are overdrawn in the carbon bank and heading towards a Northern Rock or Bear Stearns situation very soon.

The economic prosperity of the modern world has been built on two deadly but energy-rich hydrocarbons: coal and oil. Over many millennia, most of Earth's carbon has been locked away in the ground.

Dead plants and animals, buried in the ground and compressed, became fossil fuels. If human activity were to extract all of this carbon from the ground and burn it, the carbon released would combine with oxygen to produce carbon dioxide, and then we wouldn't have to worry about global warming any more: we'd already be dead from asphyxiation. There wouldn't be enough oxygen left for us to breathe.

In July 2005, the Stern Review on climate change was announced by Gordon Brown, then the UK's Chancellor of Exchequer. Sir Nicholas Stern, who was former chief economist at the World Bank, wanted to assess the economic benefits of moving to a low-carbon economy, and the potential for adapting to climate change. The review was published in October 2006 and I found it an impressive addition to the debate. He reported that the atmospheric concentration of greenhouse gases were already up from 280ppm during the Industrial Revolution to 430ppm. This is set to rise to 550ppm by 2035, bringing at least a 77 per cent chance that the average global temperature will increase by more than two degrees. A rise of two degrees is the maximum that scientists believe we can tolerate, before our current climate suffers a runaway collapse.

Most alarming was Stern's warning that with no action on emissions, the world's temperature could go up by more than five degrees by the end of the twenty-first century. This kind of rise would send human life on Earth into unknown territory. He pointed out that even a three- or four-degree rise would cause a serious decline in crop yields, and sea level rises that would threaten London, New York, Shanghai, Hong Kong and Cairo. It would also mean the collapse of the Amazon rainforest and the possible shutting down of the Gulf Stream – the ocean current delivering temperate climates to much of Europe.

Stern calculated that the overall costs and risks of climate change would be the equivalent of losing at least 5 per cent of global GDP. But if a wider range of risks was taken into account, such as the spread of disease, then this could rise to 20 per cent or more. On purely technical grounds, this is a risk to business that now has to be taken seriously – and factored into every part of commercial thinking.

In order to stabilise atmospheric gases at around 500 to 550ppm, global emissions at 2006 levels would have to be reduced by 80 per cent. The challenge is that emissions must peak, then fall by 1 to 3 per cent a year for the foreseeable future. Among Stern's proposals there were four sets of measures that were of particular interest to the Virgin Group: reducing demand for goods and services that produced a great deal of emissions; an increased efficiency in any engines when we did use carbon; swifter action on non-energy emissions, such as the burning and clearing of tropical forest land; and switching to low-carbon technologies for power, heat and transport.

Some global businesses are making an effort to tackle the issue, but piecemeal efforts are not going to be enough. Our war against carbon dioxide needs to be expanded by government and by business into every product, every application and every design. We also need to do something to extract as much existing carbon dioxide as possible from the atmosphere. That was the challenge that drew my immediate attention.

Steve Howard, the CEO of the Climate Change Group, believes we have a few years to make a massive global difference – or human life as we know it could cease to exist within a couple of hundred. I am an optimist and I believe that business can – and will – find the solutions to this massive problem. But for our children's sake, we have to embrace this challenge, every day, from now on.

Perhaps I took nature too much for granted. I was brought up in stunning English countryside, surrounded by wildlife, birds and trees. A love of the natural environment has been a big part of my life. But it was a visit to my London home by a former US presidential candidate that was the tipping point for my view of how that love should inform the way businesses are run.

The former US vice president, Al Gore, came to visit me in Holland Park. I had never met him before. He asked to see me because he was looking for a business leader who was recognised on a global basis. It seemed that I fitted the bill. He thought I could make a gesture that might bring other business leaders along too. He spent two hours giving me, Will Whitehorn and Jean Oelwang a guided tour of the issues surrounding climate change – a presentation that was later to reach many millions as his Oscar-winning documentary, *An Inconvenient Truth*.

Prior to Al Gore's visit, I had read a book called *The Skeptical Environmentalist*, which was dangerously convenient reading for someone in business! It argued that global warming could even be a positive thing that would stop the world heading for the next ice age. But as a result of meeting Al Gore, I went back to other scientists and other thinkers. I rediscovered the work of Crispin Tickell and James Lovelock. And by the end of my reading, I had reached an inconvenient truth of my own: that I had to do something rather than be passive.

Finally I was handed a book that stopped me in my tracks. It was Tim Flannery's *The Weather Makers*. Tim's thesis was fascinating – and alarming. It put flesh on the bones of the concept of global warming. It gave concrete examples of what was happening and why. I devoured its many beautifully written stories. One in particular sticks in my mind: how the American pioneers cut and burnt the great eastern forests and burnt and grazed the western plains and deserts. Eventually, the vegetation grew back – which is why most of America's forests are less than sixty years old and regrowing vigorously in the process, absorbing half a billion tonnes of CO_2 a year. This has helped cool the planet. Once this vegetation matures, however, it will stop extracting as much CO_2, just when we need its assistance most.

Tim's book was a gem, and I noticed that he returned again and again to the work of James Lovelock. Tim was greatly influenced by Lovelock's book *Gaia*, which talked persuasively about the Earth as a single, living entity.

I had to meet James Lovelock and find out what he thought. One of the privileges of my life is that I get to meet many brilliant people. Jim is an independent thinker, inventor and scientist. In his late eighties, he is sharp and lucid. An honorary professor at Oxford University, he has won many medals and accolades for his original environmental thinking.

As a young mathematician and scientist, James Lovelock regularly visited the Jet Propulsion Laboratories in Pasadena. The laboratory was closely connected with NASA and the American space programme, and undertook work for unmanned space missions. Jim's inventions have gone into several of the interplanetary probes NASA has launched over the years to explore other planets. Jim also worked on a remote-controlled microbiological laboratory, which was to be dispatched in a rocket to Mars to test whether the planet could sustain bacteria, fungi and other microorganisms. It was then that Jim began to pose the basic question: What is life – and how can we recognise it?

Working with his acclaimed colleague Dian Hitchcock, he began to study the potential for life on Mars. And as they worked, the scientists naturally turned back, for comparison, to Earth – its biosphere and atmosphere. They came to the conclusion that the only feasible explanation of our planet's atmosphere was that it was being manipulated on a daily basis from the surface. The constant flux of all the different gases in the Earth's atmosphere was itself proof of living activity.

Jim's emerging theory was that the world and its atmosphere were one living and breathing system. It was a radical view for its time and rejected by the scientific consensus. However, Carl Sagan, the editor of the astronomy journal *Icarus*, was intrigued enough to publish Jim's views.

When, in 1965, the US government abandoned the Martian exploration project that Jim had been working on, he went to work for Shell Research, to consider the effects of air pollution and its global consequences. This was in 1966, and three years before the foundation of Friends of the Earth. Jim warned about the build-up of particles which were then depleting the ozone layer – a thin skin of gas which protects us from the sun's radiation. One of his many inventions was the electron capture device which was essential for detecting and measuring the atmospheric concentration of chlorofluorocarbons (or CFCs) – the chemicals responsible for breaking down the ozone layer.

It was his friend, the writer William Golding, author of the *Lord of the Flies*, who gave him the name. Golding suggested 'Gaia' after the Greek goddess of the Earth. (It's from her that we get the root of words like geography and geology.) Jim put forward his 'Gaia hypothesis' at a scientific meeting about the origins of life on Earth at Princeton, New Jersey, in 1968. Gaia is Jim's shorthand for the complex interactions between the Earth's biosphere, atmosphere, oceans, rocks and soils. Earth, in his view, is effectively a self-regulating mechanism – a machine for life.

When I first spoke to Jim he told me that in the 1970s, he had no clear idea how that machine worked, but as a scientist he knew that the Earth was different from our nearest neighbours in our solar system, and he was fascinated by how the Earth, unlike Mars and Venus, constantly managed to make itself a fit and healthy place to live.

Jim Lovelock has become a great friend, and he has shared with me his work on his long-overdue follow-up book – a soliloquy for his beloved Gaia. Even in his advancing years, his freedom of thought and mind is astounding. I'm not an academic and I struggle with some of the detailed scientific technical stuff, but Jim's descriptions are poignant, beautiful and understandable.

Jim knows he isn't going to live for ever, and that his ideas will disappear unless we capture them now. So he has been sending me a host of ideas in the hope that I can turn at least some of them into businesses. He talks about dropping pipes into the ocean, about burying algae at sea, about putting extra sulphur into the atmosphere. He is not a crank, or a lone voice in the wilderness. He is an internationally celebrated and revered figure and his ideas have a lot of currency. What is lacking, however, is the sort of serious, heavily funded research necessary to show which of his ideas are most worth pursuing.

In April 2006, almost in the same post as the letter from the charity Starfish, I found a letter from former US president Bill Clinton, inviting me to the Clinton Global Initiative, to be held in New York that September. I fully respect the work that Bill is doing to tackle social and environmental issues, so a few days later I agreed to participate. Bill also phoned me and asked if there was any gesture that I would be willing to make.

I was sitting in the bath when it occurred to me: why not just divert all the profits made by the Virgin Group from our carbon-creating businesses – such as the airlines and trains – and invest it in developing the cleaner technologies of the future? I'd also look at business research on wind power and solar power and anything that could replace the fossil fuels. When I briefed him beforehand, Bill was excited. He wanted to make it the centrepiece of the meeting in September. I said I would like Al Gore, Bill's former vice president, to be there as well. I said that without Al visiting me I wouldn't have come up with the idea in the first place. Bill Clinton's introduction went like this:

'I've had the privilege in my increasingly long life to know a lot of amazing people and Richard Branson is one of the most interesting, creative, genuinely committed people I have ever known.'

I gulped with embarrassment when I heard about this. Thanks, Bill – but then you expected me to *speak*?

Happily for me, I wasn't in the hall. An aide shouted up to him: 'He's not here yet. He's on his way.' As ever, I had missed my cue. I was in the loo.

Bill coolly segued into the next item. Well, I made it – eventually. And I outlined my plans for the Virgin Group. 'What we've decided to do is to put any proceeds received by the Virgin Group from our transportation businesses into tackling environmental issues, and hopefully it will be something like $3 billion over a number of years ... Like Al Gore, I don't believe it is too late. I think we do have a handful, two handfuls of years to get the ball rolling, to address the problem. And if we can develop alternative fuels, if people can take risks on developing enzymes, if we can try to get cellulose ethanol, then replace the dirty fuels that we're using at the moment, then I think we've got a great future.'

Al stepped up. 'Richard,' he said, 'I have one question. I didn't hear it on the list, and I want to make sure. Are the expected profits from the rocket ships also going into this?' I nodded and said: 'By the way, they are environmentally friendly rocket ships!'

The conference was well received, and my announcement did what Al Gore wanted. That a business leader in the transport industry admitted there were problems with global warming and that something had to be done about it made the headlines. And this would make it more difficult for the oil and coal companies to continue to deny their responsibilities. But I decided I needed to help make a further step – and this time, a prize made the best sense. We set up a prize to encourage every inventive thinker to try to come up with a way of extracting carbon dioxide out of the Earth's atmosphere. If that could be achieved, the temperature of our planet could be regulated by mankind, extracting carbon dioxide from the atmosphere when it gets too hot.

On 9 February 2007, we announced the Virgin Earth Challenge. To win the $25 million prize, participants will have to demonstrate a provable, commercially viable design which will result in the removal or displacement of a significant amount of environmental greenhouse gases from the atmosphere. The challenge will run for ten years.

Al Gore agreed to be a judge; so too did Tim Flannery and James Lovelock. I also asked two other distinguished people to join the panel – Sir Crispin Tickell, the director of the Policy Foresight Programme at the James Martin Institute for Science and Civilisation at Oxford University, and Dr James Hansen, professor at the Columbia University Earth Institute and head of the NASA Goddard Institute for Space Studies in New York City. This was a heavyweight group of assessors.

The judges will decide whether a scheme has the potential to make a significant difference to global warming, and whether the prize should be awarded to one winner or shared between two or three. We found that setting more prescriptive targets was pointless, because there are so many ways to address the greenhouse gas problem. This point was very well put by James Lovelock, who was as sharp as ever when commenting on our early suggestions:

> *I was surprised to read in the outline of the Virgin Earth Challenge that the requirement for the prizewinner was the removal of at least one billion tonnes of CO_2 per year. This seems*

small compared with the near 30 billion tonnes we add yearly. In fact, 6.3 billion humans breathe out yearly nearly two billion tonnes of CO_2 – trying to restore the Earth by removing one or even two billion tonnes a year is a bit like trying to bail out a leaky rowing boat with a teaspoon . . .

He said we should keep in mind that a billion tonnes of carbon could be taken out of the atmosphere if we synthesised our food, which would release huge areas of farmland to revert to natural vegetation.

Is it too late to make the conditions harder and at the same time more general? It would be a shame to have to turn down a good proposal for a method for making tasty and nutritious food by biochemical synthesis directly from air and water.

I knew I had to get Jim more involved, and Will Whitehorn offered to go and see him. Returning from a climate change meeting in France with former president Jacques Chirac, he agreed to complete the line-up of judges for the prize. 'It's a grand idea,' he wrote, 'and who knows, it might just promote the discovery of an answer. We have all spent far too long sleepwalking towards extinction and need an incentive.'

I think that all business people need to have sceptical scientific friends who can challenge, prod and stimulate. Jim was certainly doing this for me.

A successful application for the Virgin Earth Challenge could very well take into account the Earth's self-regulating ability. In September 2007, Jim and his colleague Chris Rapley wrote to the science journal *Nature*: 'The removal of 500 gigatonnes of carbon dioxide from the air by human endeavour is beyond our current technological capability. If we can't "heal the planet" directly, we may be able to help the planet heal itself.'

One way to do this would be to lower vertical pipes into the ocean. Wave power could enable a simple pump to drive cold, nutrient-rich waters up from the depths to the relatively barren ocean surface. This would promote the growth of algae, which would consume CO_2 and produce dimethyl sulphide, the chemical that turns humid air into clouds.

Jim mentioned this example to me because he was attending a meeting in Washington the following week and wanted to discuss the idea with scientists and engineers there. He recently wrote to me with a new idea:

More and more I think our best chance of reversing global heating lies in the burial of charcoal on land and in the ocean. If most farm waste were turned into charcoal yearly on the farms and then ploughed in, this alone would do much more than anything otherwise proposed. More than this, the preparation of charcoal yields a modest amount of biofuel and the total could be quite large. It would take longer to establish the same scheme with ocean farms but if we really intend to do something this is the way to go.

It's an ingenious notion – and might even become a successful business proposition.

Within the first year, the Virgin Earth Challenge attracted more than 3,000 notes of interest – and this was very exciting. But one thing began to dawn on me: prizes do take time to produce results. Peter Diamandis came up with the X Prize concept for commercial space flight in 1994 and over the course of several years had presented it to numerous people for funding – including Virgin – but it wasn't won by Burt Rutan and Paul Allen until ten years later. As fighters in the war against global warming, we were all too well aware that time was one thing in very short supply.

A prize of $25 million was an incentive for departments at a lot of universities – but I began to ask what if there was a bounty ten or even twenty times this size? Perhaps this would attract the major industries to divert significant research and development into the project. A prize of this magnitude would do a great deal to stimulate the large corporates with their massive R&D spending power.

With this in mind, early in 2008, I accepted an invitation to address the UN's two-day workshop on climate change, where I was made UN Citizen of the Year by the Secretary General Ban Ki-moon for my work on climate change. As the owner of several airlines, even I can see the irony in that!

I already had a lot of sympathy for the views of Jeffrey Sachs, outlined in his book, *Common Wealth: Economics for a Crowded Planet*, when he stated: 'When it comes to problem-solving on a global scale, we remain weighed down by cynicism, defeatism and outdated institutions. A world of untrammelled market forces and competing nation states offers no automatic solutions to these challenges. The key will lie in developing new sustainable technologies and ensuring that they rapidly reach all those who need them.'

So I arrived in New York with Jackie McQuillan and Jean Oelwang, determined to make a public plea for the creation of an Environmental War Room. I intended opening with a Cousteau quotation: 'There are no boundaries in the real Planet Earth. No United States, no Russia, no China, no Taiwan. Rivers flow unimpeded across the swathes of continents. The persistent tides, the pulse of the sea do not discriminate; they push against all the varied shores on Earth.'

The president of the UN General Assembly, Srgjan Kerim, the former Minister of Foreign Affairs for Macedonia, chaired the session. As I remember it, this went under the banner 'Addressing Climate Change: The United Nations and the World at Work'. Srgjan was a gracious host. Among the other participants were the Secretary-General and Michael Bloomberg, the mayor of New York. Also with me at the conference was the actress Daryl Hannah, a perceptive campaigner on climate change issues.

On 11 February, Srgjan introduced the session: 'I am very much encouraged in that the climate is changing – in terms of the political climate at least – and that people have replaced ignorance with awareness. Awareness is now our ally but that's not enough. We are not talking about long-term planning and the world of tomorrow. We're talking about the emergencies of today.'

He explained that the United Nations was talking about partnerships and that a negotiation process was going on among member nations on setting up targets on greenhouse gases. But he said that only partnerships that included the business world, the media, the non-governmental organisations, and academics (such as those who made a contribution with the IPCC, which was awarded the Nobel Peace Prize in 2007 and helped politicians understand the magnitude of the problem) would work. He stressed that the UN could not do it all by itself. The chairman said that when he was preparing for his role as president of the General Assembly he had read about climate change – and he acknowledged the creation of the Virgin Earth Challenge. 'It is not by chance that they are here; they inspired me,' he said. 'I invited them ... this is why we are here together.'

I started in a sombre tone. At the last minute I dispensed with the poetic Cousteau intro and went straight for the jugular. 'There are some eminent scientists who already believe that we have gone through the tipping point, that there is nothing mankind can now do to stop the Earth heating up by five degrees, with all the dire consequences that will come with that.'

I then cited Jim Lovelock, saying that he went further than the UN report and he predicted we would lose all the floating ice in the summer months in the Arctic Ocean within ten years and that the five-degree rise is likely within forty years, rather than the eighty years that had been predicted by the United Nations. However, unlike the UN report, he believes that the world will then stabilise at this five-degree rise and that there will be survivors. But much of the lush, comfortable world that we now enjoy will be gone. It will erode into a largely featureless desert. The loss of life is likely to be gigantic, and we will be in a world where not nearly enough food is grown, or enough fresh water is available, to support a large population.

'Whether you believe we have gone through the tipping point or not, most scientists are in agreement that we are extremely close to it and it doesn't look particularly good. History has taught us that in times of peril, when all seems lost, bringing together the minds of the greatest to work together with one common goal – survival – is the most effective way to prevail. I'm convinced a winning strategy can be devised. The great minds are out there – but they are fighting in isolation.

'We all need to play a role to bring all the scientists, engineers and inventors worldwide together to come up with innovative, radical approaches to the issue, including finding a way to extract carbon out of the Earth's atmosphere. If such a breakthrough could be made, mankind would be able to regulate the Earth's temperature. By extracting carbon when it's getting too hot – and by adding carbon when it's too cold. We have certainly sorted how to add carbon – we just need to sort out how to extract it. But it cannot be beyond the wit of man to crack this problem.'

Then I made a strong offer of partnership to anyone out there really concerned about this. 'Virgin has put up a $25 million prize to encourage scientists and inventors to put their mind to it. Today we'd like to urge the twenty wealthiest governments to match us in this endeavour so we can make this the largest scientific prize in history – a half-a-billion-dollar prize.' Surely, this would get some traction! I'm still waiting for a call.

I feel that with enough determination the world can pull together to fight this common enemy. I believe that man's ingenuity – driven in many cases by business acumen – can get on top of these catastrophic issues. And so I have begun to think of the way dark times focus great minds to a common goal. This is exactly what we need now: everyone has to work together and find the best solution. When Britain was faced with the prospect of war in Europe in the late 1930s, the Royal Air Force's Operational Requirements Branch determined the specification for a monoplane design to take on the Nazis. They had two projects competing against each other. Reginald Mitchell's Spitfire and the Hawker Hurricane, designed by Camm, had to be able to hit an all-metal bomber 266 times to lethally damage it. The designers had to meet this challenge by firing 1,000 rounds a minute. Both succeeded. There are countless examples of new technologies emerging to overcome the odds in wartime – from the invention of cannons powerful enough to bombard castle walls, to the birth of modern computing among the Enigma code breakers at Bletchley Park in England, a team led by Alan Turing. So why not create a peacetime war room to fight the new common enemy – runaway climate change?

The Environmental War Room will be a unique combination of entrepreneurial muscle, the best possible data and the power to mobilise resources and inspire innovation. Representatives from big business and finance will work alongside representatives from 'green' organisations with whom they may previously have been at odds. It will be a collection of 'best of class' thinking, brought together for the good of all – and it will be truly global. The plan is to have a small, indepedent team that works closely with partners to ensure we don't duplicate, but instead connect the dots on what is already happening, provide reliable information and help speed up the solutions.

The war room will identify all the best (and in some cases radical) ideas, map who is doing what, track and prioritise the impact of existing solutions on carbon reduction and the conservation of ecological systems. It will provide analyses of all the data collected, and identify and prioritise the best options.

Leadership is paramount here. During the questions and answers at the UN conference, the journalists were intrigued to find out who would lead our troops into battle – and I was asked several times about Al Gore. I deflected the questions because we were still considering who we should appoint – I acknowledged he would be a great person to lead us in such a battle, but I wasn't sure how he might take it. We need a Winston Churchill or a Franklin D. Roosevelt figure – someone with the respect, stature and voice to assert their authority.

So just as Virgin Unite is now in the process of setting up a war room to tackle disease in sub-Saharan Africa, they are also in the process of creating a war room to tackle carbon.

Should we fail to find a technological solution then we must start to prepare the world for the consequences of a five-degree rise in temperature and look at ways of mitigating the worst effects. The war room must find radical ideas and win the global community's backing, as happened when CFC gases were banned worldwide to deal with the hole in the ozone layer.

At the session in New York, I introduced one idea as an example. 'It is now widely accepted that rising sea levels, as a result of global warming, will destroy hundreds of thousands of homes in coastal towns all over the world and displace millions of the world's population. But what if today we start planning to create massive inland lakes in Africa, Asia, Australia, North Canada and South America, using fresh water from rivers that would otherwise have gone into the sea? These inland seas can be created as sea levels start to rise with the aim of keeping sea levels as they are at present. They will also – as water – have an added benefit in helping to cool the Earth down. They will help create more rain in desert regions, which in turn will create more trees – which in turn will absorb more carbon.'

The Environmental War Room would be able to place a cost on such large ideas, negotiating compensation 'costs' with individual countries. But I stressed that the United Nations would need to work in partnership with the war room to ensure implementation happens. I had prepared a quote from Sir Winston Churchill, who created his famous War Room in London, during the Second World War. 'One ought never to turn one's back on a threatened danger and try to run away from it. If you do that, you will double the danger. But if you meet it promptly and without flinching, you will reduce the danger by half. Never run away from anything. Never!'

In March 2008, at the suggestion of Richard Stromback, a former professional hockey player who struck gold as a clean-technology entrepreneur, we decided to have a small gathering of people who were addressing the issue to see how we might be able to join forces. Richard, the chief executive of Ecology Coatings, the Climate Group and Virgin Unite invited a group of like-minded business people and former political figures to the event to consider further opportunities. Larry Page, from Google, venture capitalist Vinod Khosla, Elon Musk, the creator of PayPal, Jimmy Wales, the creator of Wikipedia, and Tony Blair – the former British prime minister, now working as a Middle East peace envoy – were among those attending.

In America, the 'clean tech' business boom has already begun, not only in Silicon Valley and the rest of California, but also in and around Boston, around Albuquerque, New Mexico, and near Austin, Texas. Already energy investments are the third largest component of all US venture capital funds, and by far the fastest growing segment. The number of companies and individuals to watch in this sector is now large, with companies like Odersun, Solyndra, Clipper Windpower and Enphase Energy moving very fast.

Shai Agassi, the former president of SAP's product and technology group, is out on his own now as the founder of Better Place of Palo Alto; he has been trying to create the infrastructure to operate a countrywide fleet of electric vehicles in Israel.

Elon Musk, the creator of PayPal and now a space entrepreneur, talked about his Tesla Motors, a Silicon Valley company that makes electric sports cars retailing for $100,000. (Larry has ordered one, but I'm holding off for the moment as I rarely even use a car now.) Hunt Ramsbottom, chief executive of the synthetic fuel technology company Rentech, talked about his plans to make biofuels for aeroplanes, while William McDonough showed us designs for a building in Abu Dhabi with solar panels built into the windows, and a Wal-Mart distribution centre with an energy-friendly grass roof.

Then Tony Blair said something that chimed with me – and made me more determined than ever to pursue the war room. He said governments are too busy firefighting to truly make a difference. 'It is frightening with the day-to-day hustle and bustle of government how little time is spent on the major issues such as carbon,' he told us. For example, the UK's environment minister would come in for a meeting with him for perhaps two hours a month if he was lucky. The Cabinet would work out some short-term project and say: 'OK, let's do this or that.'

If this is typical, then there is a truly desperate need for the Environmental War Room – and I see the green entrepreneurial community playing a central role in its operations.

To run a business ethically, *you have to consider the effect of your operations on others*. You would never tolerate bribery; by the same token, you must not tolerate casual damage to the environment.

It took me a while to realise this. I was half afraid to look the problem of climate change in the eye. It daunted me. I thought it was too big for me – too big for anyone. And so I tried to persuade myself that it didn't exist.

Like one that, on a lonesome road
Doth walk in fear and dread,
And having once turned round walks on,
And turns no more his head;

Because he knows, a frightful fiend
Doth close behind him tread.

But unlike the outlook of Coleridge's Ancient Mariner, business is about facing up to realities. Real problems – even ones as gigantic as climate change – are never as frightening as the spectres in our minds. We can do something about global warming. We just have to lose our fear of it. We have been frozen in horror and denial for too long. We have to act.

No one is asking you to save the planet. *Just dream up and work on a couple of good ideas.* No one expects you to find a global solution to everything. *Just make a difference where you can.* Local solutions have a value in themselves, and some can be scaled up, so it doesn't matter how modest your budget, you can and will make a difference.

That's the good news.

Now comes the frightening bit.

If you don't do this, then you will almost certainly go out of business, if not next year, then in five years' time, or ten or twenty. The climate is changing and the population is rocketing. As a consequence the price of everything is fluctuating. The insurance market is in chaos. Unpredictable, unexpected shortages are disturbing production. Changing weather patterns are imperilling whole populations and disrupting the economies of entire nations.

And it's going to get a lot worse before it gets better.

You'll recall that when I was describing our development of biofuels and spacecraft, I said that there was no such thing as an overnight success in a new market: that Virgin's early emergence in these sectors was the consequence of years of reading and research.

The sector we might as well call 'responses to climate change' is not a sector we can choose whether or not to do business in. It's a sector that now embraces all of us, whether we like it or not. Big or small, we have to do business in this area because our failure to do so will ruin us.

If you're not ahead of the game, if you're not researching the solutions to problems that may affect your business a decade from now, then you run the serious risk that you will haemorrhage and fail.

But why look at this through the gloomy end of the telescope? The reverse is equally true: make a success of yourself in this sector, and you will find yourself turning something that advantages everyone into a handsome profit for your company.

With that profit, you can then dream up and experiment with bigger and bigger scale solutions. Addressing climate change is good business; and I guarantee that once you bite the bullet and start work in this sector, you won't want to stop.

HIV/Aids and climate change are issues that I have a personal passion for and that make sense for the Virgin Group to get behind. We are working on other social and environmental investments, but the one thing all of our efforts in this area have in common is that they leverage Virgin's biggest asset – the entrepreneurial spirit of our people. This spirit, coupled with the right partners and great ideas, can truly help us make a difference, help communities thrive and help our planet.

If we want a world that we can be proud to leave to the next seven generations, every business needs to look at how they can drive change in every aspect of their operations. One last point: *don't forget to listen* – as some of the best ideas will come from your staff, customers and people on the front lines!

If you ever fancy joining us as a partner in any of our endeavours to make the world a better place, please contact us at Virgin Unite: www.virginunite.com.

Epilogue

Success

If I hadn't badly damaged my knee as a teenager I would likely have been a sportsman. If I hadn't been dyslexic I wouldn't have left school at sixteen and created a magazine, which means I wouldn't have ended up running *Student*, which means Virgin Records would never have been born, which means . . .

There are different paths that you can take in this life, and choosing the correct path is supremely important. And as if that weren't pressure enough, it's no good choosing *not* to choose, because that approach to life absolutely guarantees failure.

I don't think there is enough attention and help given to young people in life to set them in the right direction. All young people deserve wise counsel. They need someone who can show them a future. They need to be able to work out what they can do with their lives, how they can enjoy their lives, how they can pay for it and how they can take responsibility for their actions.

I think it's a shame that we teach children everything *about* the world, but we don't teach them how to take part in the world, how to realise an idea, how to measure the consequences of their actions, how to take a knock, or how to share their success. What kind of world have we built, that people can use the phrase 'it's just business' without challenge or contradiction?

Entrepreneurship is business's beating heart. Entrepreneurship isn't about capital; it's about ideas. A great deal of entrepreneurship can be taught, and we desperately need to teach it, as we confront the huge global challenges of the twenty-first century.

Entrepreneurship is also about excellence – not excellence measured in awards, or other people's approval, but the sort one achieves for oneself, by exploring what the world has to offer. I wrote to someone recently who, like me, is dyslexic. I said that it is important to look for one's strengths – to try to excel at what you're good at.

What you're bad at actually doesn't interest people, and it certainly shouldn't interest you. However accomplished you become in life, the things you are bad at will always outnumber the things you're good at. *So don't let your limits knock your self-confidence.* Put them to one side and push yourself towards your strengths.

This, I think, is sound advice for the young. For those of you who've left youth behind, my advice would be: reread the paragraph above, adding exclamation marks after every sentence.

Because, in business, you always have a choice, and you always have an obligation to choose. With the right attitude, business will keep your mind eternally young, because business is always changing, changes always bring opportunities, and you can never hide from the changes that are round the corner.

In entrepreneurial business, a conservative mindset will hamstring you, defensiveness will weaken you and a failure to face facts will kill you. Entrepreneurial business favours the open mind. It favours people whose optimism drives them to prepare for many possible futures, pretty much purely for the joy of doing so. It favours people with a humane and engaged view of the world; people who can imagine themselves into the skin of their customers, their workers and the people who are affected by their operations. Business favours people who, when they see a problem or an injustice, try to do something about it. It favours pragmatists over perfectionists, adventurers over fantasists.

Done well and in the right spirit, business will also bring you success – whatever that is.

Indeed, how do you measure who's truly successful? My list of the world's most successful people includes Sir Freddie Laker – hardly an obvious choice, to go by the headlines, the rich lists and all the other paraphernalia of business celebrity. So let's strip this particular business bare once and for all: when we talk about success, what are we really talking about?

Are we talking about money? As a measure of success, money's a crude one at best. People are always inquisitive about how wealthy other people are. It's a fascinating subject and one that produces endless reams of copy and discussion. But the reality is that wealth is like a running stream of water. During some seasons the flow of money is a torrent and you're inundated with cash. The next moment, you've put money in to develop a business and your cash flow dries up overnight leaving a barren riverbed.

So even the more well-researched rich lists have to take a bit of a potshot when arriving at their figures. There have been times I was almost bankrupt, and I was very glad to see my name in the *Sunday Times* Rich List, because I thought it would assuage the bank manager. (The figures were often wildly off the mark both ways – but I wasn't complaining.) In the last few years things have gone well for the Virgin Group. In 2008, it had a reach of nearly £12 billion.

And me? I'm rich. There – I said it. It's quite an American thing to talk about wealth. In Britain we're still sort of slightly embarrassed about it, and I think that's a good thing. When I go to a party I see people, not bank statements, and I'd like to think that when people get chatting to me they feel the same. To be perfectly honest I hated the word 'billionaire' going into the title of that show I did for Fox. It was a great title, but it wasn't my style at all. Money's only interesting for what it lets you do. On paper, if I was to sell up my shareholdings in the companies tomorrow, I would have considerable wealth. But where would be the fun in that?

If money's a poor guide to success in life, celebrity is worse. The media likes to personalise and simplify matters – and that's understandable. It's much easier to talk about Steve Jobs at Apple, Bill Gates at Microsoft or Richard Branson at Virgin, but that doesn't really acknowledge that there's a legion of senior people doing significant jobs and making major decisions every day. Everyone wants to make business 'simple' and that's one of my constant goals, but in reality there are certain complexities about running a media company, a space-tourism business or an airline. And the financial implications of running a global business across many jurisdictions require a substantial level of expert knowledge in accountancy, taxation and legal affairs, not forgetting the IT, marketing and HR functions too. I've never met a CEO who had all of those skills. Of course, the figurehead at the top does make significant strategic decisions but this is based on the work and capabilities of other people within the business. We all still have the same number of hours in the working week. In successful businesses, working hard is never confined to one or two people – you'll usually find a strong work ethic runs right through the company.

If neither money nor celebrity really encapsulate what success is about, what about personal power? I've been asked what happens if Richard Branson's own balloon bursts: isn't the Virgin Group far too reliant on one individual? I have jokingly replied that during our spell running Virgin Records, we always found that when a major rock-music artist died the records sales went through the roof.

I have spent over thirty-five years building the Virgin brand, and if I do get run over tomorrow, I think it will live on without me, just as

Google will live on without its founders, and Microsoft will live on without Bill Gates. For me, the major job has been done. A lot of people worked exceptionally hard in the early years to build the brand. With or without me, Virgin will be around for many years to come.

Is this power? In a sense, I suppose it is. But the idea that I somehow 'control' the brand is a bit sinister and silly. I gave birth to the brand. I've nurtured and I continue to nurture it. I brought it into being, and I champion it. Thinking about it is one of the things that gets me up in the morning. But you can't really control ideas.

The other thing that gets me up in the morning is the idea of making a difference. It's why I've never wanted to run a big company, and it's why I get huge enjoyment out of creating and tending to lots of smaller ones. (I have to be careful of my terms here, because airlines are hardly small companies! But I hope by now that you know what I'm getting at.) Virgin, by remembering what it is to be a small entrepreneur, has made large amounts of positive difference in many diverse business areas.

I think that the more you're actively and practically engaged, the more successful you will feel. Actually, that might even be my definition of success. Right now, I find myself doing more and more to help safeguard our future on this planet. Does that make me successful? It certainly makes me happy.

I hope you've found the thinking and the stories in this book useful. I think you can see that my definition of success in business has nothing to do with profits solely for their own sake. This is very important. *Success for me is whether you have created something that you can be really proud of.* Profits are necessary to invest in the next project – and pay the bills, repay investors and reward all the hard work – but that's all. Nobody should be remembered for how much money they have made in life. Whether you die with a billion dollars in your bank account or $20 under your pillow is actually not that interesting. That's not what you've achieved in life. What matters is whether you've created something special – and whether you've made a real difference to other people's lives. Entrepreneurs, scientists and artists who died as paupers are often the heroes.

Successful people aren't in possession of secrets known only to themselves. Don't obsess over people who appear to you to be 'winners', but listen instead to the wisdom of people who've led enriching lives – people, for instance, who've found time for friends and family. Be generous in your interpretation of what success looks like. The best and most meaningful lives don't always end happily. My friend Madiba spent twenty-seven years of his life in prison. If he had died there, would his life hold no lessons for us?

In business, as in life, all that matters is that you do something positive. Thanks for reading – and enjoy your life. You only get one.

IF -

If you can keep your head when all about you
    Are losing theirs and blaming it on you,
If you can trust yourself when all men doubt you,
    But make allowance for their doubting too;
If you can wait and not be tired by waiting,
    Or being lied about, don't deal in lies,
Or being hated, don't give way to hating,
    And yet don't look too good, nor talk too wise:

If you can dream – and not make dreams your master;
    If you can think – and not make thoughts your aim;
If you can meet with Triumph and Disaster
    And treat those two impostors just the same;
If you can bear to hear the truth you've spoken
    Twisted by knaves to make a trap for fools,
Or watch the things you gave your life to, broken,
    And stoop and build 'em up with worn-out tools:

If you can make one heap of all your winnings
    And risk it on one turn of pitch-and-toss,
And lose, and start again at your beginnings
    And never breathe a word about your loss;
If you can force your heart and nerve and sinew
    To serve your turn long after they are gone,
And so hold on when there is nothing in you
    Except the Will which says to them: 'Hold on!'

If you can talk with crowds and keep your virtue,
    Or walk with Kings – nor lose the common touch,
If neither foes nor loving friends can hurt you,
    If all men count with you, but none too much;
If you can fill the unforgiving minute
    With sixty seconds' worth of distance run,
Yours is the Earth and everything that's in it,
    And – which is more – you'll be a Man, my son!

Rudyard Kipling

Copyright Acknowledgements

Index